# Consumer Value

'Serving the customer' and 'customer satisfaction' are central to every formulation of the marketing concept, yet few books delve with sufficient depth into issues concerning the dimensions that such service to the customer entails.

This comprehensive volume fills the gap by bringing together leading US and UK scholars to explore this contentious issue – the nature and types of *consumer value*. Various contrasting methodological and theoretical domains are employed to provide a comprehensive analytical framework that is applied to the full range of consumption-related phenomena.

The framework provides eight interrelated ways to think about these issues:

- efficiency
- excellence
- status
- esteem
- play
- aesthetics
- ethics
- spirituality

With an international range of contributors and a highly individual approach, *Consumer Value* offers a useful teaching supplement to anyone studying a course on marketing in general or consumer behaviour in particular.

**Morris B. Holbrook** is Professor of Marketing at The Graduate School of Business, Columbia University. His previous publications include *Consumer Research* (1995) and he's the co-author of *The Semiotics of Consumption* (1993) and *Postmodern Consumer Research* (1992).

**Routledge interpretive marketing research series**
Edited by Stephen Brown
*University of Ulster, Northern Ireland*
and Barbara B. Stern
*State University of New Jersey*

Recent years have witnessed an 'interpretive turn' in marketing and consumer research. Methodologies from the humanities are taking their place alongside those drawn from the traditional social sciences. Qualitative and literary modes of marketing discourse are growing in popularity. Art and aesthetics are increasingly firing the marketing imagination.

This series of scholarly monographs and edited volumes brings together the most innovative work in the burgeoning interpretative marketing research tradition. It ranges across the methodological spectrum from grounded theory to personal introspection, covers all aspects of the postmodern marketing 'mix', from advertising to product development, and embraces marketing's principal sub-disciplines.

**Representing Consumers**
Voices, views and visions
*Edited by Barbara B. Stern*

**Romancing the Market**
*Edited by Stephen Brown, Anne Marie Doherty and Bill Clarke*

**Consumer Value**
A framework for analysis and research
*Edited by Morris B. Holbrook*

# Consumer Value

A framework for analysis and research

Edited by
**Morris B. Holbrook**

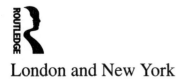

London and New York

658.8342
C7582

First published 1999 by Routledge
11 New Fetter Lane, London EC4P 4EE

Simultaneously published in the USA and Canada
by Routledge
29 West 35th Street, New York, NY 10001

Typeset in Times by Keystroke, Jacaranda Lodge, Wolverhampton
Printed and bound in Great Britain by Creative Print and Design (Wales) Ebbw Vale

*British Library Cataloguing in Publication Data*
A catalogue record for this book is available from the British Library

*Library of Congress Cataloguing in Publication Data*
Consumer value: a framework for analysis and research / Morris B.
    Holbrook [editor].
        p.    cm. — (Routledge interpretive market research series)
    Includes bibliographical references and index.
    1. Consumer behavior.  2. Consumers—Research—Methodology.
    I. Holbrook, Morris B.  II. Series.
    HF5415.32.C6593   1999
    658.8'342—dc21                                    98–33544
                                                        CIP

ISBN 0–415–19192–0 (hbk)
ISBN 0–415–19193–9 (pbk)

For John O'Shaughnessy –
philosopher and friend

# Contents

# Figures and tables

**Figures**

**Tables**

# List of contributors

**Stephen Brown** is Professor of Retailing at the University of Ulster, Northern Ireland. His books include *Postmodern Marketing* (Routledge); *Marketing Apocalypse*, co-edited with Jim Bell and David Carson (Routledge); *Postmodern Marketing Two: Telling Tales* (International Thomson Business Press); *Consumer Research: Postcards from the Edge*, co-edited with Darach Turley (Routledge); and *Romancing the Market* (Routledge). Brown wishes to assure his readers that 'these works are available from all good second-hand bookstores, charity shops, and remainder bins everywhere.'

**Kent Grayson** is an Assistant Professor of Marketing at the London Business School. His research focuses on two general areas. The first centers on issues of truth and deception in consumer behavior. The second examines network-marketing organizations, which are sometimes called pyramid-selling companies or multi-level marketing organizations. Before earning his doctorate at Northwestern University's Kellogg Graduate School of Management, Grayson worked for several years in advertising and public relations. He has published articles in the *Journal of Consumer Research*, *International Journal of Research in Marketing*, *Journal of Consumer Psychology*, and *Sloan Management Review*.

**Morris B. Holbrook** is the W. T. Dillard Professor of Marketing in the Graduate School of Business at Columbia University. Holbrook graduated from Harvard College with a BA degree in English (1965) and received his MBA (1967) and PhD (1975) in Marketing from Columbia University. Since 1975, he has taught courses at the Columbia Business School in such areas as Marketing Strategy, Sales Management, Research Methods, Consumer Behavior, and Commercial Communication in the Culture of Consumption. His research has covered a wide variety of topics in marketing and consumer behavior with a special focus on issues related to communication in general and to aesthetics, semiotics, hermeneutics, art, entertainment, and advertising in particular. Holbrook pursues such hobbies as playing the piano, attending jazz and classical concerts, going to movies and the theater, collecting musical recordings, taking stereographic photos, and being kind to cats.

**France Leclerc** earned her PhD in Marketing from Cornell University and is currently an Assistant Professor in the Graduate School of Business at the University of Chicago where she teaches MBA courses on Advertising and International Marketing. Her research interests include the psychology of time (waiting and delays), consumer promotions, and brand loyalty. Leclerc has published articles on these themes in the *Journal of Consumer Research*, *Journal of Marketing Research, Journal of Applied Psychology*, and *Journal of Personality and Social Psychology*.

**Richard L. Oliver** is the Valere Blair Potter Professor of Management and Area Head of Marketing in the Owen Graduate School of Management at Vanderbilt University. Oliver received a BSME degree from Purdue and the MBA and PhD from the University of Wisconsin-Madison. His research interests are in the area of consumer psychology with a special focus on customer satisfaction and postpurchase processes. Oliver is the author of *Satisfaction: A Behavioral Perspective on the Consumer* (Irwin/McGraw-Hill) and co-editor with Roland Rust of *Service Quality: New Directions in Theory and Practice* (Sage). In recognition of his work on the satisfaction response, he was elected a fellow of the American Psychological Association and the Society for Consumer Psychology. Oliver teaches buyer behavior and customer-satisfaction theory at Vanderbilt. He has served on the review boards of several journals and, previously, has taught at the University of Pennsylvania's Wharton School and at Washington University in St. Louis. He is the only member of the value team who rides a Harley-Davidson.

**Marsha L. Richins** is Professor of Marketing at the University of Missouri, Columbia. Richins received a Masters degree in Social Psychology and a PhD in Marketing from the University of Texas, Austin. Her early work dealt with customer responses to dissatisfaction in the marketplace. More recent research has investigated consumers' relationships with their possessions, the influence of advertising on consumers' self-perceptions, and materialism. Her articles have appeared in the *Journal of Consumer Research, Journal of Marketing, American Behavioral Scientist, Journal of Economic Psychology*, and elsewhere. Richins has served as Associate Editor for the *Journal of Consumer Research* and co-chaired an international conference on materialism in 1992.

**Bernd H. Schmitt** holds a PhD in Psychology from Cornell University. Schmitt is an Associate Professor at Columbia University's Graduate School of Business in New York, where he has taught courses on marketing strategy, consumer behavior, advertising management, and corporate identity. His research interests include branding, identity and image management, time perceptions, and international marketing. He has published numerous articles in academic and management journals, including the *Journal of Consumer Research, Journal of Marketing Research*, and *Journal of Consumer Psychology*, among others. He is the co-author with Alex Simonson of the recent book entitled *Marketing Aesthetics: The Strategic Management of Brands, Identity, and Image* (The Free Press).

**N. Craig Smith** is an Associate Professor at the School of Business, Georgetown University, Washington, DC. Smith joined Georgetown in 1991, after serving on the faculties of Harvard University's Graduate School of Business Administration and the Cranfield School of Management in the UK. His research on marketing ethics, corporate social responsibility, and related issues has appeared in a variety of business journals, including the *Journal of Marketing*, *Harvard Business Review*, *Sloan Management Review*, *Journal of Retailing*, *Journal of Consumer Policy*, *Journal of Business Research*, *European Management Journal*, and *European Journal of Marketing*. Smith is the author of *Morality and the Market: Consumer Pressure for Corporate Accountability* (Routledge), the co-editor with Paul Dainty of the *Management Research Handbook* (Routledge), and the co-author with John A. Quelch of *Ethics in Marketing* (Irwin). He consults with firms on problems of good marketing practice, including marketing ethics.

**Michael R. Solomon** is the Human Sciences Professor of Consumer Behavior in the School of Human Sciences at Auburn University. Prior to joining Auburn in 1995, Solomon was Chairman of the Department of Marketing in the School of Business at Rutgers University. He earned a BA degree in Psychology and Sociology from Brandeis University in 1977 and a PhD in Social Psychology from the University of North Carolina at Chapel Hill in 1981. In 1996, he was named to the Fulbright/FLAD Chair in Market Globalization at The Technical University of Lisbon. Solomon's primary research interests include consumer behavior and lifestyle issues; the psychology of fashion, decoration, and image; and services marketing. He has published numerous articles on these and related topics in the *Journal of Consumer Research*, *Journal of Marketing*, *Journal of Advertising*, and other journals. In addition, he is editor of *The Psychology of Fashion* (Lexington); co-editor of *The Service Encounter: Managing Employee/Customer Interaction in Services Businesses* (Lexington); and author of two leading textbooks – *Consumer Behavior: Buying, Having, and Being* (Prentice Hall) and *Marketing: Real People, Real Choices* (Prentice Hall).

**Janet Wagner** is an Associate Professor of Marketing at the University of Maryland where she teaches retailing, direct marketing, and consumer behavior. Wagner's research interests are in consumer behavior – particularly consumer responses to product design and factors affecting consumer expenditures for fashion goods. Her research has been published in major marketing journals, including the *Journal of Consumer Research* and *Journal of Retailing*, and she has served on the editorial boards of both journals. Wagner has been an active member of the Association for Consumer Research, serving as a member of the Advisory Council for six years. She has also been active in the American Marketing Association, where she is currently on the executive board of the Retailing Special Interest Group.

# Preface

Arguably, the nature and types of consumer value constitute the essential foundation and fundamental basis for both the academic study and the managerial practice of marketing. Yet, paradoxically, remarkably little attention has been devoted to the problem of understanding the philosophical and empirical underpinnings of a concept that plays such a critical role in the formulation of our discipline. The present volume pursues the goal of addressing the relevant issues in a format that will prove helpful to a variety of audiences.

Specifically, this book represents a collaborative effort that begins with an introductory framework covering the nature and relevant types of consumer value, followed by eight chapters by a group of distinguished scholars addressing each of the various types of value, as related to their own individual areas of special expertise. Toward this end, the Introduction describes a Typology of Consumer Value used to structure the remainder of the book. In this connection, my earlier work has proposed a *framework* that distinguishes among *eight key types* of consumer value, each of which appears to deserve consideration in the analysis of consumer behavior. These eight types refer to different aspects of consumption that have attracted the attention of various scholars in the field. To encapsulate these diverse areas of scholarship, I have managed to enlist *the* (or one of the) most distinguished researcher(s) in each area of inquiry to discuss whether, how, and why his or her special area of interest does or does not *fit* into the proposed framework; to provide a background overview of the *key issues* represented by his or her own specialized domain; and to offer further insights and speculations as to the directions in which that particular specialty appears to be headed in terms of future research initiatives. In other words, rather than merely rehashing old material, the book presents a tone of lively debate, prompts some penetrating insights, and even floats a few fearless prophesies on further developments of importance to the relevant issues involved. Thus, the Introduction is followed by eight chapters, authored by seminal thinkers in the field who have agreed to consider each of the main types of value:

1 Efficiency (France Leclerc, University of Chicago; Bernd H. Schmitt, Columbia University);
2 Excellence (Richard L. Oliver, Vanderbilt University);

3  Status (Michael R. Solomon, Auburn University);
4  Esteem (Marsha L. Richins, University of Missouri);
5  Play (Kent Grayson, London Business School);
6  Aesthetics (Janet Wagner, University of Maryland);
7  Ethics (N. Craig Smith, Georgetown University);
8  Spirituality (Stephen Brown, University of Ulster).

In our view, *Consumer Value* should attract the attention of many readers who have a special interest in one or another area as presented by a leader in that domain, but who peruse the remaining chapters to find out how that particular area is connected to other fields of exploration and who thereby gain a breadth of perspective that will help to enhance their understanding of the overall field of consumer research and its relevance to marketing management. Further, we believe that this book contributes an overview and a synthesizing perspective that will help to elucidate both structure and content in the field of consumer research. Specifically, the audience for the book will include at least three major components:

1  Students in Business and the Social Sciences at the BA, MBA, and PhD Levels
2  Academic marketing and consumer researchers
3  Marketing practitioners

First, the book can serve as a supplement to the material taught in many under-graduate and graduate courses in Marketing Strategy and/or Consumer Behavior. The theme of "serving the customer" is one of the most tried-and-true prescriptions preached in conjunction with the so-called "marketing orientation." Yet few courses delve with sufficient depth into issues concerning the dimensions that this service to the customer entails. When teaching such a course, almost every instructor eventually arrives at the difficult moment of answering the question, "OK, so if I want to please the customer, just exactly how do I *do* that?" The relevant Typology of Consumer Value and its elaboration in the various chapters provide at least eight interrelated ways to think about this problem and therefore offer a useful teaching supplement to anyone designing a course on marketing in general or on the marketing-relevant study of consumer behavior in particular.

Second, scholars in the disciplines of Marketing and Consumer Research must constantly struggle to keep abreast of developments in their specialized areas of research and must vigilantly consider how these developments interconnect with other areas of specialization in various related subfields. The present volume provides a cutting-edge overview of the state-of-the-art in various interrelated subdisciplines and thereby provides valuable resource materials for professional marketing and consumer researchers wishing to remain current in their fields of interest. To illustrate the plausibility of this claim, when a special session devoted to this topic was presented at the annual conference of the Association for Consumer Research in 1995 (with all but two of the participants included in the present volume making brief presentations), it was officially recognized as the highest attended session ever recorded since the Association had begun keeping score five years earlier. In other words, we have found substantial interest in this theme among the members of the academic marketing-research community in general and among consumer researchers in particular.

Third, the material covered by *Consumer Value* appears to represent one aspect of our scholarly research that practitioners in the field of marketing management find important and relevant to their work. In making presentations to various groups of practitioners from time to time, I have found this to be *the* area of my own studies in which marketing managers consistently display the greatest interest. This fascination with the topic is hardly surprising when one considers the pressure placed upon marketers constantly to find newer and better ways to appeal to the customer. The proposed Typology of Consumer Value and its various ramifications provide a coherent framework in which such searches for the bases of market success can proceed apace. In effect, the integrative typology offers a checklist of issues to consider in the quest for loyalty-maximizing customer appeals.

Innumerable friends and colleagues have contributed to the creation of *Consumer Value*. Foremost among these, of course, I owe a tremendous debt of gratitude to the nine authors who have labored mightily to give birth to the eight chapters that form the main body of the text. Further, two additional close associates – John Deighton and John Sherry – made powerful contributions to the conference session in which the project got its start but, unfortunately, were not able to participate in the more drawn-out writing project that followed. Indeed, it was John Deighton himself who deserves credit and thanks for suggesting the idea of compiling a comprehensive volume based on the collective work of the scholars involved.

I have been pursuing the theme of consumer value since a sabbatical in 1983 during which I first began delving into this issue in earnest. In the earliest stages, I was blessed by the collaborative efforts of Kim Corfman, with whom I co-authored the first piece aimed in this direction, and by the encouragement of Jack Jacoby and Jerry Olson, who co-edited the book on *Perceived Quality* wherein our ruminations first appeared. (References to this and other works mentioned in the Preface may be found at the end of the Introduction.) Soon thereafter, I got a second chance to hone my conception of consumer value by virtue of a kind invitation to participate in a conference on *Affect in Consumer Behavior* hosted by Bob Peterson, Wayne Hoyer, and Bill Wilson. By the time my work on the Typology of Consumer Value had reached this stage, I had grown so enamored of the topic that I could not bear to see my efforts subjected to the ravages of the review process as practiced at our typical journals of marketing and consumer research. I therefore delayed and delayed until, finally, I was fortunate enough to contribute my main scholarly statement on this theme to a volume on *Service Quality* compiled by Roland Rust and Rich Oliver, who graciously consented to impose only the most reasonable and helpful editorial restrictions on my flights of fancy. Realizing that my chapter for that book was perhaps a bit too "learned" for some readers to bother with, I gladly accepted the fortuitous suggestion by Marilyn DeLong and Anne Marie Fiore that I write a more "popular" version for their co-edited work on the *Aesthetics of Textiles and Clothing*. At about the time this "reader-friendly" version appeared, the critical facilitating moment arrived when Kim Corfman and John Lynch permitted me to organize a Special Topic Session on Consumer Value for the 1995 ACR Conference mentioned earlier. As already noted, the enthusiasm of the participants and the attendance at this session by the ACR members were more than sufficient to move us collectively toward thinking about the creation of a book-length text. This and the other efforts just recounted have received the generous support of the Columbia Business School's Faculty Research Fund, for which I am grateful. I am further grateful to the staff at Routledge – especially Maggy Hendry, Michelle Gallagher, Jody Ball, and Stuart Hay – for their help and encouragement at every phase of this project.

Though the friends, colleagues, and collaborators just mentioned – as well as many others too numerous to name individually – deserve my heartfelt thanks for their inputs into the present volume, there is one individual to whom I must express my deepest and most sincere appreciation. I refer to John O'Shaughnessy, who over the course of three decades has played a role of profound importance in my life – first, as my teacher; later, as my colleague; and always, as my dear friend. More than any other influence, by virtue of his massive command of a literature that I have by comparison managed to assimilate to only the tiniest degree, John has shown me the relevance of philosophy to our marketing-related studies. John's work is a shining embodiment of what the philosophical mind can accomplish when applied with dedicated diligence and brilliant imagination to marketing and consumer research. To John, with boundless gratitude and in my humble capacity as editor of this collective work by other stellar scholars, I affectionately dedicate *Consumer Value – a framework for analysis and research*.

Morris B. Holbrook
Columbia University
Spring 1998

# Introduction to consumer value

*Morris B. Holbrook*

## Introduction

This chapter introduces a volume that brings together scholars from diverse areas to address the nature and types of consumer value. Specifically, the Introduction proposes a framework to distinguish among eight key types of consumer value that appear to deserve consideration in the analysis of consumption-related behavior. These eight types refer to different aspects of consumption that have attracted the attention of various scholars in the field. Subsequently, distinguished researchers in these areas of inquiry will discuss whether and how their concerns fit into the proposed framework, offering further insights into the applicability of the Typology of Consumer Value across a broad range of research topics. In sum, this Introduction presents a systematic consideration of the proposed framework and thereby provides the basis for a subsequent critical evaluation of the framework's usefulness as an integrative scheme and for a further development in succeeding chapters of its relevance to issues concerning more specific types of consumer value.

## Background

### The marketing context

If we follow Kotler (1991) by viewing *marketing* as a managerial process concerned with the facilitation and consummation of *exchanges* and by defining the exchange of interest as a *transaction* between two parties in which each party gives up *something of value* in return for something of *greater value*, we recognize immediately that *consumer value* plays a crucial role at the heart of all marketing activity and therefore clearly deserves the attention of every consumer researcher. First, if we ignore potential externalities or possible third-party effects created by marketing exchanges (as in the case of noise pollution from one's Harley-Davidson disturbing other residents on the block, second-hand smoke from one's Marlborough choking other diners at the restaurant, or pollution from one's gasoline making the planet uninhabitable by other members of the human species), the Kotlerian perspective just described provides a built-in *ethical justification* for our activities as marketers, in the sense that if each party to an exchange has gained "greater value" through the transaction, then (by definition) both parties are *better off* than they were before so that an *increase in social welfare* has therefore occurred. Clearly, such a viewpoint helps marketers as well as consumer or marketing researchers feel good about what they do by justifying their behavior as a socially worthwhile activity. But second and more importantly in the present context, the Kotlerian conception indicates that implications concerning consumer value are *central* to our understanding of marketing and, indeed, that the Concept of Consumer Value constitutes the *foundation*, defining *basis*, or underlying *rationale* for the Marketing Concept in the sense that each party to a transaction gives up one thing in return for something else of greater *value*.

As an example to drive home the central importance of consumer value to the marketing concept, consider an issue that many would regard as *the* critical problem in the formulation of marketing strategy – namely, the problem of *product positioning*. One way to view the positioning problem for a brand is to conceive it as directed toward attaining an *optimal location* in a *market space*, where this market space represents the perceived positions for the set of competing brands in the relevant product category as well as the locations of ideal points for the various customer segments of interest. In this conceptualization, the prescription for success is to appeal to a target segment whose needs and wants are not being satisfied by the available array of competing offerings. In other words, we can attain a *differential advantage* for our brand by locating its perceived position closer to the ideal point of a target segment than the perceived locations of other available offerings. Accordingly, we should design all communicative aspects of the *marketing mix* for that brand (the product itself, the list price, the channels of distribution, the advertising and sales pitches – in short, the "Four P's" of product, price, place, and promotion) to achieve perceptions of the brand that will place it in the optimal position relative to its competitors (see Woodruff and Gardial 1996: 124).

Implicitly, this familiar strategic prescription – which, arguably, is the basis for many if not most of our insights into effective marketing management – raises at least two important questions that underlie the formulation of marketing strategy as just envisioned:

(1) Where do the *dimensions* of the market space come from?
(2) What determines the *locations* of the *ideal point(s)* for the target segment(s) in the market space?

The answers to these crucial questions, I believe, are directly related to the topic at hand. Specifically, first, the *dimensions* of the market space represent the *characteristics* that consumers seek from the relevant product category, the *attributes* of the category that provide these characteristics, and/or the *features* of the brands that embody these attributes – in short:

(1) the *dimensions* of the market space represent those characteristics, attributes, or features of brands in the product class that provide *consumer value.*

Further, second, the location of each *ideal point* represents the *combination* of characteristics, attributes, or features that the relevant market segment finds *maximally appealing* so that:

(2) an *ideal point* indicates a position of *maximum consumer value* for the customer segment of interest.

From these considerations, the critical importance to marketers of understanding the *nature* and *types* of consumer value appears to follow immediately. Only by grasping the underlying determinants of the market space as just described can we hope to design maximally effective marketing strategies aimed at addressing the positioning problem by communicating a position for our offering that wins it a differential advantage. Given the importance of this topic, one might expect that a vast marketing-related literature would be devoted to exploring the nature and types of consumer value. Indeed, some work posing these questions has begun to appear (Gale 1994; Broydrick 1996; Woodruff and Gardial 1996). Yet my impression is that such emerging attempts have thus far failed to investigate the nature and types of consumer value with anything like the degree of comprehensiveness and systematization needed to make telling conceptual inroads into the issues of concern. The purpose of this introduction and the collective work that follows is to begin the construction of such a comprehensive and systematic approach.

## *Key sources on the theory of value*

Basically, the challenging questions just raised belong to a branch of philosophical inquiry known as *axiology* or *the theory of value* (Lewis 1946; Hilliard 1950; Perry 1954; Taylor 1961; Brightman 1962; Frankena 1962, 1967, 1973; Von Wright 1963; Morris 1964; Hartman 1967; Olson 1967; Frondizi 1971). Though the theory of value is of tremendous potential relevance to the fields of marketing and consumer research – as just argued – it appears fair to say that axiology represents a body of knowledge habitually neglected by scholars in the marketing-related disciplines. Symptomatically, with some intentionally irreverent humor, a learned colleague once introduced my talk on axiology as having a title that sounded as if it had something to do with the mechanical device that connects the wheels of an automobile. Indeed, it turns out that the theory of value is a topic neglected not only by marketers but even by axiologists themselves.

The latter conclusion stems from my experiences when I first became interested in the theory of value. Ordinarily, when some topic catches my eye – for example multiattribute attitude models during the 1960s, multidimensional scaling during the 1970s, or semiotics during the 1980s – I visit the library in search of the relevant literature only to find that every single book on that particular subject has disappeared from the shelves, checked out or otherwise removed by others, a little swifter than I, who have beaten me to the punch. But when I suddenly saw the light, developed an interest in axiology, and visited the stacks of the Columbia University library, I found that all the books on the theory of value listed in the catalog sat there on the shelves, gathering dust. By examining the check-out cards in the backs of these volumes, I discovered that books donated to the University by John Dewey decades earlier had never been read. Similarly, many of their companions appeared never even to have been opened; their pages were connected at the edges and still needed to be cut apart by their first reader – me.

Braving the assault on my allergies arising from the heavy layer of dust and stench of mildew embodied by this ancient literature, I took it as a suitable if sneeze-inducing point of entry for my examination of questions axiological. During the ensuing investigation, for over a decade, I have wrestled with issues concerning (1) the general *nature* of consumer value and (2) the specific *types* of consumer value. The first attempt in this direction appeared in a chapter by Holbrook and Corfman (1985). The theme of value was revisited briefly by Holbrook (1986) and has subsequently been elaborated in a "learned" treatise (Holbrook 1994c) and in two more "reader-friendly" versions (Holbrook 1994a, 1996).

Accordingly, in the present introductory chapter, I shall content myself with an account of concepts that have already surfaced elsewhere. Toward this end, I shall review my conclusions on the nature and types of consumer value to provide a general structure as the basis for the more specific issues addressed by various contributors to this volume. In other words, I shall focus on providing an integrative *framework* that will tie together the more detailed contributions still to come.

In this connection, a crucial point – one that sounds amazingly simple when articulated, but one that appears to have eluded most of those who have previously commented on various aspects of consumer value – is that one can understand a given type of value *only* by considering its relationship to *other* types of value. One cannot comprehend Quality without comparing it to Beauty; nor Beauty without considering how it differs from Fun; nor Fun without regarding it in contrast to Ethics. In short, we can understand one type of value only by comparing it with other types of value to which it is closely or not-so-closely related. Thus, we can comprehend Quality only by comparison with Beauty, Convenience, and Reputation; we can comprehend Beauty only by contrast with Quality, Fun, and Ecstasy. In a sense, this means that the construction of a full-length work devoted to considering all these different types of value is needed before we can lay claim to understanding any of the specific types considered separately. This guiding principle explains the purpose and structure of the present volume.

# The framework – the nature and types of consumer value

## *The nature of consumer value*

I define *consumer value* as an *interactive relativistic preference experience* (see Hilliard 1950: 42). Typically, such consumer value refers to the *evaluation* of some *object* by some *subject*. Here, for our purposes, the "subject" in question is usually a consumer or other customer, whereas the "object" of interest could be any product – a manufactured good, a service, a political candidate, a vacation destination, a musical concert, a social cause, and so on (see Taylor 1961: 23). Notice that each of the aforementioned facets of consumer value – interactivity, relativism, affectivity, and a grounding in the consumption experience – is intimately interrelated with the other three. In no way do I mean to imply that the four are independent or mutually exclusive. Rather they compose an interconnected system of related aspects that overlap and combine to constitute the emergent phenomenon known as consumer value. However, for clarity of exposition, I shall now consider each separately.

## *1 Consumer value is interactive*

By *interactive*, I mean that consumer value entails an *interaction* between some *subject* (a consumer or customer) and some *object* (a product). This collaboration of *both* a subject *and* an object in the constitution of value, leaves plenty of room for debate among those who would emphasize either the subjectivist or objectivist side of the interaction at the expense of the other (Brightman 1962).

For example, extreme *subjectivism* holds that value depends entirely on the nature of subjective experience (Perry 1954; see Frondizi 1971: 51). Colloquially, those who adopt this view claim, with Protagoras, that "man is the measure of all things" (Hare 1982: 5); that "de gustibus non est disputandum" or "there is no arguing in matters of taste" (Frondizi 1971: 17); or that "beauty is in the eye of the beholder" (Frondizi 1971: 40; Nozick 1981: 400). In marketing, the foremost disciple of this viewpoint has been Levitt (1960), whose *customer orientation* assumes that a product has value only if it pleases some customer – in other words, that customers and no one else are the final arbiters of consumer value (Gale 1994: 46, 71).

By contrast, extreme *objectivism* holds that value resides in the object itself as one of its properties (Osborne 1933: 93; Lewis 1946: 434; Lee 1957: 185; Hall 1961: 179; Brightman 1962: 31; Loring 1966: 17; Hartman 1967: 42). Such philosophers argue that value is present in the relevant object whether anyone happens to recognize it or not (Osborne 1933: 78; Brightman 1962: 33; Frondizi 1971: 20). For example, Tuchman (1980: 39) viewed "quality" as "something inherent in a given work"; Osborne (1933: 124) contended that "beauty" is "a formal property of [the] beautiful"; and Adler (1981: 117) described "admirable beauty" as "objective, not subjective." In marketing, the objectivist orientation typifies those who pursue the oft-criticized *product orientation* (Levitt 1960) in assuming that – by virtue of certain resources, skills, or manufacturing efficiencies – they have managed to put value into their offerings. Along similar lines, classical economists as well as Karl Marx subscribed to a *labor theory of value* according to which the value of an object depends on the amount of work invested in producing it. This sort of extreme objectivism invites rather easy refutation via such examples as tearing a sheet of paper to shreds or breaking a piece of chalk to bits. In these cases, one invests ever greater amounts of labor in the product while simultaneously destroying its value.

A more reasonable, intermediate position suggests that value involves an interaction between some subject and an object (Parker 1957: 34; Morris 1964: 18; Frondizi 1971: 26; Woodruff and Gardial 1996: 54). Essentially, this inter-actionist perspective maintains that value depends on the characteristics of some physical or mental object but cannot occur without the involvement of some subject who appreciates these characteristics (Pepper 1958: 402; Frondizi 1971: 146). In this light, recall the old conundrum about the tree that falls in the forest without anyone there to hear it. We might argue that the tree makes a noise (objectively emitted) but no sound (subjectively experienced). However, the point of the interactionist view of value is that – whether the tree does or does not make a noise or sound – that noise or sound can have no value if there is no one there to experience it. Along similar lines, the economist Alfred Marshall compared the subjective and objective aspects of value to the two blades in a pair of scissors (Fallon 1971: 47): You need both, working together, to get results. A single blade, working alone, is like the sound of one hand clapping.

## 2 Consumer value is relativistic

By *relativistic*, I mean that consumer value is (a) *comparative* (involving prefer-ences among objects); (b) *personal* (varying across people); and (c) *situational* (specific to the context).

(a) Value is *comparative* in that we can state the value of one object only in reference to that of another object as evaluated by the same individual. In other words legitimate value judgments involve relative preferences among objects for a given person rather than utility comparisons among people (Lewis 1946: 5, 543; Hilliard 1950: 57; Frondizi 1971: 11; Laudan 1977: 120; Alicke 1983: 20; Hyde 1983: 60; Pettit 1983: 32). *Inter*personal utility comparisons of the form "I like ice cream better than you like ice cream" are *illegitimate* (Luce and Raiffa 1957; Becker and McClintock 1967; Bass and Wilkie 1973). Rather, *legitimate* value statements involve intrapersonal comparisons among different objects assessed by the *same individual* (Lamont 1955: 182). In other words, I can legitimately claim that "I like vanilla ice cream better than I like chocolate ice cream" (but not that I like any kind of ice cream better than you do). This contention that legitimate value statements involve comparisons among objects provides fuel for comedy, as in the work of the New Yorker cartoonist who suggested that we should stop worrying about whether Coke is better than Pepsi and admit that beer is better than both. In other words, changing the set of objects compared (Coke versus Pepsi as opposed to cola versus beer) changes our conclusions about whether the value of a given object (say, Coke) is high or low. Thus, as often stated by the gurus of managerial strategy, customer value must be assessed and stated as relative to the relevant competition (Gale 1994: 13, 183; Woodruff and Gardial 1996: 124, 262).

(b) Value is *personal* in the sense that it varies from one individual to another (Lewis 1946: 421; Hilliard 1950: 168; Von Wright 1963: 104). A subjectivist is necessarily committed to this personal relativity of value (Osborne 1933: 61; e.g., Parker 1957: 237). But even an objectivist may make room for a difference in objective value from one evaluator to the next (Bond 1983: 56–61, 97). Thus, subjectively, I may validly claim to like vanilla better than chocolate ice cream even while you claim with equal validity to like chocolate better than vanilla. Or, objectively, a particular medicine might have value to you as a cure for some ailment, but not to me because I am allergic to it. Thus, the personal relativity of value prompts wide agreement among axiologists with both subjectivist and objectivist inclinations. Colloquially, we agree that "one man's meat is another man's poison" (Lewis 1946: 526). Further, we should note that this personal relativity of consumer value accounts for why the world needs marketing in the first place. Specifically, a First Principle of Marketing is that *customers differ*. Such differences in valuations lie at the heart of market segmentation. Thus, the personal relativity of consumer value commands our attention as marketers, shapes the logic of *market segmentation*, and thereby holds the key to marketing effectiveness. If consumer value is the foundation for all marketing, as argued earlier, then its personal relativity is the fundamental basis for marketing successfully.

(c) Further, consumer value is *situational* in that it depends on the context in which the evaluative judgment is made (Lewis 1946: 426; Hilliard 1950: 207; Morris 1964: 41; Von Wright 1963: 13). This situation-specific nature of value occurs because the standards on which evaluative judgments hinge tend to be context-dependent, changing from one set of circumstances or one time frame or one location to another (Taylor 1961: 11). To a marketer, this means that preference functions, which relate liking to product attributes, tend to vary from moment to moment and from place to place (Woodruff and Gardial 1996: 59). For example, on a cold winter's morning I might think nothing tastes better than a nice hot cup of Earl Grey tea, whereas on a sweltering summer afternoon I might favor a frosty glass of iced Snapple. In this case, my preference function for the temperature of tea is conditional on the weather. One could represent the context-based nature of my preferences by means of situation-specific ideal points (Holbrook 1984). When applied to the aforementioned concept of the market space, such refinements could have further implications for segment-targeted situationally sensitive marketing strategy.

## 3   Consumer value is preferential

Perhaps the most fundamental point we can make about the nature of consumer value – more fundamental even than those points made thus far – is that it embodies a *preference* judgment (Lamont 1955: 189; Morris 1956: 187, 1964: 17; Rokeach 1973: 9). Among axiologists, this general focus on preference typifies the so-called "interest theory of value" (Perry 1954: 2–7; also, Alicke 1983).

As also noted by many axiologists (Moore 1957: 10; Parker 1957: 27; Hall 1961: 164; Frankena 1967: 229), the general concept of preference embraces a wide variety of value-related terms prominent in various disciplines and including (but not limited to) such nomenclature as *affect* (pleasing vs. displeasing), *attitude* (like vs. dislike), *evaluation* (good vs. bad), *predisposition* (favorable vs. unfavorable), *opinion* (pro vs. con), *response tendency* (approach vs. avoid), or *valence* (positive vs. negative). What all such expressions of value share in common is that they represent a unidimensional index of preference order (Lamont 1955: 189; Brandt 1967: 24).

Further, such preference assessments all refer to value (singular) as opposed to values (plural), raising a question as to whether there is a difference between the singular and plural concepts. Indeed, it appears that we generally use the former (value, singular) to designate the *outcome of an evaluative judgment* (that is, the *summary valuation*), whereas the latter (value*s*, plural) typically refers to the *standards* (Taylor 1961; Kahle and Timmer 1983), *rules* (Arrow 1967), *criteria* (Baylis 1958; Pepper 1958; Rokeach 1973), *norms* (Pepper 1958), *goals* (Veroff 1983), or *ideals* (Abbott 1955; Pepper 1958; Cowan 1964; Hartman 1967) on the basis of which evaluative judgments get made (that is, the underlying *evaluative criteria*).

Among axiologists, Taylor (1961) has been especially careful in spelling out the difference between value-as-singular (a preferential judgment) and values-as-plural (the relevant criteria on which such a summary judgment rests). Accordingly, notice that our focus here on consumer value (singular) differs substantially from that which deals with various types of values (VALS, LOV, AIO, and other types of psychographically oriented lifestyle research) (Rokeach 1973; Kahle 1983). The latter focus raises issues concerning individual differ-ences due to personality, education, or culture that – however interesting in their own right – are not of direct concern to the questions pursued here concerning the nature of consumer value (singular). (However, issues concerning individual differences will resurface in later chapters where the effects of personality, education, culture, and other customer characteristics become relevant.)

## 4   Consumer value is an experience

Finally, by *experience*, I mean that consumer value resides *not* in the product purchased, *not* in the brand chosen, *not* in the object possessed, but *rather* in the *consumption experience(s)* derived therefrom (Holbrook and Hirschman 1982; Woodruff and Gardial 1996: 55). This claim is critical to my own line of research

(Holbrook and Hirschman 1982), is inherent in the concept of an interactive relativistic preference (Moore 1957: 10), and has received support from any number of philosophically inclined thinkers (Lewis 1946: 387; Hilliard 1950: 92; Abbott 1955: 40; Parker 1957: 6; Baylis 1958: 490; Taylor 1961: 26; Mukerjee 1964: 108). In essence, the argument in this direction boils down to the proposition that all *products* provide *services* in their capacity to create need- or want-satisfying *experiences* (Morris 1941: 136). In this sense, all marketing is "services marketing." This places the role of experience at a central position in the creation of consumer value. As articulated long ago by Abbott (1955: 40):

> The thesis . . . may be stated quite simply. What people really desire are not products but satisfying *experiences*. Experiences are attained through activities. In order that activities may be carried out, physical objects or the services of human beings are usually needed. . . . People want products because they want the experience-bringing services which they hope the products will render.

## *Summary*

In sum, the treatment of consumer value developed herein is *radical*, but only in the sense that a radish is a "radical" plant. Specifically, it has *roots*. It is firmly *grounded* in axiology. It *springs* from a century's tradition of economic theory. And it *flowers* in a concept of value that offers insights to current marketing thought. When we say that consumer value is an *interactive relativistic preference experience*, we mean that the relationship of consumers to products (subjects to objects) operates relativistically (depending on relevant comparisons, varying between people, changing among situations) to determine preferences that lie at the heart of the consumption experience. In this sense, prescriptively as well as descriptively, Consumer Value shapes the design of Marketing Strategy.

## *The types of consumer value*

The preceding discussion describes a conceptualization intended to capture the *nature* of consumer value, but says little about differences that occur among the various *types* of value to be found in consumption experiences. In the latter connection, I propose a *framework* designed to categorize or classify the various *types of value in the consumption experience* – that is, a Typology of Consumer Value. This framework, which serves as the basis for the structure of the present volume, reflects *three key dimensions* of consumer value: (1) Extrinsic versus intrinsic value; (2) Self-oriented versus other-oriented value; and (3) Active versus reactive value. I shall now explain each in turn. For clarity, they are presented as simple dichotomies, though one can and should envision a set of continua running, in each case, from one extreme to the other with various gradations in between.

## 1 Extrinsic versus intrinsic value

*Extrinsic* value pertains to a means–end relationship wherein consumption is prized for its functional, utilitarian, or banausic instrumentality in serving as a means to accomplishing some further purpose, aim, goal, or objective (Parsons 1937: 121; Hilliard 1950: 45, 120; Lamont 1955: 88; Diesing 1962: 62; Von Wright 1963: 10, 20; Bond 1983: 20). Obvious examples would include a hammer, a drill, a screwdriver, or some other tool – valued not for itself but for its power to drive in a nail, to open up a hole, to screw in a screw, or to play some comparable instrumental role. Similarly, most of us prize money primarily as a means to the accomplishment of goals viewed as desirable – buying a newspaper, paying for a meal, or purchasing an automobile.

By contrast, *intrinsic* value occurs when some consumption experience is appreciated as an end in itself – for its own sake – as self-justifying, ludic, or autotelic (Baylis 1958: 491; Pepper 1958: 309; Von Wright 1963: 5; Frankena 1967: 231; Bond 1983: 98–108). A day at the beach serves little useful purpose beyond an enjoyment of the experience itself. Listening to Bruckner's Seventh Symphony achieves no end beyond the experience appreciated for its own sake. In the latter connection, axiologists are adamant on the point that *only an experience* – and *not* some object – can be *appreciated as an end in itself* (Lewis 1946: 414; Abbott 1955: 40; Taylor 1961: 23). Hence, only a consumption experience can confer intrinsic value. The object serving as the means to such an experience – for example, the bus that takes us to the beach or the ticket that gains us admission to the Bruckner concert – can, at best, possess only extrinsic value as the means to some desired experiential end-in-itself. (Besides those already referenced, see Osborne 1933; Perry 1954; Lee 1957; Brightman 1962; Frankena 1962, 1967; Loring 1966; Brandt 1967; Olson 1967; Fallon 1971; Rokeach 1973; Deci 1975; Nozick 1982.)

## 2 Self-oriented versus other-oriented value

A further dimension or distinction – namely, that between *self-oriented* and *other-oriented* value – has also prompted a broad consensus among axiologists and others concerned with the theory of value (see Buber 1923; Parsons 1937, 1951; Fromm 1941; Riesman 1950; Lamont 1951; Morris 1956, 1964; Parker 1957; Brandt 1967; Ladd 1967; Rokeach 1973; Siegel 1981; Hyde 1983; Kahle 1983; Von Wright 1983; and especially Mukerjee 1964). Indeed, it might be fair to say that, among those mentioned here, this dimension commands the greatest agreement.

Value is *self-oriented* (for myself) when I prize some aspect of consumption selfishly or prudently for *my own* sake, for how *I* react to it, or for the effect it has on *me*. For example, my sweater has value at least partly because it keeps me warm. My IBM Aptiva personal computer has value because it helps me process words, analyze data, and create pretty pictures. My collection of 1950s west-coast jazz recordings has value because – despite protests from my neighbors (for whom it has *dis*value) – it provides me with enjoyable listening experiences. In short, though my sweater, computer, or record collection may also provide further types of value involving others, one primary source of value derived from these objects lies in their capacities to contribute to *my own* consumption experiences.

Conversely, *other-oriented* value looks beyond the self to someone or something else, where my consumption experience or the product on which it depends is valued for *their* sake, for how *they* react to it, or for the effect it has on *them*. Here, the "other(s)" in question could range from the more *micro* level (family, friends, colleagues) to an *intermediate* level (community, country, world) to the most *macro* level (the Cosmos, Mother Nature, the Deity). Or, at the most *micro* level of all and typical of certain Eastern religions as well as Freudian psychoanalysis, the "other" could refer to some inaccessible "inner self" or to some "unconscious" part of the mind with which one seeks to "get in touch." Clearly, many cases of consumer value refer to experiences oriented toward these relevant "others," large or small. For example, I might practice Transcendental Meditation in an effort to communicate with the "Inner Me" (which, however paradoxically, must be regarded as one form of "other"). I might purchase a Lexus for the sake of impressing my neighbors. I might give up the use of products in aerosol containers because I hope thereby to help save the planet. I might attend church in order to experience an ecstatic sense of spiritual union with the Deity. In all such cases, the primary source of value would be other-oriented rather than self-oriented.

### 3 Active versus reactive value

Value is *active* when it entails a physical or mental manipulation of some tangible or intangible object – that is, when it involves things *done by* a consumer *to* or *with* a product as part of some consumption experience. This active consumer value could involve the physical manipulation of a tangible object (driving a car); the mental manipulation of an intangible object (solving a crossword puzzle); the physical manipulation of an intangible object (taking a mind-altering or consciousness-expanding drug); or even the mental manipulation of a tangible object (telekinesis). All such cases involve something done *by* the subject *to* the object in that *I* act upon *it* or *I* move *it* (Diesing 1962).

Conversely, consumer value is *reactive* when it results from apprehending, appreciating, admiring, or otherwise responding to some object – that is, when it involves things *done by* a product *to* or *with* a consumer as part of some consumption experience. Here, rather than I (the subject) doing something to it (the object), the situation is reversed: *It* acts upon *me* or *it* moves *me* (Hall 1961). Such reactive responses might, for example, involve appreciatively examining an abstract expressionist painting; enthusiastically assessing a camera as high in quality; or rapturously opening oneself to a spiritual awakening.

The distinction or continuum between active and reactive value has appeared less frequently in the literature than those between intrinsic and extrinsic or between self- and other-oriented value. However, searching carefully, we do find an emphasis placed on the contrast between activity and passivity (Parker 1957: 92; also Pepper 1958; Rokeach 1973); between control and dependence or receptivity (Morris 1956, 1964: 22); between potency and lack thereof (Osgood *et al.* 1957); between dominating and being dominated (Mehrabian and Russell 1974); or between moving and being moved by (Harré and Secord 1973).

### The Typology of Consumer Value

By treating each of the potentially continuous dimensions just described as a simple dichotomy and combining these three dichotomies into a 2×2×2 cross-classification, we may produce the eight-celled *Typology of Consumer Value* that appears in Table 1. Each cell of this taxonomy represents a logically distinct *type* of value in the consumption experience (EFFICIENCY, EXCELLENCE, STATUS, ESTEEM, PLAY, AESTHETICS, ETHICS, and SPIRITUALITY) with key *examples* of each major type shown parenthetically (convenience, quality, success, reputation, fun, beauty, morality, ecstasy, and so on). Collectively, these eight categories provide the framework for the issues of concern to this book dealing comprehensively with the nature and types of consumer value. In other words, Table 1 presents a compact summary of the structure for the present volume.

*Table 1* A Typology of Consumer Value

|  |  | Extrinsic | Intrinsic |
| --- | --- | --- | --- |
| Self-oriented | Active | EFFICIENCY (O/I, Convenience) | PLAY (Fun) |
|  | Reactive | EXCELLENCE (Quality) | AESTHETICS (Beauty) |
| Other-oriented | Active | STATUS (Success, Impression Management) | ETHICS (Virtue, Justice, Morality) |
|  | Reactive | ESTEEM (Reputation, Materialism, Possessions) | SPIRITUALITY (Faith, Ecstasy, Sacredness, Magic) |

## Types of consumer value as topics for subsequent chapters

The Typology of Consumer Value just described suggests an outline for organizing the presentations in the chapters that follow. Their order reflects the structure implied by the typology – first, from top left (EFFICIENCY and

EXCELLENCE) to bottom left (STATUS and ESTEEM); then, from top right (PLAY and AESTHETICS) to bottom right (ETHICS and SPIRITUALITY). A brief summary of each focus follows, both from the viewpoint of the typological framework in general and from the more specific perspective of the particular chapter that appears in the main body of the text. Further details occupy the subsequent chapters that constitute the remainder of this book.

## *Chapter 1 – EFFICIENCY (O/I, Convenience)*

From the perspective of the present framework, efficiency involves extrinsic value that results from the active use of a product or consumption experience as a means to achieve some self-oriented purpose (Bond 1983: 42; also Lamont 1955). Obvious examples would include many of the objects that I typically carry around in my pockets such as keys to open my doors, Kleenex to blow my nose, and coins to get candy bars out of the vending machine.

Often, efficiency is measured as a ratio of outputs to inputs or an *O/I ratio* (Hilliard 1950; Pepper 1958: 312; Diesing 1962: 12). For example, we might assess the efficiency of an automobile as some ratio of miles traveled to gallons of gasoline expended. Or we might assess the value of a meal as the number of calories consumed per dollar spent. Frequently, however, the key example of efficiency that holds greatest interest for consumers might be viewed as *convenience* – in which case, the relevant O/I ratio has *time* as a denominator representing the key input of concern.

Obvious cases emphasizing the role of time as a key resource or input in the O/I ratio would include the "psychotemporal" value associated with "convenience foods" – which can hardly be viewed as appetizing, delicious, healthy, or nutritious, but which have the advantage of being extremely quick to fix, especially when a microwave oven is involved in their preparation. Along similar lines, "convenience stores" offer only the most narrow selections of merchandise, unappealing atmospherics, and surly service, but remain open during off-hours that suit people's hectic time schedules.

Further, though not necessarily obvious on the surface, many other examples of consumer value should be interpreted as cases of efficiency in general and convenience in particular by virtue of their relevance to time as the key resource input of interest. Thus, consumer credit could be viewed as a time-shifting device, allowing us to enjoy a consumption experience now but to pay for it later; for example, a charge card lets us dine today and cover the expense tomorrow; a mortgage lets us own a home this year and expend money over a period of subsequent years. Similarly, an ordinary refrigerator helps us economize on our use of time and therefore confers psychotemporal value based on convenience; unlike a caveman who dragged home a dinosaur and had to eat the whole thing right then and there before it spoiled, we can cut a side of beef into little pieces, store them in the freezer, and eat them when we are good and ready. Indeed, along related lines, the genius of Sony was to convince the US Supreme Court that a video cassette recorder is not so much a gadget for pirating copyrighted movies and other program content as a time-shifting device – something like a refrigerator for entertainment – that permits us to store material in a sort of inventory until we are ready to consume it.

One might expect that the convenience-enhancing value of such time-manipulating products would increase as economic conditions improve, as dual careers multiply, as job responsibilities escalate, and as we consequently find ourselves with more and more products to consume but less and less free time in which to consume them. Capitalizing on this trend and striving toward the veritable apotheosis of time-shifting convenience, McDonald's has recently introduced a chain of play centers where overworked parents can take their latch-key children for the purpose of spending some "quality time" with them. Here, the young ones visit a room filled with enticing toys, while their weary parents retreat to a quiet chamber where they can relax, watch their kids on closed-circuit television, and presumably drink lots and lots of McDonald's coffee to stay awake. If desired, mom or dad can relive this family event or share it with other loved ones by purchasing a videotape to commemorate the experience. Better yet, the stressed-out parent can economize even further on time by taking a nap during the actual play episode and viewing the whole thing later on a VCR set at fast-forward.

Relevant implications concerning the consumption of temporal resources and the time-dependent aspects of consumer value figure prominently in the work by France Leclerc, Bernd Schmitt, and their colleagues on decisions regarding the use of time, on time-related perceptions, and on experiences associated with time spent waiting in lines. In Chapter 1, Leclerc and Schmitt review this research stream and place it into the context of the value typology. Specifically, these authors report findings pertinent to the relativistic sense in which time-related decisions show a risk-averse tendency that contrasts with the risk-taking orientation of money-related decisions. They further show that time perceptions depend relativistically on the environmental situation, as when delays are experienced as more disturbing if they occur near the beginning or end of a service encounter. Finally, consistent with an argument that the time-related aspects of consumer value are not merely self-oriented in nature but also entail a significant other-oriented component, Leclerc and Schmitt show that intrusions into waiting lines prompt reactions associated with the violation of social norms – in other words, with a regard for others rather than with purely selfish or personal concerns.

### *Chapter 2 – EXCELLENCE (Quality)*

As conceived here, *excellence* involves a reactive appreciation of some object's or experience's potential ability to serve as an extrinsic means to some personal self-oriented end. In other words, in the case of excellence, one admires some object or prizes some experience for its capacity to accomplish some goal or to perform some function. Such a utilitarian emphasis on the appreciation of instrumentality relates closely to the concept of *satisfaction* based on a comparison of performance with expectations and appears to constitute the essence of what we mean by *quality* (Abbott 1955: 27; Tuchman 1980: 38; Bond 1983: 121; Pettijohn 1986; Garvin 1988: 50; Juran 1988; Zeithaml 1988: 3; Steenkamp 1989: 105; Zeithaml *et al.* 1990).

Elsewhere, I have addressed the nature of *quality* at some length (Holbrook and Corfman 1985). Here, I might summarize by suggesting that quality arises as a salient type of consumer value when I admire a product for its capacity to achieve some self-oriented want but do so *without* actually using it for that purpose – in other words, reactively rather than actively (as in the case of efficiency). Thus, I might value a knife – by virtue of its quality – because it is very sharp and, potentially, could do a good job of cutting; but I do not need to go out and slash something or someone with it in order reactively to appreciate this aspect of its quality. Along similar lines, I might appreciate the quality in a Ferrari knowing that, potentially, this car could accelerate from zero to 60 mph in 4.32 seconds flat; but I do not need to go out and break the traffic laws in order to value this aspect of its quality. In this spirit, a recent print advertisement for a Kenwood stereo amplifier bragged: "With this system, you could change the treble from your bathroom. We don't know why you would. But you could."

Clearly, as one type and a related example of consumer value, excellence in general and quality in particular are closely connected to the experience of customer satisfaction. Indeed, Rich Oliver – an acknowledged expert on satis-faction – has recently co-edited a book on *Service Quality* (with Roland Rust). In the context of excellence, his chapter for the present volume explores these themes in a degree of depth that only he could provide. Specifically, Chapter 2 extends his previous work to explore the excellence component of consumer value for its many interpretations. In this direction, the various meanings of value-as-excellence are studied, the temporal primacy of each concept is debated, and a network of consumption constructs containing value is proposed. In Chapter 2, Oliver concludes that consumption value involves a judgment of receipts compared to sacrifices and that the former properly includes such valued out-comes as excellence. Ultimately, Oliver constructs a network of value-related concepts that move hierarchically from a basic level (cost-based value) to an intermediate level (consumption satisfaction or value-based satisfaction) to a higher or more exalted level (extended value involving the quality of life).

### *Chapter 3 – STATUS (Success, Impression Management)*

As employed here, the term *status* designates the active manipulation of one's own consumption behavior as an extrinsic means toward the other-oriented end of achieving a favorable response from someone else. In the broadest sense, such status-directed value can be viewed as essentially *political* in nature (Nozick 1981: 503), where "politics" involves the adoption of suitable means aimed at the accomplishment of interpersonal objectives (Perry 1954). In other words, politically, we seek status by adjusting our consumption in a manner that affects those whom we wish to influence.

As an example, consider the case of *impression management* in which I consume products or engage in consumption experiences so as to project the sort of image I wish to create. In other words, I consume so as to communicate about myself to others in ways that contribute to my *success*. In this direction, I might choose clothing that makes a fashion statement intended to impress a job interviewer. In short, I might *dress for success*. Indeed, I might choose not only my wardrobe but my briefcase, eye glasses, fountain pen, and aftershave or cologne with an eye toward conveying a favorable image to my business associates. In the latter connection, recent research has demonstrated the effect of one's fragrance on one's perceived competence and aggressiveness (Fiore and Kim 1997). A floral scent suggests weakness and passivity. Thus, one should *not* wear "White Shoulders" perfume to one's next job interview with an investment-banking firm. In other words, one should be sure to *smell for success*.

In sum, consumers choose the products they consume and the consumption experiences they pursue, in part, as a set of *symbols* intended to construct a persona that achieves *success* in the form of *status* in the eyes of others. Addressing this theme of *impression management*, for many years, Mike Solomon has employed insights from symbolic interactionism and other disciplinary orientations to elucidate the role of symbolic consumption and to emphasize the importance of product constellations as aspects of symbolically oriented consumer behavior. His chapter for the present volume develops these themes in the context of status-oriented consumption. Specifically, Chapter 3 treats status as an ongoing process of social construction, whereby an individual is motivated to identify a desirable location or locations in the social nexus and to engage in consumption activities that will support this placement. In this sense, status involves a positioning strategy for people. Here, status-as-value is viewed as a multiple-stage process of (1) determining the social persona(e) one can or should adopt (status definition); (2) acquiring products or pursuing experiences instrumental to attaining that goal (status seeking); and (3) evaluating the efficacy of that consumption in service of the chosen persona(e) (status validation).

## *Chapter 4 – ESTEEM (Reputation, Materialism, Possessions)*

Of all the distinctions in the Typology of Consumer Value, that between *status* (Chapter 3) and *esteem* (Chapter 4) is the most difficult to articulate. Indeed, it appears clear that, as defined here, status and esteem are intimately interrelated with only the fuzziest demarcation lying in a grey area somewhere in between. Specifically, I envision esteem as the reactive counterpart to status in that *esteem* tends to result from a somewhat passive ownership of *possessions* appreciated as a means to building one's *reputation* with others. In other words, under the heading of esteem-as-value, I reactively appreciate my own consumption or lifestyle in a somewhat passive way as a potential extrinsic means to enhancing my other-oriented public image.

As discussed by axiologists (Bond 1983: 161) and economists (Scitovsky 1976: 115–20), this reactive side of extrinsically motivated other-oriented value bears a close resemblance to the concept of *conspicuous consumption* (Veblen 1899) as up-dated by the so-called *demonstration effect* (Duesenberry 1949). Being reactive rather than active in nature, such a penchant might manifest itself in the form of a personality trait such as *materialism* – that is, an individual characteristic that leans toward the celebrative contemplation of one's own *possessions* viewed collectively as an indicant of one's own prestige or as an index of one's own social position. Of course, the "esteem" in question could also take the form of *self*-esteem, in which case the "other" of interest would be some sort of "inner self" that one is concerned with impressing favorably.

Examples of such esteem-as-value would properly include lifestyle-defining patterns of consumption – mutually reinforcing combinations of products owned and experiences enjoyed – or "taste cultures" as they are sometimes called. For example, if we had a beautifully manicured lawn around our house in the country (which we do not), the sole satisfaction I can imagine deriving therefrom would result from the gratification of keeping up with the neighbors – a pleasure that I could contemplate while rocking on the front porch, if we had a rocker or a front porch (which we also do not). Similarly, if we had a white picket fence around our house (also not true), it might cohere with the pattern of ownership implied by the beautiful lawn – as might the Mercedes parked in our driveway (alas, also not the case). Along similar lines, some people (again, not we) enjoy the ownership of expensive art objects or other collectibles neither because they are pleasing to one's aesthetic sensibilities nor because they embody sacred spiritual meanings but rather because they imply a standard of living, a materialistic inclination toward owning prestigious possessions, consistent with an elite reputation in the community or an enhancement of self-respect (still keeping in mind that the "self" can, in this case, also be regarded as an "other" that one wishes to impress).

In part, the contrast between (reactive) esteem and (active) status parallels the difference between two distinct styles of self-presentation that Slama and Wolfe (1997) refer to as "getting along" and "getting ahead" (Wolfe *et al.* 1986; Celuch and Slama 1995). The former involves a self-protective tendency toward conforming; the latter entails an acquisitive manipulation intended to influence others. Thus, one is more reactive, the other more active in nature: "Conformity and/or compliance often suffice for getting along; but in order to get ahead, one has to be more assertive, acquisitive, or manipulative" (Slama and Wolfe 1997: 2).

The difficult task of clarifying such points, while preserving the admittedly fuzzy distinction between status and esteem, falls to Marsha Richins, who has previously written with great conviction on the undesirable social consequences of such acquisitive preoccupations and who has done extensive empirical work on developing indices for the measurement of materialism. In Chapter 4, Richins begins with a discussion of how materialism fits into the Typology of Consumer Value and then focuses on the role of esteem, whereby possessions shape and/ or reflect a person's identity and thereby provide the consumer with a positive sense of self. Clearly, both cultural and personal factors influence the extent to which material possessions play this role. In particular, the individual characteristic of other-directedness appears closely related to the maintenance of a possessions-based sense of identity. Accordingly, Chapter 4 further explores the relationship between other-directedness, materialism, and the ownership-oriented construction of a self-image.

## Chapter 5 – PLAY (Fun)

In turning to *play*, we pursue a major shift from the left- to the right-hand side of the Typology of Consumer Value. Specifically, we recognize the crucial but often overlooked distinction between extrinsic and intrinsic value. Efficiency, Excellence, Status, and Esteem exemplify the former; Play, Aesthetics, Ethics, and Spirituality represent the latter. And, in my view, this contrast is the aspect of the typology to which we must attend with the greatest care.

As a self-oriented experience – actively sought and enjoyed for its own sake – *play* typically involves having *fun* and thereby characterizes the intrinsically motivated side of the familiar distinction often made between work and *leisure* (Huizinga 1938: 27; Dearden 1967: 84; Stephenson 1967: 192; Berlyne 1969: 840; Bond 1983: 142). For at least a century, foremost among the characteristics of play, axiologists have recognized its nature as an experience pursued as an end in itself (Santayana 1896: 19). To this, we must add its self-oriented focus (Stephenson 1967: 192; Bond 1983: 113) and its active nature associated with the display of what is variously called "competence" (White 1959), "mastery" (Csikszentmihalyi 1975), "galumphing" (Miller 1973), or "triumph" (Pepper 1958).

For example, when I "play" the piano on a Sunday afternoon – actively engaged in an experience pursued for the sake of my own pleasure (certainly not that of the neighbors, my family, or even the cat, all of whom tend to complain vociferously if the concertizing continues for longer than a few minutes) – I clearly engage in a leisure activity valued for the fun of it. By contrast, while living at Claremont Avenue on the Upper West Side of New York City next door to the Juilliard School of Music, we once inhabited an apartment one floor below that of the celebrated classical pianist Mischa Dichter. This gifted virtuoso had just won a prestigious piano competition and was busily preparing for his debut with the New York Philharmonic under the baton of Leonard Bernstein. Toward this end, Dichter had set himself the task of perfecting his performance of Rachmaninoff's "Variations on a Theme by Paganini." With a mind-boggling devotion to this project, he found it necessary to practice that particular piece, day in and day out, for roughly twelve hours at a time. Suffice it to say that, by the end of six months, I knew Rocky's Variations like the back of my own hand and that, in the meantime, I had built a healthy respect for Dichter's powers of persistence. One could safely characterize his experience as one of intense work rather than leisure; as a utilitarian quest for efficiency in hitting the maximum number of right notes with the minimum frequency of mistakes; or as the quintessence of instrumentality as opposed to fun. (Given that I had myself just embarked upon a very difficult course of study in a master's degree program, a description of my own neighborly experience of value would require the use of several expletives. But, fortunately, that's another story.)

Comparable examples of the difference between efficiency and play, between instrumentality and fun, or between work and leisure abound in our everyday experience. If I shoot a few baskets on Saturday afternoon with my kid, I'm having fun; if Patrick Ewing shoots a few baskets on Saturday afternoon with the New York Knicks at Madison Square Garden, as he so often tells reporters, he is "getting the job done." If I hit some tennis balls (mostly over the fence) with my wife on the weekend, I am engaging in a leisure activity; if Pete Sampras battles Michael Chang for the men's championship at the US Open or Wimbledon, he is working hard. If someone more courageous than I engages in skydiving just for the sport of it, that person does something playful; when the US Marines parachute into enemy territory, they are at war.

Recalling my Mischa Dichter example, the gifted jazz guitarist Stanley Jordan recently emerged from a four-year period of self-imposed exile that hinged on exactly the contrast of present concern. As he explained to a reporter for the *New York Times*,

> The main reason I play isn't for my work but because music is essential, like a spiritual food. . . . I got to the point that I was so caught up in obligations in my career that it started to feel like a job. I wanted to get away from the music business and remember why I really play. . . . When I compare the music on this record to the last couple of albums before this, I hear more joy in the music.
>
> (Rule 1994: C24)

As a contributor to the present volume, Kent Grayson has studied aspects of play as both manifest and metaphorical components of consumer behavior and marketing research. Along these lines, with John Deighton, he has also chaired a special topic session on play at the 1994 conference of the Association for Consumer Research and has written a definitive analysis of play as opposed to seduction in the shaping of consumer behavior for the *Journal of Consumer Research*. In Chapter 5 on the dangers and opportunities of playful consumption, Grayson raises some fundamental questions similar to those just voiced and proceeds to argue that a key characteristic of play involves the influence of rules. Here, he suggests that play-as-value can be attained either by following rules or by challenging them. If a consumer follows rules set by the marketer, the consumption experience becomes predictable with satisfaction relatively easy to achieve. By contrast, if a consumer pursues playful value by challenging rules set by the marketer, various uncertainties or breakdowns may occur. Grayson explores a number of ways in which consumers may gain value in the following or challenging of rules and addresses strategies by which marketers can cope with such challenges in the general context of consumption-oriented playfulness.

### *Chapter 6 – AESTHETICS (Beauty)*

On the reactive side of play, *aesthetics* refers to an appreciation of some consumption experience valued intrinsically as a self-oriented end in itself (Perry

1954; Hampshire 1982). As one type of aesthetic value, the experience of *beauty* depends on a self-oriented perspective (Hilliard 1950: 284; Morris 1956: 172; Von Wright 1963: 73) and is reactive in nature (Von Wright 1963: 64, 78). However, the hallmark of aesthetic value in general or beauty in particular is that it is enjoyed purely for its own sake – as a self-justifying, ludic, or autotelic form of intrinsic value – without regard to any further practical purpose that it might serve as a means to any other end (Perry 1954; Lee 1957; see Holbrook and Zirlin 1985).

This view of aesthetic experience as hinging on intrinsic value as an end in itself can be traced back to the work of Shaftesbury in 1709 (Beardsley 1967), but found its most influential exposition via Immanuel Kant's treatment of "dis- interestedness" in his *Critique of Judgment* from 1790 (Rader 1979: 331). Kant's formulation received further support from Bullough (1912) through the concept of "psychical distance" wherein the essence of aesthetic appreciation lies in a sort of detachment from worldly concerns with practicality. This strong emphasis on the role of disinterest, distance, or detachment from utilitarian concerns – in short, intrinsic value appreciated for its own sake rather than for some extrinsic purpose – has played a dominant role in axiological discussions of aesthetics ever since (Lewis 1946: 438; Hilliard 1950: 276; Hospers 1967: 36; Hampshire 1982: 119, 244; see also Perry 1954; Lee 1957; Olscamp 1965; Coleman 1966; McGregor 1974; Iseminger 1981; Budd 1983).

Emphatically, then, my aesthetic appreciation for a work of art has nothing to do with any practical purpose that the artwork might serve as a means to some other end beyond the consumption experience itself valued for its own sake. Clearly, a person *could* prize an artwork by virtue of some instrumental function that it might perform (Budd 1983: 153). For example, if taken outside during a rain storm, an oil painting by Rembrandt might serve quite efficiently as a sort of impromptu umbrella. Or a gleaming stainless steel sculpture by Jean Arp might make an excellent doorstop. But the moment that one used or admired an artwork for such utilitarian reasons, the relevant type of consumer value would cease being aesthetic (e.g., beauty) and would become efficiency (e.g., convenience) or excellence (e.g., quality) instead (Hartman 1967: 114).

As one example of a product associated with aesthetics along with other aspects of consumer value, *fashion* is often prized for the beauty of its *product design* – that is, on the grounds of a pleasing appearance – as well as for (say) the ability of clothes to keep us warm (efficiency), the role of self-decoration in conveying the impression of prestige (status), or the rules of decorum that involve covering oneself up for ethical reasons (virtue). In this connection, as at the conferences of the Association for Consumer Research in 1993 and 1994, Janet Wagner has frequently focused on the aesthetic aspects of product design in general and on the links between beauty and fashion in particular. In Chapter 6, she applies this expertise to a consideration of how these themes fit into our broader concern with the nature and types of consumer value. Specifically, Wagner suggests that, in the consumption experience, aesthetic value appears in its purest form in the case of the *fine arts* – music, dance, painting, sculpture, and poetry – through the experience of beauty. However, in the case of an *applied art* such as product design – appliances, furniture, automobiles, and (of course) clothing – the role of aesthetic value becomes more problematic. Specifically, with respect to fashion, Wagner suggests that beauty depends on a consumer's perception of a form that not only is attractive, but that also meets some set of utilitarian and social needs or wants. Hence, in her view, the value of fashion objects is both intrinsic and extrinsic, both self- and other-oriented, and both reactive and active in nature.

## *Chapter 7 – ETHICS (Virtue, Justice, and Morality)*

The active and other-oriented pursuit of *ethics* involves doing something for the sake of others – that is, with a concern for how it will affect them or how they will react to it – where such consumption experiences are valued for their own sake as ends in themselves (Von Wright 1963: 128, 1983: 80; Nozick 1981: 451; Alicke 1983: 4). Thus, axiologists agree on the other-oriented aspects of ethics (Lewis 1946: 546; Hilliard 1950: 246, 258; Morris 1956: 171; Parker 1957: 52, 243; Von Wright 1963: 119, 182; Frankena 1973: 15, 42); on the active nature of ethical conduct (Lewis 1946: 439, 482; Lamont 1955: 310; Mukerjee 1964: 48; Frankena 1973: 63; Hampshire 1982: 90); and, above all, on the quintessential nature of ethics as a form of intrinsic value (Parker 1957: 79; Frankena 1973: 87; see also Perry 1954; Brightman 1962; Von Wright 1963; Harré and Secord 1973; Bond 1983). Colloquially, in the latter connection, we say that "virtue is its own reward" (Parker 1957: 272; Frankena 1973: 94; Scruton 1981: 118).

Elsewhere (Holbrook 1994b), I have taken pains to distinguish among the *natural* as concerned with a person's *character* (governed by some disposition or personality trait); the *right* as dictated by *deontology* (determined by various principles embodied in various rules, laws, duties, or maxims); and the *good* as reflected by *teleology* (concerned with the consequences or results of behaving in a certain way). I have further suggested that *virtue, justice,* and *morality* involve various sorts of matches or correspondences between the natural, the right, and the good. Specifically, in the case of a match between the natural and the right, we speak of *virtue* – that is, the tendency for an individual's character to lead toward actions that follow the laws, obey the rules, or fulfill prescribed duties. When the right aligns with the good, we pronounce in favor of *justice* – that is, a situation in which the laws that govern society tend to produce beneficent consequences. And when a person's nature corresponds with the good, we proclaim the existence of *morality* – that is, the tendency of that person's character to work toward outcomes that enhance the welfare of others.

For the reasons just mentioned, the Typology of Consumer Value includes *virtue, justice,* and *morality* as key examples under the general heading of *ethics.* Virtue might appear among consumers whose conscience habitually leads them to obey the traffic regulations even when no one is looking; some people refrain from crossing against the "No Walk" sign even in the middle of the night when there is not another person or vehicle for miles around – in which case, if nothing else, they presumably rack up points for entry into heaven. Justice might occur when the court system actually manages to convict the guilty or to protect the innocent – which presumably happened in either the criminal or the civil version of the O. J. Simpson trial, depending on your point of view. Morality shines forth when an individual tends by temperament to engage in selfless devotion to the cause of helping others – which undoubtedly explains why some citizens un-hesitatingly give money to beggars even though their generosity might encourage the recipients to keep on begging.

Here, as elsewhere, we must remember that a consumption experience involving some action toward others which appears to confer ethical value by virtue of its intrinsic motivation might instead stem from disguised or hidden extrinsic purposes that, if known, would remove it from the sphere of ethical value. For example, if a person donates blood to the Red Cross for the pleasure of saving lives, bestows a generous financial gift upon Yale University in order to further the cause of learning, or warmly embraces a child for the sake of bonding in a loving parental relationship, few would deny that the relevant other-oriented actions involve the experience of ethical value. However, the story would change completely if one donates blood for the satisfaction of receiving grateful recog-nition, bestows a gift in order to get a son or daughter into college, or kisses babies for the sake of winning votes in an election. All such examples have lost the essence of virtue as its own reward and instead involve aspects of consumer value associated with efficiency or status. Put differently, the same identical behavior (donating, bestowing, embracing) may have the intrinsically motivated other-oriented character of ethical action for one consumer but the extrinsically motivated character of efficiency or status for another, *depending* on whether the relevant consumption experience is valued as a means to some other end (extrinsic value) or as an end in itself (intrinsic and therefore ethical value).

In his extensive work on ethics in marketing and consumer behavior, Craig Smith has literally "written the books" on *Morality and the Market* and on *Ethics in Marketing* (with John Quelch). He is therefore uniquely well-situated to comment on these issues as they relate to the Typology of Consumer Value. In Chapter 7, Smith examines ethics as a consumer value, its relationship to the other of types consumer value, and its place in the typological framework as a whole. In particular, Smith pursues a distinction between consumption experiences that have entirely altruistic motivations and those experiences that, in addition, have a less selfless or more extrinsically motivated aspect. Illustrations of ethics as a type of consumer value are provided, including the consumption of charity services and participation in consumer boycotts. Suggestions are also made for future research that may benefit from the integration provided by the overarching typological framework.

## Chapter 8 – SPIRITUALITY (Faith, Ecstasy, Sacredness, Magic)

As a more reactive counterpart to ethics, *spirituality* entails an intrinsically motivated acceptance, adoption, appreciation, admiration, or adoration of an Other where this "Other" may constitute some Divine Power, some Cosmic

Force, some Mystical Entity, or even some otherwise inaccessible Inner Being and where such an experience is sought not as a means to an ulterior end but rather as an end in itself prized for its own sake. Here, the reactive as opposed to active nature of *spirituality* corresponds to the oft-noted distinction between *faith* (sacred experience) and *works* (good deeds). The former involves a receptive form of devotion or worship (reactive other-oriented intrinsic value); the latter entails some manipulative intervention, thereby placing it under our category of ethics (active other-oriented intrinsic value). In this connection, *faith* is viewed as involving an orientation toward some Other in the form of God, a Divine Spirit, or a Cosmic Force (Parker 1957: 20), whereas *ecstasy* involves a mystical disappearance of the self–other dichotomy in a manner that seems to merge the self with the Other, to permit one to lose oneself in the Other, or to achieve a union with the Other and that thereby produces a sense of exaltation or rapture (Perry 1954: 488; Frondizi 1971: 118). Further, axiologists agree that – via such sacred or magical experiences – spiritual value is pursued for its own sake as an end in itself (Perry 1954: 464; Pepper 1958: 585; Brightman 1962; Mukerjee 1964: 86; Hartman 1967: 116).

Notice that some experiences that would appear as spiritual under one guise might take on other aspects of consumer value under different scenarios. For example, consider the role of prayer. If one pursues prayer or meditation as a vehicle for adoring the Deity, for absorbing some source of Cosmic Energy, or for achieving union with one's Inner Self, where such an experience is valued for its own sake as an end in itself, clearly the relevant type of consumer value is spiritual in nature – that is, faithful, ecstatic, sacred, or magical. By contrast, if one prays or meditates for the purpose of asking for favors or accomplishing some ulterior purpose, then one's prayer or meditation takes on aspects of value associated with status or efficiency. Thus, Janis Joplin's song asking "O, Lord, won't you buy me a Mercedes Benz" exemplifies the use of prayer in the pursuit of success. The practice of meditation for the sake of achieving mental health or physical well-being constitutes a form of extrinsically motivated self-oriented action that some believers regard as more efficient than (say) conventional medicine.

Clearly, as broadly conceptualized here, many forms of consumption experiences are imbued with aspects of spirituality in the form of faith, ecstasy, sacredness, or magic. These and other aspects of numinous consumption have served as unifying themes in recent studies by Stephen Brown. As the premier literary stylist in marketing and consumer research – without equal in our discipline as a story teller and raconteur – Brown commands our attention whenever, wherever, and on whatever topic he chooses to speak or write. In Chapter 8, he turns his inimitable wit and insights toward the exploration of themes related to spirituality in general and to the numinous aspects of shopping in particular. Characteristic of Brown is his desire, at every turn, to surprise the reader as well as the editor. In the latter direction, Chapter 8 suggests that the value of the Typology of Consumer Value derives from its apophatic character – that is, from its helpfulness in directing our attention to its own valuelessness. After this rather jolting start – to which I shall return for further discussion in the "Conclusions" – Brown settles down to a penetrating account of essays written by his students on the subject of their shopping experiences. As he shows in depth, it turns out that these shopping experiences ring with meanings that might be described as spiritual in nature.

## Envoi

This introductory overview has suggested that the nature and types of consumer value can best be understood by placing them in a context that juxtaposes their differences and similarities so as to shed light on their underlying structure. Toward this end, I have proposed a Typology of Consumer Value to provide a general framework that serves to integrate contributions on specific topics by a group of acknowledged experts in each of the various areas under consideration. In the chapters that follow, these individual contributors will pursue a critical evaluation of the typology, will assess its applicability across diverse issues of interest to consumer researchers, and will treat related topics in a degree of depth barely hinted at in the preceding introductory remarks. In short, Chapters 1 through 8 will unfold the scholarly ramifications of the structural framework presented thus far. After this, I shall return with some "Conclusions" intended to sum up the intervening voyage of discovery.

## References

Abbott, Lawrence (1955) *Quality and Competition*, New York: Columbia University Press.
Adler, Mortimer J. (1981) *Six Great Ideas*, New York: Macmillan.
Alicke, Mark (1983) "Philosophical Investigations of Values," in L. R. Kahle (ed.) *Social Values and Social Change*, New York: Praeger, 3–23.
Arrow, Kenneth J. (1967) "Public and Private Values," in S. Hook (ed.) *Human Values and Economic Policy*, New York: New York University Press, 3–21.
Bass, Frank M. and Wilkie, William L. (1973) "A Comparative Analysis of Attitudinal Predictions of Brand Preference," *Journal of Marketing Research* 10, August: 262–9.
Baylis, C. A. (1958) "Grading, Values, and Choice," *Mind* 67: 485–501.
Beardsley, Monroe C. (1967) "History of Aesthetics," in P. Edwards (ed.) *Encyclopedia of Philosophy*, Vol. 1., New York: Macmillan and Free Press, 18–35.
Becker, Gordon M. and McClintock, Charles G. (1967) "Value: Behavioral Decision Theory," *Annual Review of Psychology* 18: 239–86.
Berlyne, Daniel E. (1969) "Laughter, Humor, and Play," in G. Lindzey and E. Aronson (eds) *The Handbook of Social Psychology*, Vol. 3, Reading, MA: Addison-Wesley Publishing Company, 795–852.
Bond, E. J. (1983) *Reason and Value*, Cambridge, UK: Cambridge University Press.
Brandt, Richard B. (1967) "Personal Values and the Justification of Institutions," in S. Hook (ed.) *Human Values and Economic Policy*, New York: New York University Press, 22–40.
Brightman, Edgar S. (1962) "Axiology," in D. D. Runes (ed.) *Dictionary of Philosophy*, Littlefield, NJ: Adams & Co., 32–3.

Broydrick, Stephen C. (1996) *The 7 Universal Laws of Customer Value: How to Win Customers & Influence Markets*, Burr Ridge, IL: Irwin.

Buber, Martin (1923) *I and Thou*, New York: Charles Scribner's Sons.

Budd, Malcolm (1983) "Belief and Sincerity in Poetry," in E. Schaper (ed.) *Pleasure, Preference and Value: Studies in Philosophical Aesthetics*, New York: Cambridge University Press, 137–57.

Bullough, Edward (1912) "'Psychical Distance' as a Factor in Art and an Aesthetic Principle," *British Journal of Psychology* 5: 87–98.

Celuch, K. and Slama, M. (1995) "Getting Along and Getting Ahead as Motives for Self-Presentation: Their Impact on Advertising Effectiveness," *Journal of Applied Social Psychology* 25: 1700–13.

Coleman, Francis J. (1966) "A Phenomenology of Aesthetic Reasoning," *Journal of Aesthetics and Art Criticism* 25: 197–203.

Cowan, Alan (1964) *Quality Control for the Manager*, Oxford: Pergamon Press.

Csikszentmihalyi, Mihaly (1975) *Beyond Boredom and Anxiety*, San Francisco: Jossey-Bass Publishers.

Dearden, R. F. (1967) "The Concept of Play," in R. S. Peters (ed.) *The Concept of Education*, New York: The Humanities Press.

Deci, Edward L. (1975) *Intrinsic Motivation*, New York: Plenum Press.

Diesing, Paul (1962) *Reason in Society: Five Types of Decisions and Their Social Conditions*, Urbana, IL: University of Illinois Press.

Duesenberry, James S. (1949) *Income, Saving and the Theory of Consumer Behavior*, Cambridge, MA: Harvard University Press.

Fallon, Carl (1971) *Value Analysis To Improve Productivity*, New York: Wiley.

Fiore, Ann Marie and Kim, Soyoung (1997) "Olfactory Cues of Appearance Affecting Impressions of Professional Image of Women," *Journal of Career Development* 23, 4: 247–64.

Frankena, William (1962) "Ethics" and "Value," in D. D. Runes (ed.) *Dictionary of Philosophy*, Totowa, NJ: Littlefield, Adams & Co., 98–100, 330–1.

—— (1967) "Value and Valuation," in P. Edwards (ed.) *The Encyclopedia of Philosophy*, Vol. 8, New York: The Macmillan Company, 229–32.

—— (1973) *Ethics*, Second Edition, Englewood Cliffs, NJ: Prentice-Hall.

Frondizi, Risieri (1971) *What Is Value? An Introduction to Axiology*, Second Edition, La Salle, IL: Open Court Publishing Company.

Fromm, Erich (1941) *Escape from Freedom*, Oxford: Farrar.

Gale, Bradley T. (1994) *Managing Customer Value: Creating Quality and Service That Customers Can See*, New York: The Free Press.

Garvin, David A. (1988) *Managing Quality: The Strategic and Competitive Edge*, New York: The Free Press.

Hall, Everett W. (1961) *Our Knowledge of Fact and Value*, Chapel Hill, NC: The University of North Carolina Press.

Hampshire, Stuart (1982) *Thought and Action*, Second Edition, Notre Dame, IN: University of Notre Dame Press.

Hare, R. M. (1982) *Plato*, New York: Oxford University Press.

Harré, R. and Secord, P. F. (1973) *The Explanation of Social Behavior*, Littlefield, NJ: Adams & Co.

Hartman, Robert S. (1967) *The Structure of Values: Foundations of Scientific Axiology*, Carbondale, IL: Southern Illinois University Press.

Hilliard, A. L. (1950) *The Forms of Value: The Extension of Hedonistic Axiology*, New York: Columbia University Press.

Holbrook, Morris B. (1984) "Situation-Specific Ideal Points and Usage of Multiple Dissimilar Brands," *Research in Consumer Behavior* 7: 93–131.

—— (1986) "Emotion in the Consumption Experience: Toward a New Model of the Human Consumer," in R. A. Peterson, W. D. Hoyer, and W. R. Wilson (eds) *The Role of Affect in Consumer Behavior: Emerging Theories and Applications*, Lexington, MA: D. C. Heath and Company, 17–52.

—— (1994a) "Axiology, Aesthetics, and Apparel: Some Reflections on the Old School Tie," in M. R. DeLong and A. M. Fiore (eds) *Aesthetics of Textiles and Clothing: Advancing Multi-Disciplinary Perspectives*, ITAA Special Publication #7, Monument, CO 80132-1360: International Textile and Apparel Association, 131–41.

—— (1994b) "Ethics in Consumer Research," in C. T. Allen and D. Roedder John (eds) *Advances in Consumer Research*, Vol. 21, Provo, UT: Association for Consumer Research, 566–71.

—— (1994c) "The Nature of Customer Value: An Axiology of Services in the Consumption Experience," in R. T. Rust and R. L. Oliver (eds) *Service Quality: New Directions in Theory and Practice*, Thousand Oaks, CA: Sage Publications, 21–71.

—— (1996) "Customer Value – A Framework For Analysis and Research," in K. P. Corfman and J. G. Lynch, Jr. (eds) *Advances in Consumer Research*, Vol. 23, Provo, UT: Association for Consumer Research, 138–42.

Holbrook, Morris B. and Corfman, Kim P. (1985) "Quality and Value in the Consumption Experience: Phaedrus Rides Again," in J. Jacoby and J. C. Olson (eds) *Perceived Quality: How Consumers View Stores and Merchandise*, Lexington, MA: D. C. Heath and Company, 31–57.

Holbrook, Morris B. and Hirschman, Elizabeth C. (1982) "The Experiential Aspects of Consumption: Consumer Fantasies, Feelings, and Fun," *Journal of Consumer Research* 9, September: 132–40.

Holbrook, Morris B. and Zirlin, Robert B. (1985) "Artistic Creation, Artworks, and Aesthetic Appreciation: Some Philosophical Contributions to Nonprofit Marketing," *Advances in Nonprofit Marketing* 1: 1–54.

Hospers, John (1967) "Problems of Aesthetics," in P. Edwards (ed.) *The Encyclopedia of Philosophy*, Vol. 1, New York: Macmillan and Free Press, 35–56.

Huizinga, Johan (1938) *Homo Ludens*, New York: Harper & Row.

Hyde, Lewis (1983) *The Gift: Imagination and the Erotic Life of Property*, New York: Vintage.

Iseminger, Gary (1981) "Aesthetic Appreciation," *Journal of Aesthetics and Art Criticism* 39: 389–97.

Juran, J. M. (1988) *Juran on Planning for Quality*, New York: The Free Press.

Kahle, Lynn R. (1983) "Dialectical Tensions in the Theory of Social Values," in L. R. Kahle (ed.) *Social Values and Social Change*, New York: Praeger, 275–83.

Kahle, Lynn R. and Timmer, S. G. (1983) "A Theory and a Method for Studying Values," in L. R. Kahle (ed.) *Social Values and Social Change*, New York: Praeger, 43–69.

Kotler, Philip J. (1991) *Marketing Management*, Seventh Edition, Englewood Cliffs, NJ: Prentice-Hall.

Ladd, John (1967) "The Use of Mechanical Models for the Solution of Ethical Problems," in S. Hook (ed.) *Human Values and Economic Policy*, New York: New York University Press, 157–69.

Lamont, W. D. (1955) *The Value Judgment*, Westport, CT: Greenwood Press.

Laudan, Larry (1977) *Progress and Its Problems: Towards a Theory of Scientific Growth*, Berkeley, CA: University of California Press.

Lee, Harold N. (1957) "The Meaning of 'Intrinsic Value,'" in R. Lepley (ed.) *The Language of Value*, New York: Columbia University Press, 178–96.

Levitt, Theodore (1960) "Marketing Myopia," *Harvard Business Review* 38, July–August: 24–47.

Lewis, C. I. (1946) *An Analysis of Knowledge and Valuation*, La Salle, IL: Open Court.

Loring, L. M. (1966) *Two Kinds of Values*, New York: The Humanities Press.

Luce, R. Duncan and Raiffa, Howard (1957) *Games and Decisions*, New York: Wiley.

McGregor, Robert (1974) "Art and the Aesthetic," *Journal of Aesthetics and Art Criticism* 32: 549–59.

Mead, George H. (1938) *The Philosophy of the Act*, C. W. Morris (ed.), Chicago, IL: University of Chicago Press.

Mehrabian, Albert and Russell, James A. (1974) *An Approach to Environmental Psychology*, Cambridge, MA: The MIT Press.

Miller, Stephan (1973) "Ends, Means, and Galumphing: Some Leitmotifs of Play," *American Anthropologist* 75: 87–98.

Moore, Willis (1957) "The Language of Values," in R. Lepley (ed.) *The Language of Value*, New York: Columbia University Press, 9–28.

Morris, Charles (1956) *Varieties of Human Value*, Chicago, IL: The University of Chicago Press.

—— (1964) *Signification and Significance*, Cambridge, MA: The MIT Press.

Morris, Ruby Turner (1941) *The Theory of Consumer's Demand*, New Haven, CT: Yale University Press.

Mukerjee, Radhakamal (1964) *The Dimensions of Values*, London: George Allen & Unwin.

Nozick, Robert (1981) *Philosophical Explanation*, Cambridge, MA: Harvard University Press.

Olscamp, Paul J. (1965) "Some Remarks about the Nature of Aesthetic Perception and Appreciation," *Journal of Aesthetics and Art Criticism* 24: 251–8.

Olson, Robert G. (1967) "The Good," in P. Edwards (ed.) *The Encyclopedia of Philosophy*, Vol. 3, New York: The Macmillan Company, 367–70.

Osborne, Harold (1933) *Foundations of the Philosophy of Value*, Cambridge, UK: Cambridge University Press.

Osgood, Charles E., Suci, George J., and Tannenbaum, Percy H. (1957) *The Measurement of Meaning*, Urbana, IL: University of Illinois Press.

Parker, Dewitt H. (1957) *The Philosophy of Value*, Ann Arbor, MI: The University of Michigan Press.

Parsons, Talcott (1937) *The Structure of Social Action*, Vol. 1, New York: The Free Press.

—— (1951) *The Social System*, Glencoe, IL: The Free Press.

Pepper, Stephen C. (1958) *The Sources of Value*, Berkeley, CA: University of California Press.

Perry, Ralph Barton (1954) *Realms of Value*, Cambridge, MA: Harvard University Press.

Pettijohn, Caryl L. (1986) "Achieving Quality in the Development Process," *AT&T Technical Journal* 65, March/April: 85–93.

Pettit, P. (1983) "The Possibility of Aesthetic Realism," in E. Schaper (ed.) *Pleasure, Preference and Value: Studies in Philosophical Aesthetics*, New York: Cambridge University Press, 17–38.

Rader, Melvin (ed.) (1979) *A Modern Book of Esthetics*, Fifth Edition, New York: Holt, Rinehart & Winston.

Riesman, David (1950) *The Lonely Crowd*, New Haven, CT: Yale University Press.

Rokeach, Milton (1973) *The Nature of Human Values*, New York: The Free Press.

Rule, Sheila (1994) "The Pop Life," *New York Times*, March 30: C24.

Santayana, George (1896) *The Sense of Beauty*, New York: Dover Publications.

Scitovsky, Tibor (1976) *The Joyless Economy*, New York: Oxford University Press.

Scruton, Roger (1981) *From Descartes to Wittgenstein*, New York: Harper Colophon Books.

Siegel, Eli (1981) *Self and World*, New York: Definition Press.

Slama, Mark and Wolfe, Raymond (1997) "Consumption as Self-Presentation: A Socioanalytic Interpretation of *Mrs. Cage*," Working Paper, College of Business, Illinois State University, Normal, IL 61790-5500.

Smith, N. Craig (1990) *Morality and the Market*, London: Routledge.

Smith, N. Craig and Quelch, John A. (eds) (1993) *Ethics in Marketing*, Boston, MA: Irwin.

Steenkamp, Jan-Benedict E. M. (1989) *Product Quality: An Investigation into the Concept and How It is Perceived by Consumers*, Assen / Maastricht, The Netherlands: Van Gorcum.

Stephenson, William (1967) *The Play Theory of Mass Communication*, Chicago, IL: University of Chicago Press.

Taylor, Paul W. (1961) *Normative Discourse*, Englewood Cliffs, NJ: Prentice-Hall.

Tuchman, Barbara W. (1980) "The Decline of Quality," *The New York Times Magazine*, November 2: 38–41, 104.

Veblen, Thorstein (ed.) (1899, 1967) *The Theory of the Leisure Class*, Harmondsworth, UK: Penguin Books.

Veroff, J. (1983) "Introduction," in L. R. Kahle (ed.) *Social Values and Social Change*, New York: Praeger, xiii–xviii.

White, R. W. (1959) "Motivation Reconsidered: The Concept of Competence," *Psychological Review* 66: 297–333.

Wolfe, R. N., Lennox, R. D., and Cutler, B. L. (1986) "Getting Along and Getting Ahead: Empirical Support for a Theory of Protective and Acquisitive Self-Presentation," *Journal of Personality and Social Psychology* 50: 356–61.

Woodruff, Robert B. and Gardial, Sarah Fisher (1996) *Know Your Customer: New Approaches to Understanding Customer Value and Satisfaction*, Cambridge, MA: Blackwell.

Von Wright, Georg Henrik (1963) *The Varieties of Goodness*, London: Routledge & Kegan Paul.

—— (1983) *Practical Reason*, Ithaca, NY: Cornell University Press.

Zeithaml, Valerie A. (1988) "Consumer Perceptions of Price, Quality, and Value: A Means–End Model and Synthesis of Evidence," *Journal of Marketing* 52, July: 2–22.

Zeithaml, Valerie A., Parasuraman, A., and Berry, Len (1990) *Delivering Quality Service: Balancing Customer Perceptions and Expectations*, New York: The Free Press.

# 1 The value of time in the context of waiting and delays

*France Leclerc* and *Bernd H. Schmitt*

## Introduction

The view of time as an economic value is common in many approaches to the study of time. For instance, in his well-known economic theory of time, Becker (1965) equates the value of time with its opportunity cost. Similarly, in discussing the perception of time in consumer research, Graham (1981) stated that people in Western culture have a "linear-separable" view of time: "Time is visualized as a straight line extending from the past into the future and separable into discrete units" (Graham 1981: 336). This view that discrete properties are associated with time implies that choices are made in terms of allocating units of time among competing activities. In other words, time is perceived as having *value* and as capable of being bought and spent as well as being saved and wasted. We can buy time, for example, when we invest in a new product designed to save us time. Alternatively, we can spend time to acquire a good, e.g., when we wait in line at a ticket counter. Time can be wasted as in situations in which we spend more time waiting or doing something than we feel should have been necessary.

What characterizes time as a consumer value? In the past decade, we have conducted research on time perceptions and on how consumers respond to waiting and delay situations. This research informs us about the value of time from a consumer's perspective, i.e., of time as a "consumer value." The present chapter reviews a subset of our research with the specific goal of evaluating the Typology of Consumer Value presented by Holbrook in the Introduction to this book. Our intent in this chapter is selective and focused. For broad reviews of the time literature in consumer behavior, we refer the reader to Jacoby, Szybillo, and Berning (1976) and Gross (1987).

Holbrook's typology has two key aspects: (1) the conceptualization of value as an interactive relativistic preference experience; and (2) the three-dimensional categorization of Consumer Value, with time being considered as extrinsic, self-oriented, and active. Hence, we examine whether it is appropriate to conceptualize the value of time as an interactive relativistic preference experience, and whether it can be considered as extrinsic, self-oriented, and active. Do the data that we collected in numerous time-related studies fit with Holbrook's theoretical framework? Or, more precisely, do the data fit with those aspects of the framework that can be construed as empirical claims?

As we will show, our research has revealed three key findings:

- Time-related decisions depend on the decision context.
- Time perceptions and, in particular, behavioral responses to waits and delays depend on situational/environmental characteristics.
- Reactions to intrusions into waiting lines involve social norms.

We first discuss the empirical findings related to these three issues, reviewing three streams of research: (1) perceptions of time in a decision context; (2) perceptions of time under different environmental/situational conditions; and (3) reactions to intrusions into waiting lines. We then examine whether or not these findings are consistent with viewing the value of time as an interactive relativistic preference experience and as extrinsic, self-oriented, and active.

## Perceptions of time in a decision context

Our research on how consumers make decisions regarding their use of time, reported in Leclerc, Schmitt, and Dubé (1995), is guided by the question, "Is time like money?" That is, can we apply what we have learned about financial decision-making to how consumers value their time?

As we said earlier, from an economic perspective, Becker (1965) treats time as if it were money. He equates the value of time with its opportunity cost – the wage rate – and assumes that the value of time is a constant, i.e., that the cost of waiting is a linear function of time. That is, the value of time is not influenced by any characteristic of the outcomes as long as the best alternative use of time is unaffected.

Becker's context-free approach seems at odds with behavioral theories of decision-making such as prospect theory. According to prospect theory, utilities and values depend on the decision context. Prospect theory defines utility as a function of gains and losses relative to a reference point (Kahneman and Tversky 1979). If the diminishing sensitivity of prospect theory's loss function holds for time, then the positive value of saving a given amount of time should be greater in the context of a short wait than for a longer one.

To test this prediction, we conducted an experiment in which subjects read a scenario describing a situation where they could save 15 minutes of travel time on a train by paying an additional $2 for a service. In one experimental condition, the saving was off a total travel time of five hours; in the other experimental condition, the saving was off a total travel time of one hour. According to Becker's economic theory, it should not matter. According to prospect theory, consumers should be more attracted to the option in which they can save 15 minutes off one hour than off five hours. As predicted by prospect theory, consumers were significantly more likely to pay $2 to save 15 minutes off one hour than five hours. In a related study, as another demonstration of context effects, consumers were willing to pay twice as much to avoid waiting for a $40 ticket than for a $15 ticket.

Moreover, because prospect theory's value function is nonlinear, the overall subjective value derived from a pair of events should differ depending on whether the events are framed as separate or combined events before they are evaluated. Consumers should prefer to have time losses integrated rather than segregated. To test this prediction, we asked consumers which situation they would find more upsetting: waiting in a bank line for 30 minutes before getting served quickly, or waiting for 20 minutes in one line and then another 10 minutes in another line. Seventy-five percent of our subjects preferred to wait only once, i.e., to have their wait loss integrated. In a related study, we extended this finding to integration/ segregation over time (namely, over a period of two days). Again confirming prospect theory, 80 percent of consumers chose to wait 30 minutes and then 15 minutes on the *same* day compared to 30 minutes on one day and another 15 minutes on a *second* day.

Finally, for decisions under uncertainty, prospect theory proposes that people are risk seeking for losses. That is, consumers prefer to gamble (i.e., be risk seeking) rather than accept a sure loss of a certain amount. If the theory applies to time perceptions, then consumers should be risk seeking for time losses, too. In contrast to these predictions, we found that consumers prefer to accept a certain time loss to a risky gamble with time. For example, consumers were asked whether they would rather take a bus that definitely leaves in 60 minutes, or take a gamble with a 50 percent chance of leaving on a bus in 30 minutes and a 50 percent chance of leaving in 90 minutes. Seventy percent selected the certainty option. This risk aversion even applies when consumers have experienced a loss (e.g., a delayed flight) of 3 hours and have a chance to make up for it with a 50 percent chance in the risky gamble. Even in such a "break-even" scenario, the majority of respondents (72 percent) chose the certainty option of adding a further delay of another 3 hours!

In sum, in risky decision-making, consumers seem to be risk seeking for money but risk-averse for time losses. This striking asymmetry was shown directly in another test in which we compared monetary decision-making and time decision-making directly. To elicit monetary values for time, and thus to make time and money values comparable, we asked our student subjects in a pretest to give an estimate of the monetary value of their time: it was $10 for one hour. For the monetary decision, we then asked subjects: "Please choose between the following options: A certain loss of $10 vs. a 50 percent chance of losing $5 and a 50 percent chance of losing $15?" For time, we asked subjects: "Please choose between the following options: Having to wait 60 minutes for sure vs. a 50 per-cent chance of waiting 30 minutes and a 50 percent chance of waiting 90 minutes?" For money, the majority of consumers (70 percent) chose the risky option; for time, the majority (53 percent) chose the risk-averse option.

In sum, our research on time perceptions in a decision context provided the following findings: (1) the value of time is context dependent; (2) consumers prefer to integrate time losses; and (3) consumers are consistently risk-averse when making time- as opposed to money-related decisions.

## Time perceptions and situational/environmental characteristics

In a second line of research, we have examined how time perceptions are affected by situational and environmental characteristics (Dubé-Rioux, Schmitt, and Leclerc 1989; Dubé, Schmitt, and Leclerc 1991). The situational/environmental characteristics that affect time perceptions may take various forms. Frequently studied environmental factors have been distracters provided in the environment. Typically, distractions and multiple activities make a wait seem shorter (Larson 1987). Examples of distractions that have been shown to affect time perceptions have included mirrors next to elevators, television screens showing news, sports events, or music (ibid.). Hornik (1984) showed that the frequency of performing an activity – say, shopping – also influences the perception of waiting time in the context of this activity.

Researchers have also suggested – though with little theoretical justification – that other situational factors can affect time perceptions. For example, the physical design of a waiting area with regard to providing comfort has been suggested as an important factor (Baum and Valins 1977; Bitner 1990). Unpleasant and uncomfortable physical environments are expected to result in longer perceived waiting times (Green, Lehmann, and Schmitt 1996). Finally, based on research in environmental psychology, one should expect that temperature, the degree of crowding, and the noise level may affect time perceptions (Sommer 1969).

In our own research, we have studied a situational factor that is directly linked to the service encounter as such – namely, the "temporal phase of a service encounter." Consumers view most service encounters in terms of a sequence of events that unfolds over time. For example, people often think of a visit to a fine-dining restaurant in terms of three temporally distinct phases: the arrival at the restaurant and the ordering and consumption of a cocktail; the ordering and consumption of the meal; and, finally, the payment of the bill and departure (Abelson 1981). Therefore, consumers may be in distinct psychological states at different phases and, as a consequence, may react differently if delays occur during one phase rather than another.

Indeed, past research has provided positive evidence for this hypothesis. Benakiva and Lerman (1985) reported that passengers perceive a minute of delay at curbside as more upsetting than a minute spent waiting inside a bus. Moreover, the time spent in a queue at fast food restaurants (the time spent between entering the queue and being able to order) had a stronger impact on customer satisfaction than service time (the time spent between ordering and receiving the order).

One theory that appropriately conceptualizes how individuals react to delays at different temporal phases – thereby allowing for precise predictions – is field theory. As developed by Kurt Lewin, field theory is one of the most prominent theories in the social sciences (Kassarjian 1973). By viewing commercial exchanges as encounters in which customers try to achieve goals and by viewing delays as barriers on the path toward goal achievement, Lewin's field theory can account for consumers' psychological reactions to waiting at moments that occur during different phases of a service encounter.

According to field theory, an individual's behavior (including his or her cognitions and feelings) is the result of the psychological forces acting upon that individual at a given time. When a person identifies a need and, as a consequence, tries to achieve a goal, tensions arise. If barriers prevent goals from being satisfied, individuals get frustrated. Barriers are perceived as less aversive, however, if they occur inside rather than outside the goal region. When the individual is inside the region of the goal, pressure is relieved and a barrier produces little frustration. On the other hand, when the individual is outside the region, tension exists, either because the individual strives for the goal (as is the case before goal achievement) or because the individual has been satiated and strives for new goals (as is the case after goal achievement).

In most services, a central phase can be conceptualized as the goal region. For example in the restaurant scenario, most consumers will perceive the consumption of the meal as the central element and consequently, as the goal of their restaurant visit. A delay in the delivery of a service should generate more intense negative responses if it occurs at the beginning of the service encounter (before the central phase of a service encounter has started) or at the end (after the central phase has been completed) than if it occurs when the core of the service is delivered. Thus, the same delay (of say 10 minutes) experienced in these three different temporal phases should be responded to quite differently.

To test the predictions of field theory, we first conducted an experiment in which we presented various delay scenarios in a restaurant setting to respondents (Dubé-Rioux, Schmitt, and Leclerc 1989). Subjects were asked to imagine that while they visited a restaurant, a delay either occurred before the core of the service (waiting for the table), during the core service-delivery (waiting for the meal), or after the core of the service (waiting for the check). As predicted by field theory and in contrast to normative models, the restaurant service was evaluated more negatively when a delay occurred at the beginning or at the end of the restaurant visit than when it occurred during the meal.

Yet, the study had one major shortcoming: it did not really examine subjects' psychological states, as required by field theory, and therefore did not address the issue of why subjects responded differently to delays at different temporal phases.

To address this shortcoming, we conducted a field experiment that investigated the underlying process that may mediate these effects. We hypothesized that waiting at different temporal phases of the delivery of a service should generate affective responses varying in intensity. This hypothesis is directly related to Kurt Lewin's field theory. As described earlier, field theory assumes that barriers may exist that prevent the individual from reaching the goal. As a result, psychological reactions of frustration and other negative affective responses will arise if the goal is positively valenced, which is the case for most consumer products and services. Yet the degree of frustration and negative affect varies depending on whether the individual is inside or outside the goal region, and field theory predicts that barriers are perceived as less aversive if they occur inside rather than outside the goal region (Lewin 1943; Karsten 1976).

In the field experiment, we investigated affective reactions in response to an interruption of a service causing a delay in the service delivery. The interruption of the service and the eight-minute delay resulting from the interruption occurred either before the service started, in the middle of the service encounter, or after the service encounter had been terminated.

A classroom session provided an appropriate setting since students are in fact consumers of a service that is produced and delivered over an extended period of time (Yekovich and Walker 1986). Students were subject to an eight-minute delay either before the beginning of a regular class session, in the middle, or at the end of the class. Results showed that they experienced more negative affect when the delay occurred at the beginning or end than if it occurred in the middle of class.

## Reactions to intrusions into waiting lines

The key question addressed in our waiting-line research is, "Why do individuals show resistance to intrusions into waiting lines?" (Schmitt, Dubé, and Leclerc 1992). This research was designed to contrast two explanations for the fact that individuals resist intrusions into waiting lines. The view that time is a resource suggests that queuers should be motivated to defend their queue position because losing it would mean encountering unexpected time costs for themselves such as additional waiting time. An alternative position, first articulated by the sociologist Charles Cooley (1964), is that individuals react by reference to a consensually shared social representation. That is, the loss of position and time may amount to a negligible cost of a few minutes or even seconds. Individuals, however, feel outraged at the intruder's violation of the norms and values on which the queue is based and which provide time allocations on a social basis. In their behaviors, queuers thus implicitly consider inconveniences and time costs for others.

As we will see, it is not easy to resolve which position is right. To put the debate in perspective, let us first review the empirical evidence that has been accumulated over the years by other researchers.

The empirical evidence originally seemed to favor the "individual costs" point of view (Mann 1970). Comparing reactions of queuers preceding the intrusion point with those following the intrusion point, individuals who preceded the intrusion point were less likely to respond to intrusions than individuals who followed the intrusion point. These findings were interpreted as evidence for the "individual costs" position, because only individuals following the intrusion point seem to encounter costs (ibid.).

As Milgram *et al.* (1986) have noted, however, there are problems with this interpretation. Individuals preceding the intrusion point may be as other-directed in their behavior as those following the intrusion point. However, they usually have their backs to the scene and therefore are less likely to notice the violation. Moreover, individuals following the intrusion point may not only respond to costs that they encounter but may also respond to the violation of the social norm, which considers the behavior of others. In other words, some of the social motivations may have been counted incorrectly as individual costs motivations.

To provide a better test of whether individuals may be motivated, in part, by concerns for others, Milgram *et al.* (1986) suggested a closer analysis of the behavioral reactions of queuers waiting behind the intrusion point. Specifically, Milgram *et al.* argued that because queuers following the intrusion point all encounter the same costs (e.g., having to wait longer for a certain period of time), any differences in their reactions cannot be explained by cost considerations. Instead, they must be explained by making reference to the values, norms, and responsibilities defined by the queuing system. They asked experimental confederates to intrude into waiting lines and recorded the behavioral reactions of queuers following the intrusion point. They found that the person in the position right behind the intrusion point was most likely to react, with the reaction gradient declining sharply right after this queue position. Milgram *et al.* concluded that individual cost considerations cannot explain this result.

There are several problems with Milgram *et al.*'s interpretation. First, the argument that all queuers behind the intrusion point encounter the same costs holds true only for absolute costs but not for relative costs. In Milgram *et al.*'s field experiment, queuers right behind the intrusion point (queuing position 4) had fewer people waiting in front of them than individuals farther down the line. Second, queuers right behind the intrusion point also must have already waited longer than those farther behind the intrusion point, who joined the line more recently. That is, queuers right behind the intrusion point had already invested more time in the queue and therefore may have been more sensitive to their individual "sunk costs."

A more convincing demonstration of the claim that queuers' behavior is other-directed required a different empirical strategy. To test whether individuals are motivated by social rather than personal concerns, the illegitimate intrusion situation had to be compared to a "control situation" in which individuals encountered the same costs but no violation of a social norm related to the structure of the queue occurred, i.e., a queuing situation in which a time delay is not considered to be inappropriate.

Several real-life consumer situations fulfill the criterion of an appropriate control situation. For example, when individuals wait in line for a service (e.g., at a bank), service personnel often cause a brief interruption of the service, e.g., by closing a service counter temporarily to count money. Occasionally, a guard blocks access to a service or event, causing unexpected waiting costs. Moreover, sometimes a person happens to join someone else who already waits in line. Although these situations result in waiting costs and, to a certain degree, violate expectations, they do not constitute illegitimate behavior in terms of the rules and norms of most queuing systems and therefore do not violate social norms related to the structure of the queue. As a result, in our research we compared intrusions to these latter types of situations.

In Study 1, we created scenarios for a setting in a bank. Subjects were asked to imagine that they were waiting at different queue positions in front of a bank counter with an average transaction time of three minutes per customer. Suddenly one of two events occurred, each causing an unexpected delay for the queuer. In one situation, an intruder who entered the line in front of the service window caused the delay. In the other situation, the service provider caused a delay by closing the only workstation in operation and putting up a sign that the service would be interrupted for three minutes. Results showed that although each subject encountered the same costs, subjects were more likely to take action if the intruder caused the delay than the service provider.

Study 1 leaves the question unanswered, however, whether subjects right behind the intrusion point in Milgram *et al.* reacted so strongly to the violation of the social norm because they were closer than others to the intruder or because they were closer to the goal of being served. That is, part of the motivational force in queue position one may not have originated from social factors but simply from individual, motivational forces "pulling" the individual to the goal – just like the Lewinian field forces discussed earlier in the context of temporal phases. Empirical support for this point of view had been provided in studies by Harris (1974) and Ahmed (1982). Intruders entered the line in front of queuers when queuers were close to the goal (two persons ahead of them in line) or far from the goal (eleven persons ahead of them in line). In both studies, those individuals closer to the goal behaved more aggressively than those farther from the goal.

Therefore, in Experiment 2, closeness to the goal and closeness to the intrusion point – which are confounded in real-life "queuing positions" – were manipulated independently. As in Study 1, the delay was either caused by an intruder or by a service provider, an employee who put up a sign informing customers that service would be interrupted for some time. Closeness to the goal was manipulated by asking subjects to imagine that they either waited close to the counter (three customers waiting in front of them) or relatively far away from the counter (eight customers waiting in front of them). Closeness to the event was operationalized by having the event in the scenario happen right in front of the customer or in front of another customer who waited three positions ahead. Results showed that subjects were more likely to take action when they witnessed an intrusion than when the service provider caused the delay. Moreover, reactions were determined by how close individuals were to the intruder rather than by how close they were to the service point. This result suggests that other, more socially motivated forces such as the intent to protect the integrity of the queuing system overrode field forces, demonstrated by Ahmed (1982).

Finally, as in other research that we conduct on time perceptions and waiting, we added a field experiment to supplement the scenario data with actual behavioral data. The field experiment was conducted in the Grand Central railroad station in New York City. Two confederates intruded into a total of 123 waiting lines that had spontaneously formed in front of the Metro North Commuter Railroad counters. Depending on the time of day, the lines varied in length between five and twelve individuals. The transaction time per customer varied between 30 seconds and 120 seconds.

In all experimental conditions, a confederate first joined the tail of a waiting line, and the behavior of the person joining the line after the confederate – the subject – was observed. After the subject had joined the line, one of two events occurred. In the Illegitimate Intrusion condition, another confederate ("the intruder") calmly approached the subject and said, "Excuse me, I'd like to get in here." The intruder did not ask the subject for permission and gave no reason for the intrusion but simply injected herself into the line. In the Legitimate Intrusion condition, the intruder looked above the counter where the departure and arrival times of trains were displayed, then looked at the confederate who waited before the subject, approached her and pretended to know her ("Hi. What are you doing here?"). She then turned to the subject and said, "Excuse me. I'd like to get in here."

As in the previous studies, naive queuers responded more strongly to an illegitimate intrusion than to a more legitimate one although they encountered identical costs.

## Time as a consumer value

Are our research findings concerning time consistent with the conceptualization of Consumer Value proposed by Holbrook in the Introduction?

Holbrook conceptualizes value as an interactive relativistic preference experience. Let us discuss each component of this noun phrase separately. First, interactive. In our opinion, the interactive nature of customer value, as conceptualized by Holbrook, is not an empirical claim but a basic assumption about the nature of the organism. Therefore, our research cannot support or refute this claim. In fact, it is a premise on which our research is based. Like Holbrook, we assume that time perceptions matter more than the objective amount of time that a consumer spends, for example, in a service system. In terms of measurement, we frequently ask subjects two different types of questions, "How long do you think the delay lasted?" and "How long did it feel?" A similar argument can be made for preferences, since our research is based on the assumption that consumers derive some "(dis)utility" for time saved (wasted). In other words, they have a preference or a valuation for time that they can equate to other resources. In our research on time and decision-making, we frequently ask subjects to indicate how much they would like to pay for a given amount of time.

Second, both our research on decision-making involving time and our research on situational/environmental characteristics confirm the relativistic nature of time as a consumer value. We provide ample evidence for two of the three types of relativism proposed by Holbrook. The first type is that value is relativistic across objects. Our research shows that consumers value the time saved in a service or in a line differently as a function of characteristics of the service. As reported previously, the subjective value of a waiting time (e.g., 10 minutes) is more negative when the overall time loss is low rather than high (e.g., 30 minutes vs. 3 hours). And the subjective value is more negative when the waiting is associated with a good or a service of low monetary value ($15 vs. $40 ticket).

The second type of relativism proposed by Holbrook is that value is situational in the sense that it depends on the situation or environment in which the evaluative judgment occurs. Again, we have shown that the temporal phase of a service encounter matters in how people assess the value of time wasted during that experience.

Finally, Holbrook claims that value is personal in the sense that it varies from one individual to another. Although, we do not investigate individual differences explicitly in our research, there are a number of personality traits that are time-related. The most relevant one is probably the type A personality syndrome (Gastorf 1980). Type A personalities feel under constant time pressure and frequently think about time. As a result, it is likely that they would assign a much higher value to time saved. Also, relevant for valuing time is Hall's culture-related distinction between monochronic time people, who prefer to do one thing at the time, and polychronic time people, who tend to engage in simultaneous activities (Kaufman, Lane, and Lindquist 1991). Monochronic time people place a higher value on schedules and promptness. Finally, cultures differ on what is called the pace of life, which is also likely to affect how people value time. Levine and Bartlett (1984) have empirically studied the pace of life in terms of walking speed, working speed, and accuracy of clocks in six countries (England, Italy, Indonesia, Japan, and the USA) and have found strong and consistent differences in all three measures among the individual countries: the highest pace of life was found in Japan, the lowest in Indonesia.

Finally, the last part of Holbrook's conceptualization of Consumer Value is that value resides not in the product purchased but rather in the consumption experience derived therefrom. In the case of time, this means that the value of using an object or a service consists of the time saved by means of this object or service. This reasoning must be extended further, however, since the value of the time saved is a function of what is done with the time since time is a resource. That is, in the same way consumers do not mainly derive utility from having a lot of money but from what they do with it, they do not derive utility from having a lot of time but from how they spend that time. Thus, we agree that the value of buying a more efficient object or service to save time resides in the consumption experience but the consumption experience can vary greatly depending on how people use the time saved. For example, the ten minutes saved by using an ATM instead of going to a branch can be allocated to family time or to household chores. The former is likely to be considered by most people to be more valuable than the latter. To use Holbrook's terminology, the value of time is extrinsic. This leads us to the first dimension discussed in the Typology of Consumer Value.

## Time as a three-dimensional value

### *Time as an extrinsic value*

In general and as discussed in the previous section, we agree with the view that the value of time is typically extrinsic. In other words, it pertains to a means–end relationship. Again, the view of time as typically extrinsic is largely equivalent to the assumption of thinking of time as a resource, which is a basic assumption of our work. However, there is a major difference between time and other resources such as money, which impacts the value of time greatly. Outcomes of times (losses or savings) cannot as easily be transferred (i.e., recouped or applied) to new situations as outcomes of money. In other words, time is less fungible or substitutable than money. The fact that time is not fungible suggests that the "time" at which the loss or saving of time occurs is relevant. In other words, two half-days each interrupted by some minutes of errands is not as valuable as one half-day non-interrupted and one half a day interrupted by a longer period. This observation seems to be well understood by professors at research universities who want to concentrate their teaching as much as they can in order to have uninterrupted time to conduct research. This non-fungibility of time leads to an aversion to uncertainty that seems to have a large impact on risk attitudes. As a result, planning is especially important for time, even more so than for money and since uncertainty makes planning difficult, uncertainty is especially aversive in this context. For example, if the taxi to the airport costs $50 more than expected, this loss can be dealt with by reducing consumption elsewhere, but if the ride to the airport takes an hour more time than expected, the hour may be difficult to recoup. Similarly, gains of time are less valuable than comparable gains of money unless there is some way to make good use of the time saved. As stressed by Gross (1987), time cannot be stored. At best, time savings may be applied immediately but they cannot be saved. That is, if the taxi arrives fifteen minutes earlier than expected at the airport, one may have a coffee before the flight but one cannot store fifteen minutes and use them to have a cup of coffee after arrival at the final destination. This combination of accentuated costs of losing time and attenuated value of gaining time makes certain outcomes, with their inherent ease of planning, particularly attractive. To summarize, even though we agree that the value of time is extrinsic, there are some clear limitations as to what the time saved can be exchanged for.

## *Time as an active value*

Holbrook classifies time as active (as opposed to reactive), defined as something that I act upon as opposed to something that acts upon me. We agree that time can be an active value (e.g., when we actively plan our time and stick to a schedule), but it can also be reactive. When consumers react to time losses as a result of waiting and delay, the locus of control is not necessarily with the consumer anymore. In fact, a lot of our work focuses on situations in which the consumer has to react to wastes of time that are not under her control such as in the case of waiting lines. One can argue that the consumer still has some degree of control since she can renege or balk. That is, it may be possible for the consumer to leave the queue (or not join at all)? However, in a number of situations, such as waiting to clear customs, there is clearly no option. Similarly, someone sitting in a plane on the runway and waiting for it to depart does not have many options to act on.

To summarize, we agree that time can be an active value and maybe it is in most cases. However, it can also be passive.

### *Time as a self-oriented value*

In the third dimension of the Typology of Value, Holbrook classifies time-related experience as providing a self-oriented (as opposed to other-oriented) type of value. On this dimension, we hold a more social, other-directed view of time, at least in the context of waiting in line. More to the point, we feel that our research on intrusions in waiting lines speaks directly to this issue. As previously described, in this research we conducted a series of experiments which, taken together, provide strong evidence that the queue constitutes a social system. Because the queue constitutes a social system, individuals waiting in a queue are motivated by concerns that transcend individual cost considerations. To summarize, we agree with the fact that in some situations, the value of time may be self-oriented. However, in the context of waiting lines, there is a clear social component.

## Conclusion

To summarize, our research on time perceptions, waiting, and delay situations is largely consistent with the Typology of Consumer Value presented in the Introduction. Our research especially supports the general view of value as being relativistic. In fact, time itself – in our case, waiting time – may have no definite value for people; its value may be constructed entirely by the context. This explains why individuals are sometimes incredibly wasteful with their time but almost stingy in other circumstances. The value of time seems to be context and situation dependent.

However, as in any comprehensive framework, certain aspects of Holbrook's Consumer-Value framework may not hold under certain conditions. Our research has identified the social context as one such condition. Our point is not to say that time is a consumer value that is never self-oriented but that it is occasionally other-oriented. The real issue may be whether time is more self-oriented than other values – a question that our research cannot answer given that it is limited to one domain.

## References

Abelson, R. P. (1981) "Psychological Status of the Script Concept," *American Psychologist* 36: 715–29.

Ahmed, S. M. (1982) "Factors Affecting Frustrating and Aggression Relationships," *Journal of Personality and Social Psychology* 16: 173–7.

Baum, A., and Valins, S. (1977) *Architecture and Social Behavior: Psychological Studies of Social Density*, Hillsdale, NJ: Erlbaum.

Becker, G. S. (1965) "A Theory of the Allocation of Time," *Economic Journal* 75, (September): 493–517.

Benakiva, M., and Lerman, S. (1985) *Discrete Choice Analysis: Theory and Application to Travel Demand*, Cambridge, MA: MIT Press.

Bitner, M. J. (1990) "Evaluating Service Encounters: The Effects of Physical Surroundings and Employee Responses," *Journal of Marketing* 54: 69–82.

Cooley, C. H. (1964) *Human Nature and Social Order*, New York: Schocken Books (originally published in 1902).

Dubé, L., Schmitt, B. H., and Leclerc, F. (1991) "'Consumers' Affective Response to Delays at Different Phases of a Service Delivery," *Journal of Applied Social Psychology* 21, 10: 810–20.

Dubé-Rioux, L., Schmitt, B. H., and Leclerc, F. (1989) "Consumers' Reaction to Waiting: When Delays Affect the Perception of Service Quality," in T. S. Srull (ed.) *Advances in Consumer Research* 15, Ann Arbor, MI: Association for Consumer Research.

Gastorf, J.W. (1980) "Time Urgency of the Type A Behavior Pattern," *Journal of Consulting and Clinical Psychology* 48: 299.

Graham, R. J. (1981) "The Role of Perception of Time in Consumer Research," *Journal of Consumer Research* 7, (March): 335–42.

Green, L. V., Lehmann, D. R., and Schmitt, B. H. (1996) "Time Perceptions in Service Systems: An Overview of the TPM Framework," in T. A. Swartz, D. E. Bowen, and S. W. Brown (eds) *Advances in Services Marketing and Management* 5, JAI Press.

Gross, B. L. (1987) "Time Scarcity: Interdisciplinary Perspectives and Implications for Consumer Behavior," in J. N. Sheth and E. Hirschman (eds) *Research in Consumer Behavior* 2, Greenwich, CT: JAI Press.

Harris, M.B. (1974) "Mediators Between Frustration and Aggression in a Field Experiment," *Journal of Experimental Social Psychology* 10: 561–71.

Hornik, J. (1984) "Subjective Versus Objective Time Measures: A Note on the Perception of Time in Consumer Behavior," *Journal of Consumer Research* 11, (June): 615–18.

Jacoby, J., Szybillo, G.J., and Berning, C.K. (1976) "Time and Consumer Behavior: An Interdisciplinary Overview," *Journal of Consumer Research* 2, (March): 320–39.

Kahneman, D., and Tversky, A. (1979) "Prospect Theory: An Analysis of Decision under Risk," *Econometrica* 47, (March): 263–91.

Karsten, A. (1976) "Mental Satiation – The Transformation of Activities," in J. De Rivera (ed.) *Field Theory as Human Science: Contributions of Lewin's Berlin Group*, New York: Gardner Press.

Kassarjian, H. H. (1973) "Field Theory in Consumer Behavior," in S. Ward and T. S. Robertson (eds) *Consumer Behavior: Theoretical Sources*, Englewood Cliffs, NJ: Prentice-Hall.

Kaufman, C. F., Lane, P.M., and Lindquist, J.D. (1991) "Exploring More than 24 Hours a Day: A Preliminary Investigation of Polychronic Time Use," *Journal of Consumer Research* 18, (December): 392–401.

Larson, R. C. (1987) "Perspectives on Queues: Social Justice and the Psychology of Queuing," *Operations Research* 35: 895–905.

Leclerc, F., Schmitt, B.H., and Dubé, L. (1995) "Waiting Time and Decision Making: Is Time Like Money?," *Journal of Consumer Research* 22, (June): 110–19.

Levine, R., and Bartlett, K. (1984) "Pace of Life, Punctuality and Coronary Heart Disease in Six Countries," *Journal of Cross-Cultural Psychology* 15: 233–55.

Lewin, K. (1943) "Defining the Field at a Given Time," *Psychological Review* 50: 292–310.

Mann, L. (1970) "The Social Psychology of Waiting Lines," *American Scientist* 58: 390–8.

Milgram, S., Liberty, H., Toledo, R., and Wackenhut, J. (1986) "Response to Intrusions into Waiting Lines," *Journal of Personality and Social Psychology* 51: 683–9.

Schmitt, B., Dubé, L., and Leclerc, F. (1992) "Intrusions into Waiting Lines: Does the Queue Constitute a Social System?," *Journal of Personality and Social Psychology* 63, 5: 806–15.

Sommer, R. (1969) *Personal Space: The Behavioral Basis of Design*, Englewood Cliffs, NJ: Prentice-Hall.

Yekovich, F.R., and Walker, C.H. (1986) "Retrieval of Scripted Concepts," *Journal of Memory and Language* 25: 627–44.

# 2 Value as excellence in the consumption experience

*Richard L. Oliver*

The provision of "value" to consumers by marketers is implicit in the exchange contract. Yet, value is a term fraught with so many interpretations that it is a wonder when consumers and marketers agree that such a contract exists. In fact, the many interpretations provide the impetus for the editor's desire to present the reader with the chapters in this volume. As an invited author, my initial reaction to having been asked to contribute a "chapter" was that this would be a well-defined task, one that would provide a reasonable set of boundaries for a narrative on the narrow topic of value-as-excellence. Unfortunately, value, even as excellence, was found to be subject to multiple interpretations in the literature. On the encouraging side, certain regularities were found to appear, nonetheless. This is so because value in its excellence form has taken on particular meanings in its many and varied uses. One purpose of this chapter is to take the reader through the many variants of value as used to imply degrees of excellence. A second purpose is to contrast and compare value with the two related concepts of quality and satisfaction.

In what follows, it will be presumed that the reader has been acquainted with the Holbrook (1994) framework. It can be found in many sources including the Introduction to this book and the conference proceedings on which the book is based (Holbrook 1996). Thus, the following discussion will presume that all references to "value" in this paper refer to the self-oriented, reactive, and extrinsic cell in Holbrook's typology. And specific types of value within this cell, as discussed here, are intended to be subtypes of this cell and hopefully not encroachments on the turf of other authors in this volume.

For the reader somewhat less familiar with the fine distinctions made in the Holbrook (1994) typology, some clarification is in order concerning the present discussion on the *reactive* extrinsic self-oriented topic of value-as-excellence as opposed to the *active* version of this same combination (value-as-efficiency). In comparing the three phases of consumer behavior, namely the prepurchase period leading to choice, the act of consumption itself, and the postpurchase period, the active period is that of consumption, while the reactive periods are those of pre- and postconsumption. The reason for the passive nature of the first and last periods is that the consumer does not actively operate on the product or service in these segments. Rather, the activity of interest is evaluation, namely evaluation of product/service cues in decision-making/choice and evaluation of performance outcomes in the postpurchase time frame. Thus, the consumer is *reacting* to two kinds of information – memory traces and new cues in the prepurchase period and observed outcomes in the post-period. For purposes of discussion, however, this "hard" distinction will be relaxed somewhat so that "reactions to action itself" can be entertained as another valuation in consumption.

As a prelude to the remainder of this chapter, it should be noted that Holbrook's theory is referred to as an axiology, or the study of value and value judgments. Two writings on this topic are Hartman (1967) and Najder (1975) wherein value is defined as a relational judgment of "good/bad," "better/worse than," and "good/ bad for." Thus, value, at its core, is a judgment of goodness/badness and better/ worse. The task here is to define these judgments in the consumable, durable, and service markets. Upon introspection, the reader will recognize that judgments of this nature are made routinely and ubiquitously. This frequent usage, unfortunately, is problematic in the context of definition, for value has come to mean just about anything marketers and consumers wish with reference to offerings in the marketplace.

As noted, value judgments of whatever ilk occur in two time frames. Value can be assessed or predicted prior to purchase or after. When assessed in the prepurchase period, it is referred to as desired value, preferred value (preference), or valuation. Assessments after the fact are referred to as delivered value, judged value, or evaluation. For a single consumer, the same criteria may be used in both periods or the criteria may differ, as consumption itself can be a form of discovery. At different points in this paper, the distinction may be less relevant and at others more so. Lest the reader grow weary, it would now be of "value" to attempt to pin down those value-related terms that are more aligned with consumption outcomes.

## Renditions of value in consumption

Like satisfaction, value, including value-as-excellence, is a human comparator response (Oliver 1997). Individuals cannot know if some thing provided value unless a standard of valuation is available. Thus, consumption events provide value to the extent that they are judged as such. This makes value a cognitive concept for, unlike attitude or pure forms of affect (e.g., pleasure), it can exist without an affective component. That is not to say that value can not cause affect and coexist with it, but is to say that affect is not necessary for a judgment of value to come into being. Later, the issue of how consumption affect (e.g., thrill) can be judged for its value will be entertained. For now, it is convenient to say that consumers are capable of doing so.

In a comprehensive work, Zeithaml (1988) provides a perspective on value as couched in a web of consumption concepts. She finds that four themes underlie the meaning of value as derived from consumers' experiences. These are: (1) low price, (2) getting what is wanted, (3) quality compared to price, and (4) what is received for what is sacrificed.

Based on further analysis, Zeithaml models value as a function of five factors. She hypothesizes that value is positively related to: (a) quality, (b) other extrinsic attributes such as functionality, (c) intrinsic attributes such as pleasure, and (d) "high-level abstractions" including personal values. Additionally, value is posited to be a negative function of (e) perceived sacrifice, defined in terms of both monetary outlays and non-monetary costs such as time and effort. In effect, value is a positive function of what is received and a negative function of what is sacrificed. This results in a value "equation," as follows:

$$\text{Value} = f \text{(Receipts/Sacrifices)}$$

Two themes are evident from the preceding perspective. One addresses single-stimulus concepts, while the second considers two, such as the receipts/sacrifices term. Single-stimulus concepts require only one, perhaps integrated, cognition and tend to be holistic. Two- or multiple-stimuli concepts ask the consumer to consider the components in a juxtaposed or comparative manner. Each of these perspectives is elaborated next.

### *Single-stimulus definitions*

Perhaps the easiest rendition of value in lay terms is the singular notion of *worth*. Price and quality, taken separately, would fit this category. Often, this is referred to as a "utility" definition, but it is more accurate to refer to it as *cardinal* utility (see Hirshleifer 1976). While it is not my intention to slight the utility literature, the term "utility" is frequently used as a convenient overarching concept that permits discussion of consumer goals without the necessity of greater formal specification. Moreover, although utility is frequently represented in axiomatic terms, there exists no semantic definition of utility receiving widespread acceptance. For example, writings variously describe utility as usefulness, hedonic quality, "pleasure," and even satisfaction (e.g., Kahneman and Varey 1991). From time to time, this fluid definition will prove to be satisfactory for the purposes addressed here, although a number of authors have recently speculated as to why utility becomes problematic when used to describe consumer outcomes in the postchoice consumption period (Huber *et al.* 1997).

Such single-stimulus definitions provide unambiguous evaluations of value and many utility investigators are relying on their use (e.g., Kemp *et al.* 1995). In fact, Kemp and Willetts (1995; see also Kemp 1991) tested many measurement variations of value in the context of public goods and services. They concluded that consumers use the term pervasively, that its meaning is consistent regardless of how it is measured, and that the closest semantic term to describe value is "worthwhileness." Moreover, Galanter (1990) provides empirical evidence that consumers can place positive and negative value on events not normally valued in monetary terms (e.g., having twins, gum sticking to one's shoe).

Thus, value is the "worthiness" number assigned to the concept. It permits comparisons to other valuations along a numeric continuum. Ignoring ideal points, an item's value is its point estimate in currency, utility, or exchange terms.

It follows that interpretations of "excellence" are defined by valuations on the high side of the continuum; items lacking excellence are positioned at the low end. For the purpose of its use, it does not matter that the concept of value can be defined in a greater dimensionality; utility estimates take these additional dimensions into account by virtue of utility's holistic nature.

Many common events benefit from the singular notion of utility-as-worth, which is frequently defined in currency terms. For example, in its many variants, worth can mean the exchange terms required for acquisition (e.g., cost), the exchange value obtained at disposition (e.g., sale price), the estimated or imagined value of the item in ownership (e.g., appraisal), what one would be willing to pay if ownership were possible (e.g., the bid), and what one would require to give up the item (e.g., the asked). For the same item at the same time, each of these could vary, sometimes measurably.

Worth has taken on specific evaluative forms in different areas. Interestingly, the discipline which has advanced this concept more than others is securities analysis. It is now generally recognized that the worth of a firm is its value to shareholders and firm valuation is now *de rigeur* in financial circles. In this area, empirical valuation models are now well developed and value estimates are now routinely made. This has prompted one set of authors to begin their book with the exploratory query "Why value value?" (Copeland *et al.* 1996). This question immediately sets the stage for further analysis as it implies that value can be elusive and requires valuation attempts beyond the simple act of pricing.

One main implication from the financial markets that seems to have eluded many marketers is that price and value are not necessarily congruent. Consumers buy and rebuy toothpaste for a price, but have no easy means of estimating the value to their dental health provided by regular usage of this substance. In actuality, the value of a dentifrice may be manyfold its cumulative cost. Thus, as in securities investing, the value in this context is the (discounted) cumulative future return of the item. Other examples include education, wellness programs, and insurance.

Perhaps the most common example of a single-stimulus value judgment is in the realm of hedonic consumption (Hirschman and Holbrook 1982). Here, the concepts of value, utility and pleasure merge, as the foremost as well as some current interpretations of utility are that of pleasure. In the earliest writings on utility, Bentham ([1823] 1968) referred to utility as the hedonic quality of experience – attaining pleasure and avoiding pain. And in recent writings, Kahneman and Snell (1990) and Kahneman and Varey (1991) reintroduce pleasure, sometimes described as satisfaction, as an equivalent descriptor of the value of experience. (The intervening years were dominated by decision utility or revealed preference – see Schoemaker 1982.)

The valuation of pleasure and its negative counterpart pain, both experienced affects, would at first appear to be a single stimulus judgment. Individuals are known to exclaim that they are happy or sad, pleased or displeased, or mirthful or sorrowful as if it were a single judgment. The qualifier "very" on any of these terms simply moves the judgment to one or the other extreme of a single continuum. Indeed, many one-item scales or rank scores of both extremes of the hedonic continuum exist and have been used for some time (e.g., Rokeach 1973; Andrews and Withey 1976; Campbell, Converse, and Rodgers 1976). Thus, it would seem that hedonic consumption could be easily valued by virtue of the "pleasure" it provides. It does not matter that variants of pleasure, such as thrill, are attained in such consumption, for thrill can be viewed as a high energy form of pleasure.

This writer sees pleasure as value or value as pleasure as an oversimplification. Taking the experience of hedonic pleasure as an ultimate outcome of life ignores the literature on subjective well-being which clearly shows that even pleasure is relative (e.g., Parducci 1968; Campbell *et al.* 1976; Crosby 1976). Individuals have both internal and external mechanisms by which to compare their current level of "pleasure." An obvious example is pain, a negative sensation that clearly is compared to the human resting state of homeostasis (Solomon and Corbit 1974). Individuals know that pain is unpleasant because their bodies have evolved to sense and display it. A medical pain scale uses this comparative notion to assess the severity of pain where the greatest extreme point is phrased as "as much as you can bear." This immediately begs the issue of degrees of pain at bearable and unbearable levels. Similarly, pleasure can be compared to its prior internally experienced levels. Thrill, ecstasy, and delight can all be compared to simple pleasure or happiness.

Use of external comparative referents to determine one's pleasure value is also common. Most have heard of the previously satisfied consumer who becomes disgruntled when it is found that others acquired a similar item for less cost or found greater value. Marketers use this innate human comparative tendency to create dissatisfaction with older models of the same brand (e.g., auto-design changes) or competitive offerings. And, on the positive side of the situation, seemingly unhappy individuals can change their state of mind by shifting the comparative referent to a lower standard as in the "satisfied poor" (Olson and Schober 1993).

Moreover, theories of worthy or ultimate life values (e.g., Scott 1965; Maslow 1970) do not list the sensation of pleasure; rather these lists are overrepresented with virtuous traits (e.g., kindness, honesty) or enduring life situations (e.g., self-esteem, self-fulfillment). Pleasure is simply too fleeting a sensation to be held out as an ultimate life experience. Further, the satisfaction literature (to be discussed), sees pleasure as one component along with other affects and cognitions.

Nonetheless, hedonic consumption is pursued by consumers and one must assume that the resulting affects and more distinct emotions provide a sense of "value" to these individuals. Unfortunately, a generally agreed-upon metric for measuring or comparing hedonic utility to other types of "value" has not been forthcoming. Generally, researchers assume that, when given a list of mixed goods, services, and aesthetics, consumers can "value" them on a common scale. For example, Kemp *et al.* (1995) measured the value to consumers of varied items from cash to chocolate to bus trips to wine on an 11-point 0–10 scale bounded by "you think this item is completely useless or valueless to you" to "very great personal use or value." Note that this is a very different question from the affect scales used for measuring pleasure or other positive affects (e.g., Watson *et al.* 1988) and still more different from scales recommended for satisfaction (Oliver 1997). Thus, hedonic value is measured empirically but the researcher takes much on faith in assuming that the as yet unknown psychophysics of valuating pleasure will manifest themselves in consumer ratings.

Another now-popular version of value has arisen in current discussions of a loyal customer base. One road to loyalty, it is said, is to provide value to customers – thus value-based loyalty (e.g., Fredericks and Salter 1995). But this implies that the value behind the loyalty to one firm be greater than that of another, itself implying a comparison. Note, that this rendition of value demands that the specific nature of the comparator be made, for it immediately begs the question of "value compared to what?" Writers are quite clear on what this comparison is – value compared to that of competitive offerings. So, what is it that is supposed to be compared? It is presumed that the consumer should know – or the marketer will inform him/her. The present discussion is now in the realm of dual-stimulus definitions, to be pursued shortly.

Before doing so, however, it is instructive to evaluate single-stimulus definitions in the context of the purpose of this chapter, to explore value-as-excellence. Can the expression of worth or utility or even pleasure connote excellence? As noted, high levels of these variables imply greater value, but is this high level of value excellence? A current teen expression of endearing performance is "Excellent, Dude." Does this phrase capture the essence of excellent value? No, excessively positive or exuberant phrases simply mean that a high level of the delivered outcome was experienced. If the outcome were truly known to be the very highest possible – the superlative outcome, excellence would be implied. To say this, a standard of comparison is needed and a dual-stimulus perspective is required.

## Dual-stimulus definitions of value in consumption

Value in the context of two stimuli is by definition a comparative process. This is not the same as saying that value is defined by two dimensions, such as the ambience and food served in a restaurant. Rather, the two stimuli do not have to be on the same conceptual plane as in the proverbial choice between what one has and the unknown behind a closed door.

There are two comparative processes consumers can take in assessing value. The first is an intra-product comparison such as when benefits are compared to costs; the second is an inter-product comparison that occurs when consumers compare the value of a product to its alternatives. The first comparison is actually a precursor to the second, but consumers do not necessarily process value comparisons in two stages. Both views are prominent in the literature, however. Most academics research the first comparison for an understanding of the underlying psychological process of value determination, while practitioners talk about the second comparison for its relation to loyalty, a inter-offering judgment. Thus, one can judge the value of a monopolistic offering, or consumers can simply state that they find more value in a product than in its competition and, because of this, will continue to rebuy it in the future. Discussion of each follows.

## Intra-product or internal value: valuing value

There is a growing body of literature on the meaning of consumption value from the perspective of the consumer, as compiled by Woodruff (1997) and Woodruff and Gardial (1996). In the latter source, the authors propose a summary definition whereby value is defined as the customer's desire for specific consequences instrumental in accomplishing an intended goal. Here, it is clear that value is a derivative of the consumer's goals in purchasing. Woodruff and Gardial elaborate on this definition by distinguishing between *value in use* and *value in possession*. Use value implies that the goal of purchasing is for the functional consequences of the product or service. The product is simply a means to an end such as when a disposable battery is used to power a toy. Possession value, in contrast, implies that the mere ownership of a product is its goal. Art, status symbols, and accomplishments such as mountain climbing qualify here.

In the first case, the value to the customer is what he/she would pay for the functional consequences and not the product itself. Thus, the same long-life battery used for a pacemaker would have greater value than when used for a watch. The fact that the battery may cost the same for both uses again illustrates the divergence of value and price. In the second case, the value is purely psychological and may differ greatly across consumers. Clearly, the owner of a unique Van Gogh places a higher value on possession of this piece than any other and may not part with it "for any price." Only when the owner desires to sell at auction, perhaps, does some correspondence between value and price materialize.

These examples illustrate the intra-product comparison process. Here the valuation is against a goal of consumption. In the case of value in use, the goal is the production of desired consequences. In the battery example, the battery's value is powering a toy. The value of the toy, in turn, is in providing enjoyment. Interestingly, the toy is typically valued more highly than the battery despite the fact that the toy would not be functional without the battery. One could say that the toy absent the battery still retains value in possession, as if to say that one's toy contains enjoyment potential despite the fact that it is not powered. For example, one could put the toy on a shelf and admire it, whereas the same sort of appreciation would be unlikely in the case of a battery.

The conundrum here is that the toy's utility can also be judged against the activity which might be pursued in its stead, including the resting state. Thus, the enjoyment of playing with the toy can be compared to the imagined enjoyment of playing with another toy, watching TV, or doing nothing at all. In this framing, the battery and the toy should have the same value, since the enjoyment of play cannot take place without both. But again, they do not.

This example, one of value in use, misses the essence of value as excellence. One cannot judge excellence without reference to directly comparable alternatives. Only by abstracting to more general categories can an excellence judgment be made. For example, one can exclaim that they have had an excellent dining experience or that playing with the aforementioned toy is excellent entertainment, but the consumer has done nothing more than broaden the category of dining and entertainment to include many diverse forms of these pastimes.

Value in possession may or may not have an excellence component to it. If one owns the finest example of a particular antiquity, its possession has excellence, uniqueness, and pride of ownership. One can own lesser forms of this same object (e.g., less excellence), but still retain uniqueness and pride of ownership. In fact, the rarest forms of an antiquity are often graded on their excellence (e.g., a rare coin). In still another example, one can have pride of ownership (i.e., possession), of a non-excellent and non-unique object. Children often covet their playthings even though they are very common.

This brings the discussion to comparisons of what is received to what is given, as in the definition of value a function of rewards versus costs. Numerous examples of this type of value assessment are available. *Consumer Reports* frequently rates products as "best buys." This means that, in their estimation, the ratio of what is received to its price is the best "value for the money." The publication typically finds that many medium and even low priced products are "best buys." In the same way, computers are rated on the basis of computing speed per dollar, common household and grocery items are rated on volume of contents per dollar, and homes on the basis of dollars per square foot of living space. As long as the something per dollar is quantifiable or nearly so, this comparison is too tempting to ignore.

Thus, one can produce a hierarchical list of the degree to which cost is embedded in the internal valuation process. At the uppermost level, cost is irrelevant. The value of the outcome (i.e., its goal) is sought at any cost. An infertile couple's desire to have children is an example of this, as is a terminally ill patient's willingness to spend and risk all to recover, as is an addict's craving for the drug of choice. Bidders at auctions will often engage in "bidding wars" over a desired object and collectors often will pay "any price" to complete a collection (or to start one). In a phrase, this type of value is "priceless" – priceless value.

Skipping to the extreme, lower level of internal value, the consequences and, perhaps, goal-related outcomes are compared to price or cost more generally. Now cost is considered in the value equation and value can be both internal and external. This is to say that the item can be assessed in isolation from any other thing as long as a value rule is known. For example, a coin can be valued for its gold content using the current price of gold as a standard. It can also be given additional valuation based on its rarity, where rarity is based on the original number of coins minted, those remaining in circulation, etc. And it can further be valued on its condition, with the degree of wear determined by the level of detail which remains. Interestingly, this same single-object valuation now permits two objects, similarly judged, to be compared.

Elaboration on the middle level of cost consideration in value, reserved until now, necessarily takes the discussion to inter-object comparisons. Thus, it provides a segue to the more formal material in the next section, presented shortly. At this middle level, cost is considered only in relation to a general category of similar pursuits. One way to look at this is to assume a fixed cost for an item or activity and examine all alternatives that fulfill this criterion. A common example is travel or vacationing. Consumers will have saved many thousands of dollars earmarked for a vacation. The travel agent is instructed to prepare alternatives that fall within this cost constraint. The cost is then considered forgone, and is not entertained further. The alternatives, however, are still considered for their value. Generally, these will be qualitatively different alternatives and compete on that basis.

Still other examples are home buying, entertainment, education, and aesthetics. In the case of home buying, the upper limit as to cost is set by the buyer's income. This puts a cap on the range of homes under consideration. As all buyers are encouraged by brokers and financial planners to "buy as much house as you can" because the mortgage payments are fixed, whereas income usually rises, the homes under consideration are in the same price range, but differ markedly in terms of architectural design, layout, location, etc. Thus, for each residence under consideration, the constellation of home facets is judged for its (intrinsic) value. This value, then, becomes the criterion on which the houses are judged against one another – an inter-object comparison as discussed next.

## Inter-object comparisons

Here the excellence judgment is now more direct. As alluded to in the preceding discussion, a direct comparative referent is needed to form the prototype against which alternatives are compared. This may be an ideal object or, absent that, "best in class." Inter-object comparisons permit an additional dimension not available to intra-object evaluations. Whereas intra-object valuations require some internal or external standard of measure, inter-object comparisons do not. As long as consumers can indicate a preference between two of these, the evaluation standards do not require specification. Oftentimes, individuals cannot state why they prefer one alternative to another (Wolfe 1998). This is particularly true in matters of aesthetics, foodstuffs, "taste," and even romance.

The desire on the part of researchers to understand the "hidden" criteria consumers use has prompted research on "preference," such as preference mapping and study of the inner workings of the brain. Whereas science may eventually discover how individuals make preference judgments when they lack the cognitive ability to do so, this does not concern the present discussion. The preferences exist, nonetheless, and the preferred item is the one consumers value most.

Writers have searched for the best way to describe the hidden evaluation function discussed previously. While many options are available including scaling, conjoint analysis, and multi-attribute attitude modeling, it would be convenient if a single concept could be studied for insight on how the consumer views the focus of this chapter, that of value-as-excellence. In both lay and business terms, this concept is typically referred to as "quality." How is quality as "excellence" related to value? As Holbrook (1994) notes, it is a component of value in broader terms. His framework presumes that the value of consumption increases as quality increases. What, then, is quality?

## *Variants of quality*

Oliver (1996, 1997) provides a summary of quality definitions based on the extant literature (e.g., Garvin 1984; Steenkamp 1990). He categorizes the terms used in various writings on the topic into three conceptual perspectives. The first, *attainment*, implies that an object has achieved a high level of technical accomplishment. Phrases describing this perspective include "innate excellence," "superiority," and "uncompromising standards." Thus, marketers wishing to bestow impressions of "quality" can suggest to consumers that their consumable is paramount on some high level standard of unspecified dimensions. Readers will recognize this as similar to the previous discussion of utility and, as will be noted, similar problems are evident.

The second perspective, *desirability*, refers to the consumer's need for attachment to the consumable. Phrases such as those used in earlier sections of this paper appear here, such as "preference" and "worth." Interestingly, Oliver (1997) includes "affordable excellence" here as if to differentiate it from "innate" excellence, reflecting the ability on the part of the consumer to actually own what s/he desires. Generally, this perspective relates to the attractiveness of the consumable and suggests a level of quality that can be possessed.

The third perspective, *usefulness*, reflects the influence of utility-based reasoning on quality definitions. Phrases such as "fitness for use" and "capacity to fulfill wants" characterize this perspective. Thus, quality can be defined in terms of the consequences of consuming as well as its attractiveness or "excellence."

Of interest is the fact that value is more akin to the desirability perspective. Like quality, value can be assessed before and after usage. One does not have to experience quality to estimate or assess it. At this point, however, the answer to the question of the role of quality in value has not been given. Part of the reason is that, like value, quality can be discussed as a single stimulus concept without a comparative referent. For example, in the three perspectives of quality, one might ask: "What is it that has been attained?," "What, exactly, does the product possess to make it so desirable?," and "For what purpose is the consumable useful?" Like value, these questions require consideration of the comparative referent – the second of the dual stimulus definitions, to be exact.

## *The comparison referent*

Some of the phrases given to illustrate the three perspectives do hint at a comparison referent. For example, "affordable excellence" implies that this virtue is achieved at a reasonable cost and, hence, represents value. Similarly, the word "superiority" implies that some other alternative must be inferior. And fulfilling wants assumes that the level of want is understood. To address these unspecified standards, writers have relied on two criteria. Both would be recognized by most as incontrovertible standards for quality assessment.

The first of these, *ideals*, derives from early interest of the part of consumer researchers in ideal point models (Green and Wind 1973). Generally it is assumed that the ideal consumable can be elicited by the consumer through the calculation of distances from current market offerings to an imagined ideal brand. Thus, quality can be defined in terms of a difference from the ideal with small distances being preferred. In the absence of an ideal or in the inability of consumers to imagine what an ideal brand would entail, consumers can be asked to compare offerings to a "best brand" (Cadotte *et al.* 1987).

The second of the quality comparators is *excellence*. Excellence is a criterion many companies and quality promoters frequently use in describing their consumables. It would appear to be one notch below an ideal product as it only requires that the consumable be rated among the top in its field. As long as consumers can imagine an excellent product, whether it exists or not, excellence or phrases similar to it can be held out as a standard. In fact, in their proposed measure of service quality, Parasuraman *et al.* (1991) ask respondents to assess performance against standards of *excellent* companies. Here, excellent companies could be either real ("best brand") or imagined (a better best brand). The ideal referent, by comparison, is one step removed in a potentially unattainable direction. And in a variant of this standard, a local seller of plants advertises itself as the "superlative florist." Not ideal, but superlative.

As noted, both variants of quality rely on a comparison referent to infer value. The value addressed here, however, does not take sacrifices into account. Like the grading of a diamond by the four "Cs" standards – cut, color, clarity, carat weight – quality, generally, is an externally mediated perception that a product or service possesses excellent levels of the key quality dimensions which define quality for that product/service. Thus, perceived levels of quality are cognitive in nature and, as such, can remain in the consumer's mind for extended periods as well as be reinforced by external cues including advertising and word-of-mouth.

Thus, quality is representative of the first examples of the value hierarchy, priceless value, where cost is not explicitly considered. In fact, market forces will determine what monetary valuation is placed on various quality grades in the manner of diamond pricing. The excellence criteria, the four Cs, are invariant and standard tables have been prepared for grading. Other factors such as inflation, availability, brand (e.g., Tiffany), and the trend in marriages will help influence the cost to the consumer.

This notwithstanding, quality *is* one of the components of value in consumption. Consumers derive value from quality; it enhances their consumption experience and, in economic terms, gives them added utility. Thus, quality is a precursor to both value and satisfaction (Oliver 1997). This brings up the issue of how value relates to satisfaction. Just what is satisfaction and how does it relate to value?

## Value as a satisfaction-like postpurchase comparison?

As noted, Holbrook (1994; Holbrook and Corfman 1985) posits that there are eight fundamental types of value in consumption. The dimensions on which they are based define the consumer's essential criteria for forming value judgments. In order, the dimensions include: (a) whether the outcomes are judged with reference to the self or others, (b) whether the outcomes are actively accomplished ("done by" the consumer) or are reactively appreciated ("done to" the consumer), and (c) whether the outcomes are valued for their relation to another goal (extrinsic) or are valued as an end in themselves (intrinsic). This allows for the emergence of the following values: efficiency, excellence, status, esteem, play, aesthetics, ethics, and spirituality.

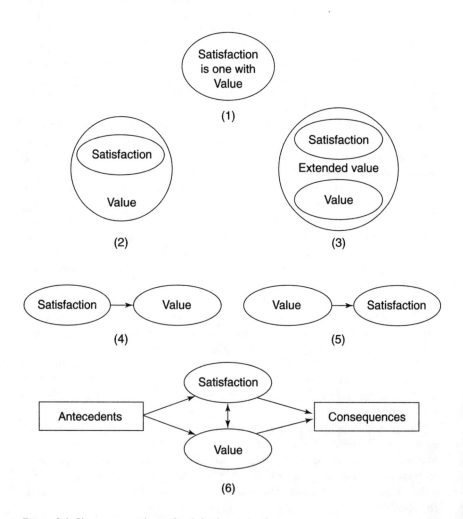

*Figure 2.1* Six representations of satisfaction and value

Elsewhere, Oliver (1996) notes that satisfaction, another frequently pursued goal of consumption, does not appear in the Holbrook typology. He raises a number of interesting questions. Namely: (1) Is satisfaction value – are they the same concept? (2) Is satisfaction one of the values in the Holbrook typology? (3) Is it an additional value defined by another dimension not considered (e.g., extended value)? Is satisfaction a related, but conceptually distinct, concept? (4) If so, is satisfaction an antecedent of value – do consumers receive value from satisfaction? (5) Alternatively, is it a consequent – do consumers receive satisfaction from value in consumption? And (6) Are satisfaction and value linked bidirectionally in a larger web of consumption constructs? See a graphical depiction of each of these alternative representations in Figure 2.1.

## *What, now, is value?*

These questions are intriguing but cannot be pursued until there is some agreement over the definitions of satisfaction and value. By now the many approaches taken here to pin down a value definition point to three possibilities, corresponding to the three representations of value as to whether or not it relates to sacrifice. The first is what the consumable gives the consumer regardless of cost. It is utility in its truest sense. It is how much the consumer would suffer – how much less the consumer would be – in its absence. This includes items that can be assessed for their worth and those that cannot – the priceless item. When an individual claims that his or her life would be "worthless" without some entity, that person's very existence is the value of that entity to him/her.

The second definition is a comparative assessment to other alternatives whether qualitatively similar or not. Here the phrase "more value than" (although the actual valuation may not have been made) comes into play. This is an ordinal assessment that may be quantifiable. When individuals drop out of the workforce to pursue an MBA, they are making an implicit judgment that their future job prospects will have more value at the end of the program than if they had stayed in the labor market and worked for the length of the MBA program. Unfortunately, the true value of this comparison can never be known, but it is projected nonetheless. Oftentimes, the cost of the interlude is substantial, involving both tuition and forgone income. The individual makes the value determination regardless.

The third definition reflects the value "equation" of outcomes compared to sacrifices and is characterized by the "best buy" moniker. Here the comparison is explicit in the definition. Which of these "values" is the real value? One way of answering this question is to look for commonalities among them.

What is apparent is that the numerator of the value equation is common to all. What the consumer has, will have, or believes they have or will have is the universal. Thus, like the notion of utility, value is the additional "worth" an entity brings to one's life. Absent the object, the consumer suffers a value decrement. Separately, it is the consumer's choice whether comparisons are made to internal or external standards, other alternatives, or to cost. If any of these comparisons are made, the value takes on other nuances, but still is value. Thus, value is what is added to the consumer's existence. This addition can be cast in terms of additional pleasure, monetary worth, or simple "utility." Or it can be cast in terms of maintaining pleasure or ensuring against loss of pleasure (e.g., insurance). Or it can be cast in terms of restoring an individual to homeostasis as in the case of a medicine restoring health. Of interest is the fact that these three perspectives on value correspond to what Oliver (1989, 1997) has called "satisfaction-as-pleasure," "satisfaction-as-contentment," and "satisfaction-as-relief." Thus, there must be some correspondence between value and satisfaction, as follows.

### What, now, is satisfaction and what is its role in value?

In Oliver (1997), satisfaction is defined as *pleasurable fulfillment*. That is, the consumer senses that consumption fulfills some need, desire, goal, etc. and that this fulfillment is pleasurable. The primary emphasis here is on pleasure, because some fulfillment is unpleasant (paying taxes, doing laundry). Even over-fulfillment can be unpleasant (overeating, too much of a good thing generally), while some underfulfillment can provide pleasure (palliatives, emergency repairs). Thus, satisfaction is the consumer's sense that consumption has provided pleasant outcomes against a standard of pleasure/displeasure. It is a singular response to a consumption event. This notion of outcomes compared to a standard suggests that the cost-based perspective on value may play a role in the value-satisfaction conundrum, as follows.

Few would disagree that a comparison of performance outcomes (i.e., quality) to sacrifices (i.e., cost-based value) is, in all likelihood, one of the antecedents of satisfaction. That would make it one of the comparative operations in satisfaction formation which can be added to those discussed in Oliver (1997). See Table 2.1. In this perspective, the "receipts compared to sacrifices" version of value is viewed as one among the other comparative operations in postpurchase judgments. In effect, it operates in parallel with the other comparators in the satisfaction response. This view is consistent with Zeithaml's (1988) position that a cost-based definition of value is an antecedent of satisfaction.

*Table 2.1* The comparative operators in consumption

| Performance Comparator | Resulting Cognition |
| --- | --- |
| Predictive expectations | Expectancy disconfirmation |
| Needs | Need fulfillment |
| Ideals/excellence | Quality |
| Fairness | Equity/inequity |
| Counterfactual alternatives | Regret |
| Nothing | Unappraised cognition |
| Sacrifices | Cost-based value |

In a seemingly tautological perspective, it may also be the case that satisfaction is a precursor to value. That is, some of the value derived from consumption could be satisfaction-based. This begs the question of where satisfaction belongs in the Holbrook typology.

Oliver (1996) notes that, for satisfaction to be an input to the value one receives in consumption, it must provide one of the outcomes in the Holbrook typology or provide an outcome not accounted for in his paradigm. Close inspection of the Holbrook (1994) cells, which include efficiency, excellence, status, esteem, play, aesthetics, ethics, and spirituality, suggests that these outcomes, if attained, would provide a sense of satisfaction to the recipient. If satisfaction is still another component of value, then what is the missing dimension on which it is defined? One conclusion from this analysis is that satisfaction and value are related but different concepts and that satisfaction is not a variant of value. More will be said of this next.

## What *is* the relation between satisfaction and value?

It is now time to answer the question of which of the frameworks in Figure 2.1 are most accurate, given the logic and analysis presented here. It should be noted at the outset that the first representation, number (1) in Figure 2.1, can be dismissed. Satisfaction emerges as a distinct construct when compared to *any* of the definitions of value discussed here. To show this, it is only necessary to provide example cases where satisfaction can exist in the absence of value and where value can exist in the absence of satisfaction, an exercise useful in distinguishing satisfaction from quality (see Oliver 1993). In what follows, two examples are given, one relating to the first perspective of value as having no bearing on cost, and a second where receipts are compared to costs.

In an example of priceless value, a consumer may own an heirloom, passed down from forebears that is of immense value on the market. Yet this hypothetical consumer exclaims that she has no need for it, stores it in a safe, and derives no satisfaction from it. It is not fulfilling in any way and is a mere possession. Alternatively, a simple possession such as a common jigsaw puzzle may be very satisfying each time it is completed, but has no value beyond its ability to challenge and satisfy.

In another example involving sacrifices, the actual cost may have been sufficiently low and even zero as in a free good. In this case, just about any level of reasonable receipts may provide immense value. The consumer, however, may find little satisfaction or even need fulfillment in this case. An unneeded or disliked gift of great value would provide yet another example. Alternatively, a needed item may come very dear (expensive), giving great satisfaction but little value in the receipts over cost sense. For example, a makeshift emergency automobile repair may be truly satisfying (i.e., satisfaction-as-relief; see Oliver 1989) if it enables a motorist to reach the nearest service station. The road mechanic may charge an exorbitant price, thereby offering poor value for this "service." The motorist's needs, however, were fulfilled nonetheless. Here, the "value" is of a higher order and must be explained without regard for cost.

These examples illustrate both the divergence and interplay between satisfaction and value. As noted previously, satisfaction is the consumer's fulfillment response. The value of this response is the end-state of the consumer after having been satisfied (fulfilled). Satisfaction provides value in what it leaves with the consumer – the satisfied state. It may also be the case that knowing that one has received value can be satisfying, as in the cost-based version; alternatively satisfaction may provide a sense of *extended* value in that the consumer values (places a high utility on) being satisfied. This may explain the basis for the conundrum of the primacy of satisfaction or value. At the same time that consumption value enhances satisfaction, satisfaction may be a valued outcome for many consumers. The extent to which satisfaction provides extended "value" awaits further research.

This brings the discussion back to Figure 2.1 and the question of which of the six representations is correct. Having previously dismissed representation (1), the preceding analysis would suggest that representation (2) is also problematic. The reason is clear from the difficulty noted earlier of positioning satisfaction in the Holbrook (1994) typology. Unless satisfaction is a *personal* value, a combination of topics that has not been extensively studied as yet, satisfaction cannot be considered to be contained in a set of values despite the fact that it may be valued.

Representation (3) goes beyond that of (2) to suggest that there is a conceptually higher plane of "extended value," alluded to previously. This would take discussion to a higher order of value in consumer consumption, approaching the issue of the quality of life. In essence, attaining and receiving elements of value as well as being satisfied would jointly contribute to the (extended) value of one's life. This too, is an under-researched issue in consumption and life quality, in general.

In contrast to the first of the six representations, there is merit to the remaining three perspectives in Figure 2.1. When value is viewed as a desirable end-state of consumption (Woodruff and Gardial 1996), satisfying consumption events are of value to consumers. Thus, being satisfied gives value. Again, the state of satisfaction is separate from the end-state of being satisfied, which is valued. Thus, there is merit to representation (4). Similarly, when value is viewed as receipts compared to costs, it becomes one of the satisfaction comparators of Table 2.1. In this case, value gives satisfaction as in representation (5).

It is now apparent that representation (6) may be the most accurate of those entertained here. Value and satisfaction mutually influence each other as value transforms and modulates between calculated states and end states. Both have common antecedents in consumption events, such as product or service performance, and both have common consequences such as loyalty. Thus, both are embedded in a web of consumption constructs, as suggested earlier.

This latter perspective also suggests the role of quality in value. In agreement with Zeithaml (1988), quality is an input to value. Value, then, becomes a super-ordinate concept subsuming quality. And, in accord with Oliver (1993, 1997), quality is an input to satisfaction through the comparison of performance to

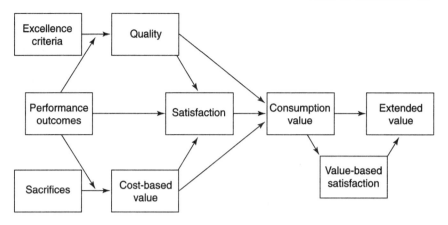

*Figure 2.2* Nomological net of value concepts in consumption

excellence standards. Then, in a seemingly circular pattern, quality enhances satisfaction and value, which provides additional satisfaction – satisfaction deriving first from quality and then from value.

It should not be overlooked that the value and satisfaction provided by quality derive from other desired purchase outcomes which, by their nature, define the essence of quality. As typically found in studies investigating the meaning of quality to consumers (e.g., Gutman and Alden 1985), quality brings reliability, durability, status, self-confidence, and ease of decision-making. For these reasons, quality is value, thereby being a "valued quality" in consumption.

These relationships have been portrayed graphically in Figure 2.2. There, one can see the "web of consumption constructs" in which quality, cost-based value, satisfaction, and higher forms of consumption value are embedded. Thus, value-as-excellence is not "one thing." Rather it is a constellation of consumption-related constructs which includes quality, an excellence-based consumer judgment. One hopes that researchers will use this framework to corroborate the reasoning presented here.

## *What of personal value?*

Because the issue of personal value has been broached earlier in this paper, the discussion would be remiss if some attempt were not made to address it. Before proceeding, however, a distinction between consumption value and personal value requires elaboration. Specifically, it is suggested that the value derived from consumption does not necessarily correspond to values desired by individuals in general which reflect desirable end states in life sought by all individuals (see Corfman *et al.* 1991). For example, the Kahle (1984) List of Values includes accomplishment, belongingness, enjoyment, excitement, fulfillment, fun, security, self-respect, and warm relationships. Note that some of these, such as enjoyment and security can be obtained through consumption while others, such as self-fulfillment, are not easily achieved in this manner. While means–end chain analysis provides a way of linking consumption to values (e.g., Gutman 1991), it does so only indirectly and without explicit consideration of satisfaction's role in the process.

Researchers are encouraged to forge ahead with a renewal of research connecting consumption events (including the attainment of value) to the contribution they make to the enhancement of personal value. More has been written on the intuition inherent in this statement than on its substance. Means–end chain analysis does efficiently show how consequences of consumption affect values directly. What it does not yet do is connect higher order consumption value to personal values. Some would say that these higher order utilities and values have been included in the various lists of values that have been proposed. This remains an empirical question, one worthy of future attention.

## Acknowledgment

Parts of this paper were reprinted from Oliver (1996) with permission from the publisher and copyright holder, the Association for Consumer Research.

## References

Andrews, F. M., and Withey, S. B. (1976) *Social Indicators of Well-Being*, New York: Plenum Press.

Bentham, J. ([1823] 1968) "An Introduction to the Principles of Morals and Legislation," in A. N. Page (ed.) *Utility Theory: A Book of Readings*, New York: Wiley, 3–29.

Cadotte, E. R., Woodruff, R. B., and Jenkins, R. L. (1987) "Expectations and Norms in Models of Consumer Satisfaction," *Journal of Marketing Research* 24, August: 305–14.

Campbell, A., Converse, P. E., and Rodgers, W. L. (1976) *The Quality of American Life*, New York: Russell Sage Foundation.

Copeland, T., Koller, T., and Murrin, J. (1996) *Valuation: Measuring and Managing the Value of Companies*, 2nd Ed., New York: John Wiley & Sons.

Corfman, K., Lehmann, D. R., and Narayanan, S. (1991) "Values, Utility, and Ownership: Modeling the Relationships for Consumer Durables," *Journal of Retailing* 67, Summer: 184–204.

Crosby, F. (1976) "A Model of Egoistical Relative Deprivation," *Psychological Review* 83, March: 85–113.

Fredericks, J. O., and Salter, J. M. II (1995) "Beyond Customer Satisfaction," *Management Review* 84, May: 29–32.

Galanter, E. (1990) "Utility Functions for Nonmonetary Events," *American Journal of Psychology* 103, Winter: 449–70.

Garvin, D. A. (1984) "What Does 'Product Quality' Really Mean?," *Sloan Management Review* 26, Fall: 25–43.

Green, P. E., and Wind, Y. (1973) *Multiattribute Decisions in Marketing: A Measurement Approach*, Hinsdale, IL: Dryden Press.

Gutman, J. (1991) "Exploring the Nature of Linkages Between Consequences and Values," *Journal of Business Research* 22, March: 143–8.

Gutman, J., and Alden, S. D. (1985) "Adolescents' Cognitive Structures of Retail Stores and Fashion Consumption: A Means–end Chain Analysis of Quality," in J. Jacoby and J. C. Olson (eds) *Perceived Quality: How Consumers View Stores and Merchandise*, Lexington, MA: Lexington Books, 99–114.

Hartman, R. S. (1967) *The Structure of Value: Foundations of Scientific Axiology*, Carbondale and Edwardsville, IL: Southern Illinois University Press.

Hirschman, E. C., and Holbrook, M. B. (1982) "Hedonic Consumption: Emerging Concepts, Methods and Propositions," *Journal of Marketing* 46, Summer: 92–101.

Hirshleifer, J. (1976) *Price Theory and Applications*, Englewood Cliffs, NJ: Prentice-Hall.

Holbrook, M. B. (1994) "The Nature of Customer Value: An Axiology of Services in the Consumption Experience," in R. T. Rust and R. L. Oliver (eds) *Service Quality: New Directions in Theory and Practice*, Thousand Oaks, CA: Sage Publications, 21–71.

—— (1996) "Customer Value – A Framework for Analysis and Research," in K. P. Corfman and J. G. Lynch, Jr. (eds) *Advances in Consumer Research*, Vol. 23, Provo, UT: Association for Consumer Research, 138–42.

Holbrook, M. B., and Corfman, K. P. (1985) "Quality and Value in the Consumption Experience: Phaedrus Rides Again," in J. Jacoby and J. C. Olson (eds) *Perceived Quality: How Consumers View Stores and Merchandise*, Lexington, MA: Lexington Books, 31–57.

Huber, J., Lynch, J., Corfman, K., Feldman, J., Holbrook, M. B., Lehmann, D., Munier, B., Schkade, D., and Simonson, I. (1997) "Thinking about Values in Prospect and Retrospect: Maximizing Experienced Utility," *Marketing Letters* 8, July: 323–34.

Kahle, L. R. (1984) *Attitudes and Social Adaptation: A Person–Situation Interaction Approach*, Oxford: Pergamon.

Kahneman, D., and Snell, J. (1990) "Predicting Utility," in R. M. Hogarth (ed.) *Insights in Decision Making*, Chicago: University of Chicago Press, 295–310.

Kahneman, D., and Varey, C. (1991) "Notes on the Psychology of Utility," in J. Elster and J. E. Roemer (eds) *Interpersonal Comparisons of Well-Being*, Cambridge: Cambridge University Press, 127–59.

Kemp, S. (1991) "Magnitude Estimation of the Utility of Public Goods," *Journal of Applied Psychology* 76, August: 533–40.

Kemp, S., Lea, S. E. G., and Fussell, S. (1995) "Experiments on Rating the Utility of Consumer Goods: Evidence Supporting Microeconomic Theory," *Journal of Economic Psychology* 16, December: 543–61.

Kemp, S., and Willetts, K. (1995) "Rating the Value of Government-funded Services: Comparison of Methods," *Journal of Economic Psychology* 16, March: 1–21.

Maslow, A. H. (1970) *Motivation and Personality*, 2nd Ed. New York: Harper & Row.

Najder, Z. (1975), *Values and Evaluations*, Oxford: Clarendon Press.

Oliver, R. L. (1989) "Processing of the Satisfaction Response in Consumption: A Suggested Framework and Research Propositions," *Journal of Consumer Satisfaction, Dissatisfaction and Complaining Behavior* 2: 1–16.

—— (1993) "A Conceptual Model of Service Quality and Service Satisfaction: Compatible Goals, Different Concepts," in T. A. Swartz, D. E. Bowen, and S. W. Brown (eds) *Advances in Services Marketing and Management: Research and Practice*, Vol. 2, Greenwich, CT: JAI Press, 65–85.

—— (1996) "Varieties of Value in the Consumption Satisfaction Response," in K. P. Corfman and J. G. Lynch, Jr. (eds) *Advances in Consumer Research*, Vol. 23, Provo, UT: Association for Consumer Research, 143–7.

—— (1997) *Satisfaction: A Behavioral Perspective on the Consumer*, New York: Irwin/McGraw-Hill.

Olson, G. I., and Schober, B. I. (1993) "The Satisfied Poor: Development of an Intervention-oriented Theoretical Framework to Explain Satisfaction with a Life in Poverty," *Social Indicators Research* 28, February: 173–93.

Parasuraman, A., Berry, L. L., and Zeithaml V. A. (1991) "Refinement and Reassessment of the SERVQUAL Scale," *Journal of Retailing* 67, Winter: 420–50.

Parducci, A. (1968) "The Relativism of Absolute Judgments," *Scientific American* 219, December: 84–90.

Rokeach, M. (1973) *The Nature of Human Values*, New York: The Free Press.

Schoemaker, P. J. H. (1982) "The Expected Utility Model: Its Variants, Purposes, Evidence and Limitations," *Journal of Economic Literature* 20, June: 529–63.

Scott, W. A. (1965) *Values and Organizations*, Chicago: Rand McNally.

Solomon, R. L., and Corbit, J. D. (1974) "An Opponent-process Theory of Motivation: I. Temporal Dynamics of Affect," *Psychological Review* 81, March: 119–45.

Steenkamp, J.-B. E. M. (1990) "Conceptual Model of the Quality Perception Process," *Journal of Business Research* 21, December: 309–33.

Watson, D., Clark, L. A., and Tellegen, A. (1988) "Development and Validation of Brief Measures of Positive and Negative Affect: The PANAS Scales," *Journal of Personality and Social Psychology* 54, June: 1063–70.

Wolfe, D. B. (1998) "What Your Customers Can't Say," *American Demographics* 20, February: 24–9.

Woodruff, R. B. (1997) "Customer Value: The Next Source for Competitive Advantage," *Journal of the Academy of Marketing Science* 25, Spring: 139–53.

Woodruff, R. B., and Gardial, S. F. (1996) *Know Your Customer: New Approaches to Understanding Customer Value and Satisfaction*, Cambridge, MA: Blackwell Publishers.

Zeithaml, V. A. (1988) "Consumer Perceptions of Price, Quality, and Value: A Means–End Model and Synthesis of Evidence," *Journal of Marketing* 52, July: 2–22.

# 3 The value of status and the status of value

*Michael R. Solomon*

## The value of status

"I don't get no respect." To echo the hallmark phrase of the comedian Rodney Dangerfield, status is a consumption activity that gets no respect compared to the other seven cells in Holbrook's Typology of Consumer Value. Status is not terribly efficient, it often does not impart other than fleeting satisfaction, status-seekers may be low in esteem, and many would argue that the pursuit of status is neither fun, beautiful, ethical, nor spiritual.

Indeed, consumers and researchers are of two minds about status; it's the phenomenon they have to acknowledge but love to hate. Status-seeking is what everyone *else* does, perhaps because the status markers sought by others may seem hollow or meaningless compared to those we ourselves value. The academic may deplore the executive's penchant for expensive luxury cars. He turns up his nose at this materialistic excess, even as he is ensconced in his study eagerly reviewing the latest Social Science Citation Index report of other scholars who have cited *his* work on decision processes underlying car purchases. Simultaneously, an automotive engineer enjoys a reverie about the aesthetically pleasing design modification she made to a concept car – and, perhaps, fantasizes about the sizeable cash bonus she will receive for this contribution. As Holbrook (1994) reminds us, virtually any consumption experience can take on the coloring of any kind of value depending upon who is doing the consuming – and perhaps, who is assigning the value. Perhaps status (like beauty) is in the eye of the beholder.

This chapter will explore the value of status as a consumption goal and will also consider the status of this value within the realm of consumer research. Holbrook's Typology of Consumer Value classifies forms of consumption using three dimensions: Intrinsic versus Extrinsic value, Self-oriented versus Other-oriented value, and Active versus Reactive value. Status occupies one of the resulting eight cells by virtue of its depiction as an extrinsic, other-oriented, and active type of value.

This chapter will consider the status of status in terms of each of these dimensions. It will then conclude with a brief assessment of current status research within the realm of the consumer-behavior discipline, identifying some gaps within this research domain that perhaps will be filled by those hardy researchers willing to brave the stigma of working in the Rodney Dangerfield cell of Holbrook's Typology.

## Defining status

Before the status of status in the Holbrook typology can be assessed, it is necessary to step back and consider precisely what is meant by this construct. This is particularly important because the term status as it will be used here does not strictly correspond to the conventional definition as embraced by sociologists. The current treatment is instead closer to that employed by consumers, who tend to view status as a form of self-expression to be striven for or eschewed, rather than as a classificatory label applied to a larger social group (Vanneman and Pampel 1977; Munson and Spivey 1981; Coleman 1983; Eastman *et al.* 1994; Mager and Kahle 1995).

### The structuralist tradition

Undoubtedly the traditional status construct is most closely associated with the work of Max Weber, a pioneer in the development of stratification theory. Sociologists who focus on the roles of power and structure argue that a process of stratification divides society into segments; all societies manifest patterns of social inequality resulting in a series of ranks that differentiate group members. The phenomenon of *social stratification* refers to the creation of artificial divisions in a society by which scarce resources are distributed unequally to status positions (Turner 1981).

Weber agreed with Karl Marx that property is the primary basis upon which classes are established. In contrast to Marx, however, he argued that the market rather than production is crucial to the generation of class distinction. The potential for class membership is not realized until resources are actually used in a market to secure access to privilege. For Weber, social classes are concrete groups constructed by and recognized by participants, and he identified four such classes in capitalist society: working class, petty bourgeoisie, propertyless intelligentsia, and specialists and classes privileged through property and education. By monopolizing access to property and to credential-granting institutions, the privileged classes further enhance their relative value by actively excluding members of less advantaged groups (Weber 1978).

Weber fully realized that the assignment of status is not solely mandated by access to economic resources. He acknowledged the crucial role of what he termed *social honor*, and he argued that status groups are composed of community members among whom social honor is differentially accorded. The way that social honor is distributed in a community is the "social order." Thus what one *does* with the resources available is even more diagnostic than the sheer amount of resources one has. This conceptualization highlights the subjective aspect of status, since it is left to both the actor and to observers to allocate social honor according to the criteria established by a specific community. One person's status symbol is another person's useless extravagance.

The structuralist tradition has more recently been carried forward by a more contemporary standard-bearer. Giddens (1973) focuses on the way the market transforms potential patterns of inequality into concrete manifestations. He calls this closure process *structuration*. For example, educational credentials divide capitalist society into upper, middle, and lower classes. However, since the market lacks formal limitations on individual mobility, there must be mechanisms to maintain the separation in micro contexts. Giddens terms these sources of *proximate structuration*, and he identifies three such sources: 1) Division of labor, 2) Division of authority, and 3) Distributive groupings or "those relationships involving common patterns of the consumption of economic goods – such as class-segregated neighborhood communities" (ibid. 1973: 109).

## *The constructivist tradition*

A static, structuralist perspective helps to appreciate the power dynamics of social groups. However, its contribution at a more micro, phenomenological level is problematic. As Weber wrote, "status honor is normally expressed by the fact that above all else a specific *style of life* can be expected from all those who wish to belong to the circle" (Weber 1978: 74, italics in original).

This pithy observation (the origin of the modern term *lifestyle*) encapsulates the basic point of departure in this chapter from conventional sociological treatments of status. We will focus more on the aspect of *wishing to belong* to a status group at the individual level than on being classified as belonging to an extant status group at a macro level. The construct of status in the present context thus actually refers to the *process of achieving status*; the consumption activities and desires related to the attainment of a certain placement in a social hierarchy by an individual. This operationalization differs from a focus on status as a structural variable used in a more abstract sense to describe (in the aggregate) the relative placement of group members – achieving *a* status.

Hopefully, this perspective gets us a step closer toward capturing the complexity and richness of status-seeking at the individual level, recognizing that the desire to be ranked in a certain way is an ongoing, dynamic process. The logic here is similar to theoretical developments in the areas of fashion diffusion and communication. In both cases, attempts at explanation began with the imposition of a positivist linear process that lacked the recognition that these processes actually are the product of a complex series of social constructions. And in each case, initial models ignored the crucial role of feedback and interactivity and the crucial role played by various cultural intermediaries (Solomon and Englis 1997).

Communications researchers now are more likely to acknowledge the decoder's contributions to textual meaning by adopting perspectives such as reader-response theory or by focusing on interactivity in hypermediated environments (Fisher 1978; Scott 1994; Hoffman and Novak 1996; Venkatesh,

Dholakia, and Dholakia 1996). Diffusion researchers have largely abandoned the static "trickle-down" approach to fashion, focusing instead upon the proactive influence exerted by consumers in defining and modifying "received" product meanings in accordance with the symbolic needs of specific subcultures (Hebdige 1979; Arnould and Wilk 1985; McCracken 1985; Costa and Bamossy 1995; Thompson and Hirschman 1995; Ger and Belk 1996; Englis and Solomon 1997).

The constructivist perspective emphasizes the central function of symbolic consumption – products often are a vehicle employed by both actor and observers to determine the actor's social identity and placement within a social nexus. The use of consumption activities as a form of self-construction is often related to strong associations between products and social roles. Whether for yuppies, sports teams, or motorcycle gangs, group identities coalesce around forms of expressive symbolism. The self-definitions of group members are derived from the common symbol system to which the group is dedicated; these symbols define the group's "personality." As a result, each social role is associated with a collection or constellation of products and activities taken by society to define that role (Solomon 1983, 1988a).

So, status can be viewed as the outcome of a social construction process that assigns meaning to the desire for, acquisition, and/or display of valued objects calculated to increase social honor in a community (Waters 1994). While engaged in this process, the individual is motivated to 1) identify a desirable location(s) in his or her particular social nexus, 2) acquire products and experiences s/he believes will attain this position, and 3) validate this standing among relevant others. Each stage of this dynamic process can be (at least roughly) linked to one of Holbrook's classificatory dimensions as shown in Table 3.1. These three consumption stages will now be considered in the order just described.

*Table 3.1* Stages of status-seeking and the Typology of Consumer Value

| *Consumption Stage* | *Consumption Focus* | *Typology Dimension* |
|---|---|---|
| Status Definition | Identifying the social identity one can or should adopt and determining the optimal strategy to achieve that identity | ACTIVE |
| Status Acquisition | Performing consumption activities instrumental to attaining that identity | EXTRINSIC |
| Status Validation | Evaluating the impact of one's consumption choices in attaining desired identity | OTHER-ORIENTED |

# Status as active

Status-seeking can be conceived as an ongoing quest for social honor (to use Weber's term). Status definition entails an identification of the social *persona(e)* one can or should adopt and a determination of the optimal strategy to achieve that identity. People have a deep-seated tendency to evaluate themselves, their professional accomplishments, their material well-being, and so on, relative to others. The need, or even passion, to accumulate and display status objects in the pursuit of self-identification affirms Holbrook's classification of this consumer value as *active*.

This value is contrasted in the typology with esteem, which Holbrook terms reactive in the sense that the mere possession of objects is sufficient to create a reputation. In this regard Holbrook's distinction may be a bit ambiguous (and overly charitable), insofar as he labels the conspicuous ownership of luxury objects as a reactive posture tending to inspire envy (Holbrook 1994). The current perspective is perhaps a bit more Machiavellian in assuming that the spectacle created by such a display often is artfully staged rather than accidental – active rather than reactive.

## *Status: trying to consume*

Indeed, in this context it is useful to regard status as a *motivational construct*. Like a basic biological drive (for food, water, or sex), a discrepancy exists between the consumer's present state and some ideal state. This gap creates a state of tension (or arousal). The magnitude of this tension determines the urgency the consumer feels to reduce it by patterning his/her consumption in a way calculated to increase the likelihood of achieving a desired status designation.

The need to relieve this arousal is perhaps most evident among the social group described as the *nouveau riches*, the members of which are chronically plagued by status anxiety. They monitor the cultural environment to ensure that they are doing the "right" thing, wearing the "right clothes," being seen at the "right" places, using the "right" caterer, and so on (Fussell 1983; DeParle 1989). Advertising directed at this group often plays on these insecurities by emphasizing the importance of "looking the part." For example, ads for *Colonial Homes* magazine feature consumers who "have worked very hard to make it look like they never had to."

## *But trying to consume what?*

If indeed people are motivated to engage in acquisition and consumption intended to accumulate social honor, this argument begs the question of just what items or activities will most likely yield the prize. The singular specification of a set of "status symbols" is problematic because the social meanings of these objects evolve over time and are accorded differential value by various reference groups.

It should be noted that this assertion departs from the traditional, rather static approach to lifestyle research, which often claims to incorporate status considerations. The psychographic perspective focused on AIO (activities, interest, and opinions) assumes that the meaning of each specific AIO-based category is singular, durable, and self-evident. Thus, simple knowledge of a person's consumption choice and its frequency is sufficient to infer an underlying set of values and purchasing priorities.

Unfortunately, this quantified, aggregated approach does not permit a relational view based on what each activity means in the context of the group (Solomon and Englis 1997). As Holt observes, for example, both poor people and counterculture youths shop at thrift stores, but for very different reasons. The psychographic approach also assumes a static self, yet consumers can and do shift lifestyle definitions periodically, whether out of whimsy or necessity (Holt 1997). Furthermore, lifestyle patterns reflect a particular collectivity in relation to alternative ones – e.g., the "skinhead" lifestyle is meaningful only when juxtaposed with those of adult middle class and working-class populations (Hebdige 1979).

A more dynamic approach implies the need for a more interactive study of status definition. Much status research is reminiscent of the one-sided view advanced with great influence by the *Frankfurt School*, which dominated mass communications research for most of the twentieth century. In this view, the media exert direct and powerful effects on individuals, and communications often are used by those in power to brainwash and exploit the masses. The receiver is basically a passive being – a "couch potato" who simply is the receptacle for many messages and who is often duped or persuaded to act based on the information he or she is "fed" by the media as "mind candy." In contrast, proponents of *uses and gratifications theory* argue that consumers are an active, goal-directed audience that draws on mass media as a resource to satisfy needs. Instead of asking what media do for or to people, they ask what people do *with* their media (Katz 1959; O'Donohoe 1994).

A similar argument can be made in the context of status definition. Instead of assuming that we "know" what social personae are positively valued and what products are interpreted as status symbols, perhaps it would be more fruitful to conceptualize the assignment of status value to products as an ongoing, dynamic process that is jointly determined by producers and consumers. As the art critic Leo Steinberg observed in another context, "May we not drop this useless, mythical distinction between – on one side – creative, forward-looking individuals whom we call artists, and – on the other side – a sullen, anonymous, uncomprehending mass, whom we call the public?" (Steinberg 1972: 3)

Most analyses of modern art and culture typically consider only the artists and the forces that motivate them. They do not consider the role of the audience in assigning value to cultural products or what accounts for the popularity of certain styles (Halle 1993). Similarly, sociological "living-room studies" make an inventory of items and then discriminate among social classes, but they seldom ask people about the meaning of the items with which they live (Laumann and House 1970; Csikszentmihalyi and Rochberg-Holton 1981; Belk, Wallendorf, and Sherry 1989).

Lifestyle marketing – which traces its roots to Weberian notions of stratification and "style of life" – is predicated on the recognition that people sort themselves into groups on the basis of the things they like to do, how they like to spend their leisure time, and how they choose to spend their disposable income (Zablocki and Kanter 1976; Bourdieu 1984; Solomon 1996). But, ultimately the notion of lifestyle only has meaning if it is meaningful to consumers themselves.

In his assessment of lifestyle research, Holt advances a somewhat similar argument as he advocates a post-structuralist perspective that allows for more nuanced description of consumption patterns than is currently afforded by dominant approaches based (more or less) on AIO inventories (Holt 1997). In the current context, an issue that is in need of additional attention is to assess the utility of status definition in terms of the role(s) it actually plays in the phenomenology of the consumer.

One consequence of adopting a more dynamic approach to the issue of inferring consumption values from consumption choices is that one must take into account the expressions of longing or loathing for the collectivity these objects have come to signify. Instead of assuming that the consumer indeed possesses a requisite assortment of appropriate status symbols (and as a result is a contented occupant of a certain social standing), a motivational perspective underscores the *desire* to acquire specific artifacts in order to better express a desired identity – a work in progress rather than a finished masterpiece.

This perspective regards lifestyle as a learned pattern of consumption activities – actual or imagined – that serves as an orienting force to a consumer who is motivated to approach, avoid, or ignore certain assortments of consumption objects. It is assumed that consumers are perceivers who are motivated to make sense of their social worlds and, as a result, are active processors of consumption information available both immediately and vicariously in the media as an aid to maximizing the efficacy of this process. Status placement, then, serves as both a classificatory mechanism at the macro level and as a motivational mechanism at the micro level.

The static AIO conception fails to recognize that consumption choices may be driven by an individual's motivation to attain membership in some (idealized) AIO category to which he/she does *not* belong – there is little room for aspiration and emulation in an AIO matrix. A status statement can be defined as much by what is *not chosen* as by what is. While the role of avoidance motivation has yet to be adequately addressed in this literature, any reader who happens to have adolescents living at home surely would appreciate the extent to which a lifestyle is constructed as a series of rebellious acts; the self defined by who it is not (Englis and Solomon 1995; Solomon and Englis 1996a).

So, where do these desires originate? Obviously, from a plenitude of sources, ranging from the personal (observation of friends) to the vicarious (socialization via mass media). However, it would appear that direct contact plays an increasingly peripheral role in shaping consumer perceptions as compared with media imagery (Solomon and Englis 1994; Englis and Solomon 1996). For example, American consumer magazines help fuel consumer desires for fashions, furnishings, and entertainment. They provide bountiful images of luxury and conspicuous consumption that are virtually inescapable in our media-saturated environment (Belk and Pollay 1985; Belk 1995). Direct observation takes a back seat to the influence of media because consumer behavior is often motivated *not* by a desire to emulate the lifestyle group to which the consumer *currently* belongs, but rather by the desire to emulate one that he or she *aspires* to join. Consumers are oriented toward a status definition representing an aspirational (and perhaps unattainable) social definition.

Paradoxically, the underlying accuracy of these simplifications of social reality may not matter – perception is paramount. As one critic noted, "Everywhere the fabricated, the inauthentic and the theatrical have gradually driven out the natural, the genuine and the spontaneous until there is no distinction between real life and stagecraft. In fact, one could argue that the theatricalization of American life is the major cultural transformation of the century" (Gabler 1991).

Indeed, from a postmodern perspective, questions concerning the "accuracy" of these social constructs miss the point altogether. What may be more important is to recognize this process of social construction as the "factory" where meaning systems are created and then to recognize that the resulting behavior of consumers will recursively create new market "realities" for marketers to analyze. This paradox was noted by the historian Daniel Boorstin over three decades ago:

> Humanist historians had aimed at an individualized portrait. The new social science historians produced a group caricature. . . . Oversimplified socio-logical concepts – "status," "other-direction," etc. – appealed because they were so helpful in building images. These wide-appealing "modes," expressed in our dominating notions of norms and averages, led us unwittingly to try to imitate ourselves. We have tried to discover what it is really like to be a junior executive or a junior executive's wife, *so we can really be the way we are supposed to be, that is, the way we are.*
>
> (Boorstin 1961: 202, emphasis added)

## Staging a status event

The value of status resides not only in the acquisition of a valued or valuable item, but also in purposefully letting others know that one has done so. Indeed, much like Veblen's classic discussion of the *potlatch* ceremony, the display or staging of a status product often contributes as much or more to the experience of status as does the object *per se*. Just as (to some amateur philosophers anyway) a falling tree does not make a sound if no one is there to hear it, perhaps the value of a status act does not fully "register" if others don't know the act has been performed. Indeed, maybe this is the litmus test of status as opposed to esteem vis a vis Holbrook's typology: Will the object retain its value if its purchase or use is unobservable or inconspicuous?

An interesting paradox to ponder in this regard is that the value of many status displays are enhanced if they *appear* to have occurred *without* instrumental action on the part of the exhibitor. Status displays often are "staged" to appear as if they were not actively undertaken, but rather were naturally occurring or bestowed upon the individual reactively by others. For example, a publicist worth his or her salt is one who can engineer a situation to ensure that an award is bestowed upon a client (Hirschman 1990). Like a movie star who "unexpectedly" wins an Oscar but who just happens to have a speech prepared, the beneficiary can feign modesty and surprise while gratefully accepting the accolade and basking in the resulting social honor.

## Status as extrinsic

Status acquisition is an extrinsic form of consumption involving a set of instrumental acts calculated to engineer a desired *persona*. Holbrook contrasts this means-to-an-end focus with the intrinsic nature of ethical behavior as an end in itself, where presumably a consumption act is satisfying (to use Milton Rokeach's familiar distinction in the context of values research) for terminal rather than instrumental reasons.

The desire to accumulate "badges of achievement" that signify social honor is summarized by the popular bumper-sticker slogan: "He who dies with the most toys, wins." Status-seeking is a significant source of motivation to procure appropriate products and services that the user hopes will let others know that he or she has "made it." As argued in the previous section, though, social honor is a moving target. We hold ourselves to a standard defined by others that is constantly changing. Today's status symbol is tomorrow's tacky relic.

The extrinsic motivation to consume was a centerpiece of Thorstein Veblen's seminal writings on this topic at the turn of the century. Veblen felt that a major role of products was for *invidious distinction* – that is, to inspire envy in others through display of wealth or power. Veblen coined the term *conspicuous consumption* to refer to people's desire to provide prominent visible evidence of their ability to afford luxury goods. For Veblen, the "currency" used to assess status evolved from skill at hunting or military exploits to the acquisition of property – this concept was later extended to include both women (in modern parlance, as "trophy wives") and money. Forms of invidiousness included *emulation* (e.g., one-upmanship of a competitor), *vicarious consumption* (e.g., a woman filling a ceremonial role to advertise her husband's wealth), and *industrial exemption* (e.g., wearing confining or impractical clothing to signal that one is sufficiently wealthy to avoid earning a living through manual labor).

Veblen's work was motivated by the excesses of his time. He wrote in the era of the robber barons, where the likes of J.P. Morgan, Henry Clay Frick, and William Vanderbilt were building massive financial empires and flaunting their wealth by throwing lavish parties. Some of these emblems of excess became legendary, as described in this account:

> There were tales, repeated in the newspapers, of dinners on horseback; of banquets for pet dogs; of hundred-dollar bills folded into guests' dinner

napkins; of a hostess who attracted attention by seating a chimpanzee at her table; of centerpieces in which lightly clad living maidens swam in glass tanks, or emerged from huge pies; of parties at which cigars were ceremoniously lighted with flaming banknotes of large denominations.

(Brooks 1981, quoted by Solomon 1999)

In modern times, the likes of Donald Trump have inherited the mantle of ostentation. While flamboyant products fell out of favor in the early part of this decade, the late 1990s are witnessing a resurgence of interest in luxury goods. Companies such as Hermès International, LVMH Hennessy Louis Vuitton, and Baccarat are enjoying sales gains of between 13–16 percent, as affluent consumers are once again indulging their desires for the finer things in life.

Some of this resurgence can be attributed to the stock market boom of the late 1990s – in 1997, the securities industry earned nearly $12 billion, twice the profit realized during the best parts of the "go-go" 1980s. This prosperity has benefitted the Wall Street moguls, but it has also trickled down to many middle-class workers, some of whom are also reaping riches from the company stock options they receive. Maybe that's why Hermès is selling out of handbags that cost up to $14,000 or why Gulfstream reports that it has back orders for about 100 luxury jets (Shnayerson 1997).

## Instrumental versus terminal consumption

The notion that some products are consumed for extrinsic rather than intrinsic reasons is central to many marketing strategies that center on the ability of our possessions to accomplish some social goal. The issue of whether a consumption object derives its value for purely terminal reasons is relevant in many consumption domains, particularly in examinations of aesthetic appreciation.

For example, numerous social scientists have ably addressed the potential utilitarian aspects of art (Halle 1993). Economists view art as an investment vehicle and as part of a drive to accumulate economic capital (though this financial perspective does not necessarily address how demand for a particular type of art or artist is derived in the first place). Art has also been regarded as a vehicle for ideological domination; the Frankfurt School viewed mass culture as a standardized commodity and an ideological tool by which large corporations and the advertising industry dominate and repress the public. The notion that art is a form of cultural capital (i.e., a status product), where high culture reproduces the class structure of the dominant and dominated classes and is used to exclude subordinate classes from circles of power and privilege, is a cornerstone of the work by Bourdieu and other sociologists (Bourdieu 1984).

Our notions of the sacrosanct nature of individual "taste" (for which "there's no accounting") and the assumption that subjective aesthetic preferences are privileged and idiosyncratic ("that's why they make chocolate and vanilla"), often are jarred when we consider the extent to which our selections of ostensibly self-expressive items are motivated by somewhat more venal considerations than beauty, truth, sweetness, and light. In reality, consumers appear to manifest the belief that many ostensibly subjective preferences – in such domains as professional clothing and home furnishings – actually are objective. They often feel there is a right way and a wrong way to consume, and the "correctness" of these decisions is externally verifiable (Solomon *et al.* 1984; Solomon and Douglas 1987; Bell *et al.* 1991).

## Status as other-oriented

A status event is hardly one to hide its light under a bushel. As an other-oriented consumption value, the reactions of others play a key role in determining the benefits derived from the experience or product. Unlike such values as fun, aesthetics, efficiency, or excellence in the consumer-value typology, status doesn't "count" unless it has an effect on one's intended audience. Status validation requires external feedback to yield its value.

Indeed, a truly venal take on status would argue that this type of value is calibrated not in terms of what I have, but rather in terms of what you don't. The quality level of a status event is derived from the extent to which it is not only good, but is also *better* than what others experience. As a result, a seemingly endless spiral of social comparison is set in motion; the status-seeker attains a certain threshold of satisfaction, only to find that the stakes are higher once others attain the same level.

### Social comparison: whose opinion matters?

Social comparison theory posits a self-evaluative drive; people engage in a process of gauging their own qualities by calibrating them relative to others – and usually to those of somewhat similar standing (Festinger 1954). Of course, our choice of comparison others depends on the circumstances. Research evidence indicates that we try to identify those of somewhat lesser standing to use as a yardstick when self-worth is threatened (Richins 1992), though more generally the inclination is to cast our eyes up rather than down.

As a general rule, then, aspirational forces impel us to compare our standing with those whom we seek to emulate. This upward process ("social climbing") is fueled to a great extent by media depictions of "the good life;" idealized (and perhaps unattainable) images of wealth or material comfort well beyond what is available to many middle-class households (Belk and Pollay 1985). Indeed, one content analysis of advertising found no old, poor, sick, or unattractive couples in 500 ads sampled (Jordan and Bryant 1979). Thus, the derivation of relative value is computed vicariously via comparisons to well-off media phantoms as well as to flesh-and-blood success stories.

Does the need for positive feedback from others motivate all consumers equally? Probably not. At the individual level, a sizeable body of research hints at personality differences in sensitivity to feedback from others. For example, *high self-monitors* are more attuned to how they present themselves in their social environments, and their product choices are influenced by their estimates of how these items will be perceived by others (Snyder 1979; Holbrook *et al.* 1990). High self-monitors are more likely to evaluate products consumed in public in terms of the impressions they make on others than are low self-monitors (Graeff 1996), and those who are more sensitive to their public *persona* are more likely to be involved with self-enhancements in the form of clothing and cosmetics (see Solomon and Schopler 1982). Similarly, some recent research has looked at aspects of *vanity*, such as a fixation on physical appearance or on the achievement of personal goals. Perhaps not surprisingly, groups like fashion models and college football players tend to score higher on this dimension (Netemeyer *et al.* 1995).

### Invidious distinction and social control

A case study of organizational culture at Disneyland provides a telling illustration of the complex relationship between the display of consumption cues and the assignment of status. The researchers found that park employees' status is expressed by the right to wear different uniforms. High-status jobs for men include ". . . the crisp, officer-like monorail operator . . . the swashbuckling Pirate of the Caribbean, the casual cowpoke of Big Thunder Mountain." These members of the Disney "cast" appear to internalize the symbolism of their costumes, thus allowing management to bestow nonmonetary reinforcement (van Maanen and Kunda 1989).

So, even low-paid service workers will find ways to differentiate among themselves. This comparative process can potentially create social instability, and its divisive qualities occasionally prompt societies to regulate product display as a form of social control (Kaiser 1997; Solomon 1998). For example, sumptuary laws (whether in Victorian England or modern-day Islamic cultures) restrict the display of certain styles or colors. They are intended to ensure that the populace will adhere to culturally desirable norms of propriety, or that status-seeking "wannabees" will not attempt to impersonate those of a higher station (e.g., in Biblical times purple was a "royal" color that was prohibited from use in garments worn by the masses). More recently, several major school districts – including Long Beach (CA), Baltimore, and New York City – have implemented or are seriously considering school uniform requirements as a way to reduce the distractions and even disciplinary problems fostered by dress competition among preening students (*New York Times* 3 Sept. 1994).

### Impression management: scripting the status event

Since the status event only "matters" if it registers with its desired audience, understandably the status-seeker is motivated to ensure that the intended outcomes are realized. This entails great diligence to the process of *impression management*, which has been defined as "any behavior that has the purpose of controlling or manipulating the attributions and impressions formed of that [a] person by others" (Tedeschi and Riess 1981: 3; cf. Schlenker 1980).

Individuals have a variety of reasons to manage their impressions, such as avoiding blame and gaining credit for their actions, maintenance of self-esteem, or strategic self-presentation where the goal is to enhance others' view of the self. The goal is to accumulate prestige (similar to Weber's concept of social honor): the "perception by the target that the source possesses material and/or political resources that can be used for purposes of rewards and punishments, and that the source has the will to utilize these resources on behalf of power" (Tedeschi and Riess 1981: 13–14).

The somewhat ephemeral nature of impression formation forces an emphasis on superficial cues, which tend to be tangible objects or physical characteristics. This process was highlighted by the sociologist Erving Goffman, whose focus on the individual as a creative executor of roles (as a key component of his dramaturgical perspective on social behavior) brought to the forefront the importance of linguistic cues, body language, gesture, dress, display of possessions, and arrangement of physical objects for the assignment of social meaning. As Goffman observed, "Whatever an individual does and however he appears, he knowingly and unknowingly makes information available concerning the attributes that might be imputed to him and hence the categories in which he might be placed. . . . The physical milieu itself conveys implications concerning the identity of those who are in it" (Goffman 1961: 102). Similarly, the more cognitive orientation of script theory, which focuses on the learning of a coherent sequence of events to orient behavior, posits that through a process of impression management we try to control the scripts people use when they think about and interact with us (Schlenker 1980).

## Consumption activities define social categories

Consumption activities – whether carefully scripted or not – often are used as data to make inferences regarding status. A product can serve as an important social reference point to fellow consumers, either as an emblem of pride or as a social stigma. The importance of products in communicating social information is well-documented, as is the level of nuance that may affect these messages (Solomon 1983). The decoding of consumption may encompass perceptions of tangible possessions (e.g., straight-leg button-fly jeans versus lime green baggies), leisure activities (e.g., rollerbladers versus football players), or services (e.g., patrons of health food restaurants versus pub crawlers).

This exercise in "applied semiotics" means that the status-conscious actor must engage in an ongoing quest to identify those specific consumption events that will successfully yield social honor. Of course, the assignment of value to products in this regard is of crucial importance to marketers, whose economic fortunes may be yoked to a brand's standing within the current pantheon of status symbols. To muddy the waters, though, the issue of just what symbols will make the desired impression on others is perhaps more problematic than it may appear.

One important consideration is whether the status-seeker already belongs to the lifestyle group s/he is aiming to please. In-group members tend to be capable of finer or more articulated discriminations within that group, while non-members tend to see members as being relatively similar (Englis and Solomon 1995). By extension, this difference may result in more idiosyncratic associations by group members due to the greater flexibility of members' knowledge structures (Solomon 1988a). Out-group members may be more likely to rely on a few prototypical product symbols of a role for their sign value and may attach more importance to ownership of these exemplars. Related phenomena have in fact been observed in work on anticipatory role acquisition, cultural assimilation and compensatory symbolism. Newcomers to a role tend to purchase more stereo-typical products, and to be brand loyal to market leaders as a way to speed acculturation (Englis and Solomon 1997).

## The self as generalized other

It seems clear that if any one cell in the consumer value typology is a candidate to be truly other-oriented, status is a frontrunner for the honor. However, that blithe assumption does need to be qualified. As with any form of consumption, the true value must come home to roost. Though admittedly a solipsistic perspective, ultimately the net effect of any consumer behavior must be assessed in terms of how it is perceived by the consumer himself.

Conveniently, the sociological tradition of symbolic interactionism stresses that relationships with other people play a large part in forming the self (Mead 1934). This perspective maintains that people exist in a symbolic environment, and the meaning attached to any situation or object is determined by the interpretation of these symbols.

Like other social objects, the meanings of individuals are themselves defined by social consensus. The consumer interprets his or her own identity, and this assessment is continually evolving as he or she encounters new situations and people. In symbolic interactionist terms, we *negotiate* these meanings over time.

Essentially the consumer poses the question: "Who am I in this situation?" The answer to this question is greatly influenced by those around us: "Who do *other people* think I am?" We tend to pattern our behavior on the perceived expectations of others in a form of *self-fulfilling prophecy*. By acting the way we assume others expect us to act, we often wind up confirming these perceptions. According to this view, our desire to define ourselves operates as a sort of psychological sonar: We take readings of our own identity by "bouncing" signals off others and trying to project what impression they have of us (Solomon 1983; Englis *et al.* 1993; Solomon and Douglas 1987).

Impression management thus does double duty as an instrument of self-perception. While status-related consumption typically is very much directed toward others, the ultimate audience is the self – external feedback from relevant others is required to validate a desired *persona*. As one researcher observed: "Performances that were once inaccurate self-reflections can become accurate as the self-concept changes" (Schlenker 1980: 40). As a result perhaps it's not surprising that there is a tendency for the inferences about the probable lifestyle of an actor by both the actor and his/her observers to converge – in a sense both parties are reading from the same page when evaluating the available evidence (Burroughs *et al.* 1991).

## The status of status

To come full circle, Holbrook's consumer-value typology regards status as extrinsic, other-oriented, and active. The current assessment of status amplifies Holbrook's conceptualization. This value is viewed as part of a process of social construction whereby an individual is motivated to identify desirable location(s) in the social nexus and then to acquire products and experiences that (s/he believes) will successfully achieve this social honor. This ongoing process of identity negotiation puts the locus of status at the dynamic, individual level, as opposed to the somewhat more static, aggregate treatment it is accorded in traditional sociological writings.

### *The status of status research*

Status is perhaps one of the best known values among both researchers and laymen; the word itself, along with such derivatives as status-seeker and status symbol, is very much a part of the common vernacular. Still, there is much more work to be done to understand how consumers navigate the process of status acquisition and display. A sampling of research questions worth addressing is offered here:

#### *Buying the world a Coke: cross-cultural dynamics of status display*

Social honor comes in many forms, and clearly the specific objects or experiences capable of bestowing this value are culturally determined. Indeed, at the risk of stating the obvious, a better understanding of this process is of import to marketing practitioners as well as academic researchers. Given the pervasiveness of positioning strategies that hinge upon this kind of consumer value, the ability to track the status value of products and services certainly offers pragmatic value.

More work is needed to identify cross-cultural aspects of status symbolism and their ramifications for diffusion of Western consumer culture. For example, fairly pedestrian American products such as Coca-Cola, Levi jeans, and Marlboro cigarettes carry major status baggage in some Third World countries and in transitional economies in Central Europe (Ger and Belk 1996; Belk 1997). Even in fully industrialized countries like Japan, the display of American products or even those with English-sounding names that (to us) border on the bizarre like Mouth Pet (breath freshener), Pocari Sweat ("refreshment water"), Armpit (electric razor), Brown Gross Foam (hair-coloring mousse), Virgin Pink Special (skin cream), Cow Brand (beauty soap), and Mymorning Water (canned water), are snapped up as status symbols (Howard and Cerio 1994; Sherry and Camargo 1987).

### The "career" of a status symbol

Even within the same culture, though, nothing is forever. It seems feasible to speak of a *status-symbol life cycle*, and to chronicle the evolution of products as they rise and fall – and perhaps rise again – as status symbols. This cyclic progression can clearly be seen, for instance, in the domain of cultural ideals of beauty – whether epitomized by Clara Bow, Marilyn Monroe, or Kate Moss – and the specific constellation of accessories, hairstyles, body shapes, and so on taken to be "elegant," "cool," or otherwise desirable by a culture at any point in time (Englis, Solomon, and Ashmore 1994).

Given that the attainment of status is a moving target, it follows that there should be an ongoing process of valuation and re-valuation of the items used to signify desired social placement. Just as we can speak of *dowager brands* that have perhaps outlived their usefulness, perhaps it is useful to think of dowager status symbols that now may have progressed into the obsolescent stage of the status life cycle. Indeed, products that serve as emblems of a lifestyle today may become stigmatized as other groups adopt or coopt them, to the extent that they may literally be "anti-emblems" tomorrow. For example, the Playboy bunny, once the totem of the "sophisticated man," now is strictly *declassé* (a bunny mirror ornament is more likely to be spotted hanging from a beat-up Chevrolet than from a sleek Lexus), and its display is passionately avoided by the bunny's original target audience.

### Status is consuming – not?

Efforts to shun outmoded status symbols remind us that status displays may be composed of what one doesn't consume as well as what one does. This process also highlights the overlooked importance of *avoidance products* – sometimes the conscious act of *not* consuming a product or service is itself part and parcel of status construction. Some research indicates that consumers are judged as much by what they don't consume as by what they do (Englis and Solomon 1995; Solomon and Englis 1996b)!

Paradoxically, as the competition to accumulate status symbols escalates, sometimes the best tactic is to reverse course. One way to do this is deliberately to *avoid* well-known or highly visible status symbols – that is, to seek status by mocking it. This sophisticated form of conspicuous consumption has been termed *parody display* (Solomon 1996). Hence the popularity in recent years of High Tech interior design (deliberately rough and austere), old and torn blue jeans, or "utility" vehicles such as Jeeps among the upper classes. Thus, "true" status is manifested by ostensibly opting out of the race for status. Of course, one aspect of this paradox is that over time the undesirable object itself becomes a status symbol, and the spiral continues (Brooks 1981).

*New and used status symbols*

Holbrook argues that value is inherently interactive, in that it requires some usage relationship between the consumer and the object. While the veracity of this argument in general is hard to dispute, ironically, within the status domain the consumer instead may place a premium on activities that *inhibit* interactivity or that move it to a purely conceptual level – s/he may instead strive to maintain the pristine nature of the object, unsullied by human hands. Whether this involves preserving priceless oil paintings, meticulously maintaining luxury cars, covering living room furniture with glossy plastic slipcovers, or hoarding unopened Barbie boxes, it seems that often objects are status symbols to the extent that they are *not* used – or at least used up.

Further work is needed to explore the more general issue of authenticity and ownership (e.g., how is value obtained, transferred, and/or compromised via the purchase of garments that once belonged to celebrities or via the practice of renting gallery art for temporary display in private homes)? In addition, we know relatively little about the extent to which the display of a status item enhances or detracts from its value – once shown, perhaps its utility as a status symbol is diminished. Consumption as anticlimax.

*Status? Says who?*

The tracking of the "career" of a status symbol raises another important question: Who or what determines what is "hot" and what is not? A relatively small number of cultural gatekeepers, including marketing executives, profoundly influence the value of objects and experiences within the "status marketplace." As one example, Ralph Lauren's advertising and merchandising campaigns have succeeded in creating a fantasy world of affluence and sophistication. He has created a quasi-mythical lifestyle – brimming with status symbols – that has become The Holy Grail for hordes of enthusiastic consumers.

But how do gatekeepers like Lauren make *their* selections, how are their preferences communicated, and just how influential are these judgments anyway? Virtually no research exists on the choice strategies or heuristics used by designers, advertising creatives, and other "reality engineers" who create or sanction status symbols. Yet, these choices exert a profound influence on the perceptions, aspirations, and acquisition patterns of consumers (Solomon 1988b).

## The value of classifying value

Although the Holbrook framework focuses on dividing consumer value into its various types, in reality it celebrates the multidimensionality of virtually all consumption experience. The possibility (and desirability) of assigning every form of value a discrete label is perhaps driven as much by the determination of the individual attempting the feat as from the phenomenon itself. To paraphrase an anonymous observation sometimes credited to Kenneth Boulding, "There are two kinds of people in this world, those who believe there are two kinds of people and those who don't!"

Holbrook's attempt at rigorous classification sits on the page and thumbs its conceptual nose at us, challenging us to come up with contravening examples. Indeed, virtually all forms of consumption are candidates to be "hijacked" by status concerns and put on display as visible markers of success. Even a "noble value" like morality can serve as a status symbol, as when Presidential candidates court the Christian Coalition vote by spotlighting their own religiosity, stable marriage, or military service.

The consumer-value typology forces us to realize how culture-and time-bound are our conceptions of value, insofar as the same product or experience can impart different types of value to different perceivers. Like the story of the blind men and the elephant, we each come away with a different meaning, depending upon which part of the animal we have been assigned. Perhaps status truly is in the eye of the beholder. No doubt Rodney Dangerfield would agree.

# References

Arnould, E. J. and Wilk, R. R. (1985) "Why Do the Natives Wear Adidas: Anthropological Approaches to Consumer Research," in *Advances in Consumer Research* 12, Provo, Utah: Association for Consumer Research.

Belk, R. W. (1995) "Specialty Magazines and Flights of Fancy: Feeding the Desire to Desire," paper presented at the Fifth Interdisciplinary Conference on Research in Consumption, Department of European Ethnology, Lund University, Sweden, August.

—— (1997) "Romanian Consumer Desires and Feelings of Deservingness," in L. Stan (ed.) *Romania in Transition*, Hanover, NH: Dartmouth Press.

Belk, R. W. and Pollay, R. W. (1985) "Images of Ourselves: The Good Life in Twentieth Century Advertising," *Journal of Consumer Research* 11, March: 887–97.

Belk, R. W., Wallendorf, M., and Sherry, Jr., J. F. (1989) "The Sacred and the Profane: Theodicy on the Odyssey," *Journal of Consumer Research* 16, June: 1–38.

Bell, S. S., Holbrook, M. B., and Solomon, M. R. (1991) "Combining Esthetic and Social Value to Explain Preferences for Product Styles with the Incorporation of Personality and Ensemble Effects," in F. W. Rudmin (ed.) *To Have Possessions: A Handbook on Ownership and Property*, special issue of the *Journal of Social Behavior and Personality* 6, 6: 243–74.

Boorstin, D. J. (1961) *The Image: A Guide to Pseudo-Events in America*, New York: Vintage.

Brooks, J. (1981) *Showing Off in America*, Boston: Little, Brown.

Bourdieu, P. (1984) *Distinction: A Social Critique of the Judgement of Taste*, Cambridge, MA: Harvard University Press.

Burroughs, W. J., Drews, D. R., and Hallman, W. K. (1991) "Predicting Personality from Personal Possessions: A Self-Presentational Analysis," in F. W. Rudmin (ed.), *To Have Possessions: A Handbook on Ownership and Property* special issue of the *Journal of Social Behavior and Personality* 6, 6: 147–63.

Coleman, R. P. (1983) "The Continuing Significance of Social Class to Marketing," *Journal of Consumer Research* 10, December: 265–80.

Costa, J. A. and Bamossy, G. J. (eds) (1995) *Marketing in a Multicultural World:*

*Ethnicity, Nationalism, and Cultural Identity*, Thousand Oaks, CA: Sage Publications, Inc.

Csikszentmihalyi, M. and Rochberg-Holton, E. (1981) *The Meaning of Things: Domestic Symbols and the Self*, Cambridge: Cambridge University Press.

DeParle, J. (1989) "Spy Anxiety: The Smart Magazine that Makes Smart People Nervous About Their Standing," *Washington Monthly*, February: 10.

Eastman, J. K., Flynn, L. R. , and Goldsmith, R. E. (1994) "Shopping for Status: The Retail Managerial Implications," *Association of Marketing Theory and Practice*, Spring: 125–30.

Englis, B. G. and Solomon, M. R. (1995) "To Be and Not to Be: Reference Group Stereotyping and *The Clustering of America*," *Journal of Advertising* 24 (Spring), 1: 13–28.

—— (1996) "Consumption Constellations: Implications for Advertising Strategies," *Journal of Business Research* 37 (November), 3: 183–92.

—— (1997) "Where Perception Meets Reality: The Social Construction of Lifestyles," in L. Kahle and L. Chiagurus (eds) *Values, Lifestyles, and Psychographics*, Hillsdale, NJ: Lawrence Erlbaum Associates, Inc., 25–44.

Englis, B. G., Solomon, M. R., and Oloffson, A. (1993) "Consumption Imagery in Music Television: A Bi-Cultural Perspective," *Journal of Advertising* 22, December: 21–34.

Englis, B. G., Solomon, M. R., and Ashmore, R. D. (1994) "Beauty Before the Eyes of Beholders: The Cultural Encoding of Beauty Types in Magazine Advertising and Music Television," *Journal of Advertising* 23, June: 49–64.

Festinger, L. (1954) "A Theory of Social Comparison Processes," *Human Relations* 7: 117–40.

Fisher, R. A. (1978) *Perspectives on Human Communication*, New York: Macmillan.

Fussell, P. (1983) *Class: A Guide Through the American Status System*, New York: Summit Books.

Gabler, N. (1991) *The New York Times*, October 20, quoted in M. Dery (1993) "Hacking, Jamming and Slashing in the Empire of Signs," *Adbusters Quarterly*, Summer: 55–61.

Ger, G. and Belk, R. W. (1996) "I'd Like to Buy the World a Coke: Consumptionscapes of the 'less affluent world'," *Journal of Consumer Policy* 19, 3: 271–304.

Giddens, A. (1973) *The Class Structure of the Advanced Societies*, New York: Harper Torchbook.

Goffman, E. (1961) *Encounters*, Indianapolis: Bobbs-Merrill.

Graeff, T. R. (1996) "Image Congruence Effects on Product Evaluations: The Role of Self-Monitoring and Public/Private Consumption', *Psychology & Marketing* 13, 5 (August): 481–99.

Halle, D. (1993) *Inside Culture: Art and Class in the American Home*, Chicago: The University of Chicago Press.

Hebdige, D. (1979) *Subcultures: The Meaning of Style*, London: Methuen.

Hirschman, E. C. (1990) "Secular Immortality and the American Ideology of Affluence," *Journal of Consumer Research* 17, June: 31–42.

Hoffman, D. L. and Novak, T. P. (1996) "Marketing in Hypermedia Computer-Mediated Environments: Conceptual Foundations," *Journal of Marketing* 60, 3 (July): 50–68.

Holbrook, M. . B. (1994) "Axiology, Aesthetics, and Apparel: Some Reflections on the Old School Tie," in M. R. DeLong and A. M. Fiore (eds) *Aesthetics of Textiles and Clothing: Advancing Multi-Disciplinary Perspectives*, Monument, CO: International Textile and Apparel Association, 131–41.

Holbrook, M. B., Solomon, M. R., and Bell, S. (1990) "A Re-Examination of Self-Monitoring and Judgments of Furniture Designs," *Home Economics Research Journal* 19, September: 6–16.

Holt, D. B. (1997) "A Poststructuralist Lifestyle Analysis: Conceptualizing the Social Patterning of Consumption in Modernity," *Journal of Consumer Research* 23, March: 326–50.

Howard, L. and Cerio, G. (1994) "Goofy Goods," *Newsweek*, August 15: 8.

Jordan, B. and Bryant, K. (1979) "The Advertised Couple: The Portrayal of the Couple and Their Relationship in Popular Magazine Advertisements," paper presented at the Popular Culture Association and American Culture Association meetings, Pittsburgh, April 28.

Kaiser, S. B. (1997) *The Social Psychology of Clothing: Symbolic Appearances in Context* 2nd Ed., New York: Fairchild Publications.

Katz, E. (1959) "Mass Communication Research and the Study of Popular Culture: An Editorial Note on a Possible Future for this Journal," *Studies in Public Communication* 2: 1–6.

Laumann, E. O. and House, J. S. (1970) "Living Room Styles and Social Attributes: The Patterning of Material Artifacts in a Modern Urban Community," *Sociology and Social Research* 54, April: 321–42.

McCracken, G. D. (1985) "The Trickle-Down Theory Rehabilitated," in M. R. Solomon (ed.) *The Psychology of Fashion*, Lexington, MA: Lexington Books, 39–54.

Mager, J. and Kahle, L. R. (1995) "Is the Whole More than the Sum of the Parts? Re-Evaluating Social Status in Marketing," *Journal of Business Psychology* 10, Fall: 3–18.

Mead, G. H. (1934) *Mind, Self and Society*, Chicago: University of Chicago Press.

Munson, J. M. and Spivey, W. A. (1981) "Product and Brand-User Stereotypes Among Social Classes: Implications for Advertising Strategy," *Journal of Advertising Research* 21, August: 37–45.

Netemeyer, R. G., Burton, S., and Lichtenstein, D. R. (1995) "Trait Aspects of Vanity: Measurement and Relevance to Consumer Behavior," *Journal of Consumer Research* 21, March: 612–26.

*New York Times* (1994) "School Uniforms Growing in Favor in California," September 3: 8.

O'Donohoe, S. (1994) "Advertising Uses and Gratifications," *European Journal of Marketing* 28, 8/9: 52–75.

Richins, M. L. (1992) "Media Images, Materialism, and What Ought to Be: The Role of Social Comparison," in F. Rudmin and M. Richins (eds) *Meaning, Measuring, and Morality of Materialism*, Provo, UT: Association for Consumer Research, 202–6.

Schlenker, B. R. (1980) *Impression Management: The Self-Concept, Social Identity, and Interpersonal Relations*, Monterey, CA: Brooks/Cole Publishing Company.

Scott, L. M. (1994) "The Bridge from Text to Mind: Adapting Reader-Response Theory to Consumer Research," *Journal of Consumer Research* 21, December: 461–80.

Sherry, J. F., Jr. and Camargo, E. G. (1987) "May Your Life Be Marvelous: English Language Labeling and the Semiotics of Japanese Promotion," *Journal of Consumer Research* 14, September: 174–88.

Shnayerson, M. (1997) "The Champagne City," *Vanity Fair*, December: 182–202.

Snyder, M. (1979) "Self-Monitoring Processes," in L. Berkowitz (ed.) *Advances in Experimental Social Psychology*, New York: Academic Press, 85–128.

Solomon, M. R. (1983) "The Role of Products as Social Stimuli: A Symbolic Interactionism Perspective," *Journal of Consumer Research* 10, December: 319–29.

—— (1988a) "Mapping Product Constellations: A Social Categorization Approach to Symbolic Consumption," *Psychology & Marketing* 5, 3: 233–58.

—— (1988b) "Building Up and Breaking Down: The Impact of Cultural Sorting on Symbolic Consumption," in J. Sheth and E. C. Hirschman (eds) *Research in Consumer Behavior* Vol. 3, Greenwich, CT: JAI Press, 325–51.

—— (1996) *Consumer Behavior: Buying, Having, and Being*, 3rd Ed., Upper Saddle River, NJ: Prentice Hall.

—— (1998) "Dressing for the Part: The Role of Costume in the Staging of the Servicescape," in J. F. Sherry, Jr. (ed.) *Servicescapes: The Concept of Place in Contemporary Markets*, Lincolnwood, IL: NTC Publishing Group and American Marketing Association, 81–108.

—— (1999) *Consumer Behavior: Buying, Having, and Being*, 4th Ed., Upper Saddle River, NJ: Prentice Hall.

Solomon, M. R. and Douglas, S. P. (1987) "Diversity in Product Symbolism: The Case of Female Executive Clothing," *Psychology & Marketing* 4, Fall: 189–212.

Solomon, M. R. and Englis, B. G. (1996a) "I Am Not, Therefore I Am: The Role of Anti-Consumption in the Process of Self-Definition," Special Session at the Association for Consumer Research meetings, October, Tucson, AZ.

—— (1996b) "Consumption Constellations: Implications for Integrated Communications Strategies," in E. Thorson and J. Moore (eds) *Integrated Communication: Synergy of Persuasive Voices*, Hillsdale, NJ: Lawrence Erlbaum Associates, Inc. , 65–86.

—— (1997) "Breaking Out of the Box: Is Lifestyle a Construct or a Construction?" in S. Brown and D. Turley (eds) *Consumer Research: Postcards from the Edge*, London: Routledge, 322–49.

Solomon, M. R., Pruitt, D. J., and Insko, C. A. (1984) "Taste Versus Fashion: The Inferred Objectivity of Aesthetic Judgments," *Empirical Studies of the Arts* 2, 2: 113–25.

Solomon, M. R. and J. Schopler (1982) "Self-Consciousness and Clothing," *Personality and Social Psychology Bulletin* 8, 3: 508–14.

Steinberg, L. (1972) "Contemporary Art and Its Public," in L. Steinberg *Other Criteria: Confrontations with Twentieth-Century Art*, New York: Oxford University Press, 3.

Tedeschi, J. T. and Riess, M. (1981) "Identities, the Phenomenal Self, and Laboratory Research," in J. T. Tedeschi (ed.) *Impression Management Theory and Social Psychological Research*, New York: Academic Press, 3–22.

Thompson, C. J. and Hirschman, E. C. (1995) "Understanding the Socialized Body: A Poststructuralist Analysis of Consumers' Self-Conceptions, Body Images, and Self-Care Practices," *Journal of Consumer Research* 22: 139–53.

Turner, J. H. (1981) *Sociology: Studying the Human System*, 2nd Ed., Santa Monica, CA: Goodyear.

Van Maanen, J. and Kunda, G. (1989) "Real Feelings: Emotional Expression and Organizational Culture," in L. L. Cummings and B. M. Straw (eds) *Research in Organizational Behavior* 43, 58–70.

Vanneman, R. and Pampel, F. C. (1977) "The American Perception of Class and Status," *American Sociological Review* 42, June: 422–37.

Venkatesh, A., Dholakia, R. R., and Dholakia, N. (1996) "New Visions of Information Technology and Postmodernism: Implications for Advertising and Marketing

Communications," in W. Brenner and L. Kolbe (eds) *The Information Superhighway and Private Households: Case Studies of Business Impacts*, Heidelberg: Physical-Verlag, 319–37.

Waters, M. (1994) *Modern Sociological Theory*, London: Sage.

—— (1970) "Class, Status, Party," in E. O. Laumann, P. M. Siegel, and R. W. Hodge (eds) *The Logic of Social Hierarchies*, Chapter 3: 67–82.

Weber, M. (1978) *Economy and Society*, Berkeley: University of California Press.

Zablocki, B. D. and Kanter, R. M. (1976) "The Differentiation of Life-Styles," *Annual Review of Sociology*, 269–97.

# 4 Possessions, materialism, and other-directedness in the expression of self

*Marsha L. Richins*

A dominant characteristic of American society is the desire for more (Bredemeier and Toby 1960; Fox and Lears 1983; Wachtel 1983). I recently spent an hour in casual conversation with a building contractor whom I had come to know reasonably well, and I spent most of that time listening. Without prompting, my contractor friend devoted the hour to describing all the things he wanted – a new computer, a new house, a new truck, better clothes for his kids, an elk hunting trip, and more. My contractor friend is not unique. Nearly everyone with whom I have broached the topic – in conversation, in research interviews, and even in surveys – can speak at some length, and sometimes with passion, about the things they would like to have. For some, the emphasis on getting and having is sufficiently strong that we might classify them as materialistic.

It is apparent that goods have an important place in most consumers' dreams, if not in their hearts. Yet it is not the goods themselves that people desire, but rather the benefits these goods provide – an increase in comfort or pleasure, the ability to accomplish new tasks, the esteem of others when they regard what we own. In the Introduction, Holbrook describes a Typology of Consumer Value to distinguish among the benefits that commercial goods can provide. This chapter examines these values, and others, as they relate to materialism. It begins by describing materialism and explaining how materialism fits with the Typology of Consumer Value. This discussion first examines materialism with respect to the typology as a whole and then proceeds to examine in more depth the value of possessions in achieving esteem, the source of value described in the fourth cell of the typology.

## Materialism and product value

There are many approaches to and conceptualizations of materialism; Belk (1983) and Fournier and Richins (1991) provide useful overviews of these conceptualizations. When I refer to materialism, it is in the way defined by Belk (1984b: 291), who described materialism as "the importance a consumer attaches to worldly possessions." As elaborated by Richins and Dawson (1992), materialism is a value orientation in which individuals 1) place possessions and their acquisition at the center of their lives and 2) believe that important life satisfactions stem from the acquisition and possession of goods. Although most consumers express a desire for more goods, materialists are distinguished by the strength of this desire and its centrality in their lives. A further element of materialism, to be discussed in more detail below, is the tendency for consumers high in materialism to judge the success of themselves and others in terms of material possessions.

From this description, it should be clear that materialists derive or expect to derive, many important types of value from the objects they own or acquire. In fact, it is likely that the value materialists receive from a good encompasses all or nearly all of the categories described in Holbrook's value framework. This is illustrated by several of the studies I have conducted.

In one study (Richins 1994a), consumers were asked to list a few of the possessions they considered to be important and to describe the sources of value for these possessions. They also completed a materialism measure. This study dealt with possessions – goods that were already owned – and was not limited to commercial goods. Many of the valued possessions identified by study participants were things not commercially available (family snapshots, trophies won in high school) or whose value comes from non-commercial sources of meanings (a wedding ring, holiday souvenirs).

A second study, still in progress, asked consumers about products they hoped to buy and is thus limited to commercial goods. This research also differs from that reported in Richins (1994a) in that it used an interview format to elicit sources of value, allowing greater depth of response and a more detailed elicitation of value sources.

Data from these two studies indicate that all consumers, whether low or high in materialism, derive value from a large variety of sources. In Figure 4.1, these sources of value are superimposed on the framework described in Holbrook's Introduction. All eight of the categories in his framework are represented among these sources of value. (Figure 4.1 differs from Holbrook's framework in two ways. First, the empirical analysis of sources of value identified more sources than the eight outlined by Holbrook. The additional sources of value have been inserted into the cells that best characterize the values on the three dimensions identified by Holbrook, although some of them differ markedly in character from the labels Holbrook applied to those cells. Second, in empirical analysis it has been difficult to distinguish between active and reactive sources of value. Where this was most difficult, adjacent cells are separated by a dashed rather than solid line in Figure 4.1. The extrinsic/intrinsic distinction was also difficult to apply in practice, and some of the distinctions made on this dimension for purposes of Figure 4.1 are somewhat arbitrary.)

The studies I carried out reveal some interesting differences between the values low and high materialists receive from the possessions they own and that they hope to obtain from possessions they wish to acquire. It appears that the values or benefits cited by those low in materialism relate most strongly to personal or self-oriented benefits. These consumers, for instance, more frequently mentioned value sources that stem from the personal enjoyment they experience using the product, the comfort it affords them, or the personal spiritual or religious benefits

| | | **Extrinsic** | **Intrinsic** |
|---|---|---|---|
| **Self-oriented** | **Active** | EFFICIENCY<br><br>• Utilitarian<br>• Freedom/independence | PLAY<br><br>• Enjoyment/fun<br>• Personal growth |
| | **Reactive** | EXCELLENCE<br><br>• Quality/performance<br>• Financial value/security | AESTHETICS<br><br>• Comfort, peace<br>• Aesthetic appearance<br>• Symbolic of personal history<br>• Symbolic of interpersonal ties |
| **Other-oriented** | **Active** | STATUS/POLITICAL<br><br>• enhance appearance<br>• enhance interpersonal ties | ETHICS<br><br>• Help or please others |
| | **Reactive** | ESTEEM<br><br>• Enhance self-esteem<br>• Enhance status<br>• Express self, identity | SPIRITUALITY<br><br>• Spiritual |

*Figure 4.1* Theoretical and observed sources of value

associated with an object. The only externally oriented value mentioned more frequently by low materialism respondents was the sentimental value associated with symbolic objects that reminded them of people important in their lives. Even these meanings, however, seem private and personal.

High materialism respondents were more likely to value objects because of their utilitarian uses or their financial value, their pleasing appearance, or their ability to enhance the status or appearance of their owners. In general, materialists more frequently mentioned sources of value that reflect public meanings or that depend on the reactions of others.

The second study revealed another difference between consumers low and high in materialism. When asked what benefits they would receive from possessing the desired object, those high in materialism described almost 50 percent more benefits than did those low in materialism. It appears that materialistic consumers have greater expectations of what a desired object can do for them than do those low in materialism.

This finding is bolstered by a survey that used a larger sample. In this study, I asked respondents to indicate how likely it was that they would experience each of a number of benefits listed on the questionnaire. Respondents high in materialism were more likely than other consumers to believe that a desired commercial good would provide *all* of the benefits (or values) listed in the survey. Thus, they were more likely to believe that the desired object would provide them with an improved sense of self-esteem, would improve the way others viewed them, would enhance their relationships with others, and the like.

In sum, materialists (compared to other consumers) seem to place higher value on, and hope to receive greater benefits from, commercial objects. What might account for this characteristic of materialism? Although a number of factors may be responsible, the remainder of this chapter examines just one of these: the possibility that low and high materialism consumers differ in the way they use possessions to define and communicate their personal identities. This discussion will examine first the role that possessions, generally, play in providing a sense of esteem through the development and communication of a personal identity. Attention will then shift to factors that encourage the use of possessions to form identity and to generate feelings of esteem, as well as the relationship of materialism to these factors.

## Identity, image, and esteem

People desire to be perceived in a positive way, both by others and in their own eyes (Schlenker 1986; Leary and Kowalsky 1990). A positive sense of self may come from many different sources. Achievements and the praise received for these achievements can be an important source of esteem. Relationships with others and the manner in which one is treated by important others also play a role.

Possessions, the focus of this chapter, provide another way to engender a positive sense of self. A classic example of the way possessions can be used for this purpose is through conspicuous consumption, in which consumers own high-priced, status-oriented goods to impress others and to convince them of their high social status (Veblen 1899; Mason 1981; LaBarbera 1988). Conspicuous consumption in the classic sense is accompanied by social comparison. That is, the individual engaging in conspicuous consumption consciously or un-consciously compares the prestige of his/her goods with the prestige of the goods owned by relevant others. If one is successful in "out-consuming" one's peers, a positive sense of self results.

However, even individuals who do not consciously engage in conspicuous consumption may use possessions to enhance their image, in their own eyes or in the eyes of others, and to develop a positive sense of self. This is because a positive image, or "looking good," can be defined in a variety of ways. For the status-oriented or conspicuous consumer, "looking good" involves owning more prestigious products than other consumers. But for someone else, "looking good" may involve an entirely different type of image.

There is great diversity in the kinds of images people desire to possess and portray. An interior designer is likely to promote a persona that communicates her creative, artistic qualities. Someone else may choose products and clothing consistent with a socially conscious, ecologically concerned self. Yet another's image may focus on athletic prowess and fitness. Some desired images may run strongly counter to American mainstream values. The image associated with "gangsta" rappers, for instance, is highly valued by some youthful segments of the population but is powerfully repugnant to others.

But whatever "looking good" is to a particular individual, that individual wants to communicate that desired (ideal) image to others. And when that individual contemplates himself and all that he possesses, he hopes to see the person he wishes to be. The possessions, in fact, may be reassurance that he *is* the person he wishes to be.

Many aspects of personal history, perceived traits, appearance, and accomplishments shape an individual's identity. In modern Western society, possessions have taken a particularly important role in defining and communicating the self (see Belk 1988, and Dittmar 1992, for reviews). In mobile, urban American society, we often don't have information about a person's personal history or accomplishments to give us information about that person's identity. So we look instead at the clothes people wear, the cars they drive, and the homes they live in to tell us something about who they are (Cherulnik and Bayless 1986; Dittmar and Pepper 1994). And having learned that habit of judging, we look at the clothes *we* wear, the cars *we* drive, and the homes in which *we* live to tell us who *we* are.

In Richins and Dawson's (1992) formulation, materialists place a higher importance on possessions when judging themselves and others (see also Hunt, Kernan, and Mitchell 1996). Thus, they are more likely to use possessions to transmit information about themselves, and also to decode the status or identity of others through their possessions, than are those low in materialism. The following discussion will examine one possible process by which objects are actively used to shape and express identity. We will then examine some of the conditions that foster the use of objects in this way and discuss how these conditions relate particularly to materialism and the use of possessions in identity formation and communication.

## Using objects to shape identity

Wicklund and Gollwitzer's (1982) theory of symbolic self-completion and McCracken's (1986) account of how advertisers attempt to develop brand or product meaning can be adapted and elaborated to explain how possessions can be used to develop self-meaning or identity.

This process, described below and in Figure 4.2, applies when a concern about one's identity leads to a desire to appropriate the meanings of objects. This may be for purposes of forging an identity (as in the case of adolescents) or modifying an established identity (as when one takes on an important new role). In such cases, in the terminology of Wicklund and Gollwitzer, an individual's

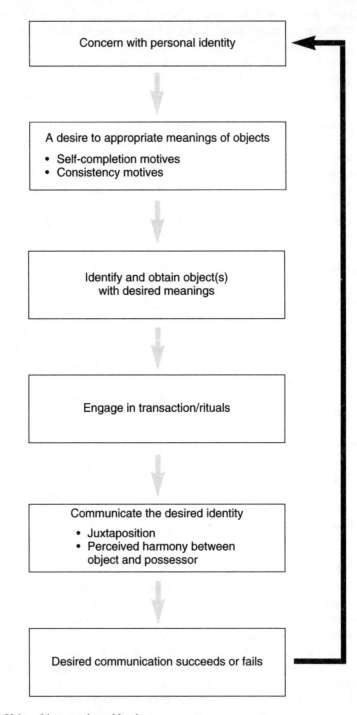

*Figure 4.2* Using objects to shape identity

self-definition is incomplete, and the individual will be motivated to use the symbolic properties of objects to move the self-definition toward completion. The meanings of objects may be appropriated for other reasons, however, perhaps simply to maintain consistency between individuals' established identities and the socially visible products by which they are judged (Grubb and Grathwohl 1967; Sirgy 1982). It is expected that individuals will differ in the extent to which they use goods to symbolically represent the self, either for completion or consistency purposes.

## *Choosing the product and meaning*

Commercial goods possess meanings (e.g., Douglas and Isherwood 1979; Mick 1986; Richins 1994b). These meanings are often widely shared and derive from a variety of sources – from advertisements featuring these goods (McCracken 1986), from information about the users and possessors of the goods, and from enculturation experiences and social interactions (Mead 1934; Solomon 1983).

The consumer consciously or unconsciously identifies products that have desirable meanings that h/she wishes to appropriate and purchases those products. For example, an adolescent male might aspire to the daring, adventuresome image portrayed in Mountain Dew commercials. Looking about in the culturally constituted world, he might come to the conclusion that snowboarding possesses the desired image of adventure and excitement. This meaning, and other meanings associated with the activity, may be particularly resonant to the individual and encourage him to purchase a K-2 Fat Bob snowboard, boots, and a plane ticket to Colorado.

## *Linking the object with self*

Simply possessing an object may not be sufficient for that object to contribute to a person's identity. Rather, the object must be linked to the individual in a meaningful way. Sartre (1953/1966, Part IV, Ch. 2; see also Belk 1988) suggested that an object may become a part of the self when the individual appropriates or controls the object for personal use, when the object was created by its possessor, or when the individual gains intimate knowledge of the object. McCracken described several possession and grooming rituals that enable the meaning of the object to flow to the individual. Such rituals as cleaning a newly acquired object, personalizing or customizing it in some way, or arranging for its display allow the consumer to "take possession of the meaning" of the consumer good (McCracken 1986: 79). Rochberg-Halton (1984) described a similar process, called cultivation, in which individuals engage in purposive transactions with certain objects through which they cultivate both the meaning of the object and the meaning of the self (see also Csikszentmihalyi and Rochberg-Halton 1981, Ch. 7).

Thus, our teenaged friend may engage in a number of activities in hopes that the active, adventurous meaning of his snowboard will become a part of his own identity. He may clean his snowboard, practice using it on the nearest hill, subscribe to a snowboarding magazine to help him learn the language of the sport, and fantasize about his planned trip to the snowy Colorado slopes.

## Communicating and affirming the identity

In some cases, private transactions with a meaningful possession are sufficient for that object to become a part of one's identity and to obtain a sense of esteem and satisfaction. But ours is a social world, and people usually wish to communicate their desired identity to others and to have this identity validated. These are the reciprocal processes of "self-symbolization" and "registering" described by Wicklund and Gollwitzer (1982), in which individuals consciously and publicly invoke symbols of their desired identities in hopes that these identities will be affirmed by others.

In some cases, the communication of identity through possessions is accidental or unavoidable. Clothing is an example. Everyone wears clothes and is judged by the clothes they wear (Holman 1981; Solomon and Anand 1985). Thus, whether we want them to or not, others make judgments about who we are by our public possessions: by what we wear, the car we drive (or the absence thereof), the neighborhood and house we live in (Cherulnik and Bayless 1986; Dittmar and Pepper 1994; Hyatt 1992).

In McCracken's analysis, juxtaposition of a meaningful object (e.g., a prop in an advertisement) with a neutral object (e.g., a new brand) causes meaning transfer to occur, but only if there is a special harmony between the two objects that the viewer grasps. The same can be said for the communication of identity. When people juxtapose themselves with a product by wearing, displaying, talking about, or using the object in public, the meaning of this object will transfer to its possessor if there is a harmony between the possession and the possessor and if observers perceive this harmony. If the adventuresome meaning of the snowboard is not in strong opposition to known characteristics of the snowboard's possessor (and, in fact, is bolstered by his other characteristics), in the eyes of observers he may come to acquire the adventuresome image he desires.

In some cases, of course, the attempted meaning transfer fails. The outrageous hat that looks so charming on a fashion model may simply look silly on a frumpy woman and may, in fact, emphasize her awkward dowdiness and lack of confidence. The shy, nerdy teenager with thick-lensed glasses whose social activity is limited to internet chat rooms and postings on alt.fan.startrek will not get an adventuresome identity simply by showing friends a picture of himself standing next to his snowboard.

## Monitoring identity

The final stage of this process is a feedback loop. This feedback consists in part of self-perceptions, as in "How convincing do I feel when I carry this snowboard? – Is it really me?" Self-perceptions are bolstered (or not) by the reactions of others. People seek information from others about how they are perceived and about the success or failure of their attempts to acquire the meanings of objects. They want to know whether their use of a symbolic product has "registered," that is, whether others are appropriately convinced by the self-symbolizing and accept the desired image as valid. If so, their personal perceptions of their own identity will be altered somewhat when they come to view themselves as others now view them (Cooley 1902; Mead 1934; Felson 1989), partially by virtue of using the product. As a result, concerns about personal identity may be quieted. This feedback will also influence future product choices and other product-related behaviors.

People's ability to use objects to shape identity is not unlimited, however. Even if the self-symbolizing attempt successfully registers with others, the feedback reinforcing this self-symbolization may not be accurately perceived by the person desiring the identity change. This is particularly true if the actor is undertaking a somewhat radical change in identity. Despite our best intentions to "become a new person," we usually are unable to accept or believe feedback that suggests an identity vastly different from our old, well-known selves (Kenny and DePaulo 1993). As Swann (1987: 1044) concludes, "for enduring changes in self-conceptions to occur . . . people must [first] undergo a major reorganization in the way they view themselves." Yet because views of ourselves are shaped by the views of others, people desiring an identity change are caught in an eternal catch-22 – others cannot see a "new you" until the "old you" has changed, but the "old you" can't become a "new you" unless others tell us we are in fact altered. For these reasons the uses of objects to achieve small or incremental identity adjustments are more likely to be successful than are attempts at major identity transformations.

The preceding discussion has described the general process by which possessions engender identity change. Yet there are cultural and individual differences in the extent to which consumers use goods in this manner. The following sections describe some of the factors that influence these differences and discuss how these factors may encourage materialistic consumers to rely on objects to develop or express their identities.

## Cultural factors that foster the use of goods to express identity

### *Large scale culture*

Observers have frequently juxtaposed the character of historical, rural communities with modern urban life in Western cultures (e.g., Boorstin 1973; Form and Stone 1957; see also Belk 1984a). In small towns, individuals and their place in the town's social structure are well-known. The community memory is long, and fellow citizens know what a person was like in high school, know the character of his/her father and mother, and probably know his/her economic status relative to other members of the community. Attempts to manipulate others' perceptions of who one is via something as superficial as a newly acquired car are likely to be fruitless and perhaps even ridiculed.

In modern urban life, however, there is little collective memory of an individual's identity. Interactions with others are often fleeting, and appraisals of identity must be made quickly and on the basis of visible signs. In large scale societies, "having becomes a substitute for doing," in part because in these more fluid environments possessions are better able to convey a (potentially false) sense of what one does; "a primary distinction in moving from small scale to large scale culture is the increased use of possessions to help regain a lost sense of self" (Belk 1984a: 758).

## Unstable meanings

In contemporary Western cultures, meaning is in a constant state of flux. As McCracken (1986) notes, the cultural categories of person that help shape identity are subject to constant manipulation by individuals, social groups, and marketing agents. Members of various demographic or cultural groups (e.g., senior citizens) work to solidify their group identities and to increase their power and status in the social hierarchy. Marketing and media institutions create new cultural categories to define market segments (e.g., Gen-Xers), and these categories then become a basis for self-definition.

At the same time, the meanings of objects that are used to make visible and stabilize the categories of culture are also subject to frequent change through their appropriation in advertising, in television programming, and among social subgroups.

This fluidity of meaning and categories requires individuals to adjust constantly the objects they use to express their identities. A possession once in harmony with one's sense of self may take on a new meaning after similar objects are appropriated by cultural subgroups whose values or behavior are in opposition to the values of the possession's owner. Thus, a prized designer shirt may lose its prestige value when its possessor, a young executive, sees an identical garment on the back of a supermarket checker. And, alas for the teenager who has just purchased his snowboard, the youthful, extreme sports image of snowboarding may soon fade as more people over 40 take up the sport (Wulf 1996). In the near future, snowboarding may no longer be quite so cool, no longer quite so congruent with the teenager's desired identity. His snowboarding activities may be abandoned, to be replaced by some new object or activity that has recently acquired an image of high adventure.

## Materialism and cultural factors

Because materialists, by definition, place more emphasis on possessions to evaluate themselves and others, they tend to be more sensitive to the signals that possessions send about their owner's identity. Thus, materialists are more likely to respond to the unstable categories of person and constantly shifting product meanings in North American culture by using goods to construct and/or express their identities.

## Individual factors that foster the use of goods to express identity

Although characteristics of culture may encourage an individual to use possessions to define identity, not all members of a culture do so to an equal extent. Some are very conscious of the relationship between their possessions and their (real or desired) identity and actively promote a congruence between the two, while others may be more likely to rely on other elements that shape identity, such as interpersonal relationships, work accomplishments, hobbies, or altruistic behaviors. Some of the individual difference variables that may encourage a reliance on goods to shape and communicate identity, and the relationship of these characteristics to materialism, are described below.

### *Other-directedness*

In 1950, David Riesman and his colleagues set out to describe the American character. In so doing, they put a name and a supporting framework to a characteristic of some Americans that had been commented upon for more than a century. Riesman identified three types of character: tradition-directed, inner-directed, and other-directed. He considered the other-directed type to be most common in the American culture of the time. Other-directed people receive their guidance from those around them, and the goals toward which these individuals strive shift with the guidance they receive from others. As might be expected, an other-directed person pays close attention to the signals from others to determine how s/he should act; s/he has "an exceptional sensitivity to the actions and wishes of others" (Riesman 1950: 22).

Although the dominant character in America may have changed in recent decades (Sennett 1977; Lasch 1979; Riesman 1980), the notion of other-directedness or other-dependence is still a useful one (Keshen 1996). It is particularly applicable in the analysis of identity. Individuals who are other-directed are concerned about how others perceive them and, as a result, are likely to be quite concerned about the visible manifestations of their identity – that is, their possessions. Consumers who possess a predominantly other-directed character are more likely to use possessions to express, and perhaps to shape, their identities.

Other-directed individuals are likely to be materialistic for two reasons. First, other-directed individuals actively cultivate the impression they make on others, and possessions are a potent mechanism for impression management. Thus, they emphasize goods as an important form of social discourse, and a heavy emphasis on goods is, in itself, an aspect of materialism. Second, other-directed individuals, so sensitive to the cues of others, are acutely aware that they are judged by their external selves (which include their possessions); and, being guided by these others, they are likely to adopt the same standards of judging. This increases the likelihood that other-directed individuals will judge both themselves and others by their possessions, a key component of materialism identified by Richins and Dawson.

The links between other-directedness and materialism have been established in empirical studies that examined constructs closely associated with other-directedness. In a small study of undergraduates, Schroeder (1991; see also Schroeder and Dugal 1995) examined the relationship between materialism (as measured by the traits of envy, possessiveness, and nongenerosity) and a number of personal characteristics that appear to reflect other-directedness. He found materialism to be positively related to self-rated susceptibility to normative influence, social anxiety, and public self-consciousness. That is, students who were high in materialism were more likely to say that they look to others to determine what they should buy, to describe themselves as anxious in their dealings with other people, and to be self-conscious about the impression they make on others. In Schroeder's study, materialism was also related to conformity. Materialistic students scored lower on a self-report measure of need for uniqueness and were judged by independent observers to be more conventional in their personal appearance.

Other empirical studies using more diverse samples of adult consumers have also examined variables that relate to other-directedness. In a survey I conducted several years ago, 235 adult consumers completed the Snyder and Gangestad (1986) version of the self-monitoring scale. Those high in self-monitoring have been described in terms very similar to those used by Riesman to describe other-directed individuals. According to Snyder (1987), high self-monitors "invest considerable effort to 'read' and understand others in search of information to aid them in choosing their own self-presentations" (p. 34), and they adapt their behavior to social situations by asking "Who does this situation want me to be and how can I be that person?" (p. 46). The two factors of the Snyder and Gangestad scale have been labeled "public performing" and "other-directedness" (Briggs and Cheek 1988). In my survey, materialism correlated significantly with both public performing ($r = .20$, $p < .01$) and other-directedness ($r = .29$, $p < .01$). Chatterjee and Hunt (1996) found a similar but stronger result among college students.

My survey of adults also included a measure of public self-consciousness, which is the "tendency to think about those self-aspects that are matters of public display . . . [and] from which impressions are formed in other people's eyes" (Scheier and Carver 1985: 687). Consistent with Schroeder and Dugal's (1995) findings among undergraduates, the larger scale study revealed a significant correlation ($r = .37$, $p < .01$) between materialism and public self-consciousness.

A final variable that may be related to both other-directedness and materialism is vanity. Netemeyer *et al.*'s (1995) definition of vanity includes "an excessive concern" for one's physical appearance or one's personal achievements. The former, and possibly the latter, indicate a preoccupation with the reactions of others to oneself and, as such, involve other-directedness. These authors reported significant correlations between vanity measures and aspects of materialism among student and nonstudent samples.

These studies provide consistent evidence that materialistic consumers are more other-directed than their less materialistic counterparts. Other-directed individuals lack an internal compass for their behavior; the constantly shifting social milieu becomes their compass, and they are very adept at making adjustments to this milieu. Such social skills are useful for advancement in business organizations or political office and for effective performance in social groups. It is likely, however, that the frequent adjustments in behavior and goals required for the other-directed individual can result in (or possibly from) an impaired sense of identity or an identity that is weakly rather than firmly held. In what follows I discuss the effects of weakly held identity on the use and display of possessions to attain a sense of self. Because a weakly held identity can result from many factors besides other-directedness, these factors are discussed in their own section.

## Weakly held identity

Self-perception theory describes how people gain knowledge from their own behaviors. When internal states such as attitudes or moods are weak or ambiguous, people must infer these states from knowledge about their own behavior (Bem 1972; Fazio 1987). For instance, if a man isn't sure whether he's in love with someone, he may look to his own behavior when asked this question. He may think, "Well, I look forward to seeing her in the evening, I try to cheer her up when she's down, I bought her an expensive necklace for Valentine's Day," and then conclude, "Yes, I guess I love her."

Since self-identity can be characterized as a set of attitudes about the self, the same processes that apply to perceptions of attitudes can apply to perceptions of one's identity. That is, if a person's attitudes about some aspect of himself (his identity) are weakly held, that person will be more likely to look to his own behavior and other external cues to determine those attitudes. Accordingly, individuals with weak or uncertain identities are more likely to use their behaviors, such as their acquisition and use of possessions, to identify who they are. Thus, a consumer can acquire a stylish wardrobe to convince herself and others that she has a good fashion sense. Or she can buy a sporty car to convince herself that she's an exciting person. And this self-convincing is easier to do if she doesn't have a strong belief that the identity she already has is counter to these images.

What factors might cause a person to have a weak identity, either temporarily or cross-situationally? The following sections describe some of these factors, but it should be noted for purposes of this discussion that all aspects of the self-concept are not held with equal strength. For instance, a person's gender identity might be firmly established but her perception of her musical abilities may be less sure. Someone may be confident that he's a good parent, but not so sure about his abilities as the family financial manager.

*Inexperience* Inexperience concerning some facet of the self is likely to result in weak perceptions concerning this facet, and this inexperience is most pervasive among the young. Adolescents are well-known for their unformed identities (Erickson 1959). Not coincidentally, this is a time of frequent and extensive experimentation with the products most closely aligned with the self, such as clothing, cosmetics, and hairstyles, as well as other identity-related products such as music. As a group, adolescents have high scores on materialism measures (National Center for Education Statistics 1988), a reflection of their emphasis on products to help them achieve their sense of identity.

Inexperience with respect to an element of the self also occurs for older individuals, particularly when an important role transition occurs. When a man marries for the first time, he has relatively little basis to form an opinion about the kind of spouse he will be. Achieving parenthood, seeing children leave the family nest, and experiencing widowhood are also important transitions that lead to uncertainty or insecurity with aspects of the self, as do other role transitions such as taking a new job or starting a new hobby. Wicklund and Gollwitzer's (1982) theory of symbolic self-completion applies specifically to the incomplete identity that exists at a time of role transition (see also Braun and Wicklund 1989; Noble and Walker 1997).

*Disruption* An unwelcome disruption in one's personal or social status might also prompt a questioning of one's identity. Divorce, losing a job, or other major upheavals are likely to cause instability in perceptions of the self and an increased reliance on objects to bolster identity. McAlexander *et al.* (1993) found that recently divorced adults use consumption and consumption objects to cope with the disruption caused by this life change. Rindfleisch *et al.* (1997) found that young adults reared in families disrupted by divorce are more materialistic.

*Low self-esteem* A particularly interesting finding in recent self-esteem research is that individuals with low self-esteem are less certain than those with high self-esteem about the extent to which they possess various trait attributes and other aspects of identity (e.g., Pelham and Swann 1989; Baumgardner 1990; Campbell 1990). The self-evaluations of people with low self-esteem also are more vulnerable to their recent experiences, including their interactions with other people, and to mood (Brown and Smart 1991; Brown and Mankowski 1993). It appears, then, that the self-concepts of those with low self-esteem are more weakly held.

*Materialism and self-esteem* Given the reasoning presented above about the relationship between uncertainty and the use of possessions to establish and communicate identity, we would expect consumers with low self-esteem to rely on possessions as a self-presentation tool and to be higher in materialism. Empirical studies, however, have revealed rather low correlations between self-esteem and materialism (e.g., Richins and Dawson 1992). An examination of the self-esteem literature suggests a potential explanation for this. Baumgardner *et al.* (1989) have argued that people high in self-esteem do not need to assert their positive qualities to others or otherwise publicly manipulate self-presentation (e.g., use possessions to impress other people) in order to have a high regard for themselves because they already hold themselves in high regard. However, people with low self-esteem do engage in more public forms of self-enhancement (e.g., public display of reassuring possessions) than those high in self-esteem. Data presented by Baumgardner *et al.* show that low self-esteem individuals more frequently manipulate their public self-presentations and that these self-presentations temporarily raise their self-esteem.

Baumgardner *et al.* have generalized their findings to all low self-esteem individuals. However, some public manipulations of self-presentation require a certain degree of skill to be successful and, thus, reinforcing. Low self-esteem individuals are not all equally adept at these manipulations. I propose that those who are low in self-esteem but are confident of their ability to publicly manipulate self-presentation would be likely to use possessions expressively (and materialistically), but low self-esteem individuals who believe they lack this ability would be less inclined to do so.

People who are high in self-monitoring are confident in their abilities to perform publicly and handle social interactions. Thus, I propose, people who are high in self-monitoring but low in self-esteem would be most likely to engage in materialistic expressions of identity. Data from the survey, described above, that measured self-monitoring and materialism also included a measure of self-esteem (Rosenberg 1965) and can be used to test this idea. Median splits were used to divide respondents into low and high self-monitoring and low and high self-esteem groups. These two classification variables were used as factors in a $2 \times 2$ analysis of variance with the status subscale of the Richins and Dawson materialism measure as the dependent variable. The status subscale is the one that most directly relates to the use of possessions to express and judge status or identity and is therefore most relevant to the hypothesis. The results appear in Figure 4.3.

As predicted, the interaction between self-esteem and self-monitoring was significant. Those low in self-esteem but high in self-monitoring had the highest

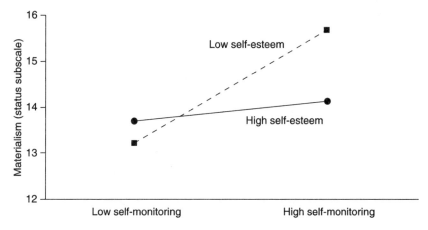

*Figure 4.3* Materialism scores of consumers low and high in self-monitoring and self-esteem

scores on the status-oriented subscale; scores in the other three cells did not differ significantly from one another. In conclusion, those high in self-monitoring but low in self-esteem are more likely to use possessions to judge themselves and others. It is likely that they also have a greater tendency to use possessions to develop and express personal identity.

## Conclusions

The literature and analyses described above suggest that other-directedness is a potentially important factor in the study of materialism. Hints of other-directedness are evident in the sources of value materialistic individuals receive from their possessions, and other-directedness is related to the expression of materialistic values directly and also indirectly through its relationship with the self-concept.

Our personal identities are central to our well-being and instrumental in our relationships with other people. Both intentionally and unintentionally, we use possessions to communicate who we are and what we wish to be. Individuals differ in the extent to which they consciously use possessions in this manner.

This chapter argues that other-directedness is a key influence on the extent to which people use objects to create, shape, and express themselves. Other-dependent people use cues from others to identify who they are and to determine the appropriate course of behavior. These cues help them identify the possessions they should own, the kind of clothes they should wear, and how they should spend their time.

All successfully functioning members of society must learn to use cues from others and to adapt their behavior appropriately. Some individuals are particularly adept at this and rely on these cues to a greater extent than others do.

This chapter has identified some of the factors that influence consumers to use possessions for identity purposes, but considerable areas for inquiry remain. For instance, it would be interesting to learn what types of objects are most likely to be used to shape and express identity, in which types of situations objects are likely to be used these ways, and for what audiences. How do consumers judge their success in these endeavors, and how do they respond when they meet with failure? What causes some individuals to redouble efforts to establish and express identity through possessions while others turn to other means such as developing new skills, collecting accomplishments, deepening their social relationships, or engaging in social service activities? The use of possessions in the formation and communication of self is a fascinating area of inquiry and one that deserves further study.

## References

Baumgardner, A. H. (1990) "To Know Oneself Is to Like Oneself: Self-Certainty and Self-Affect," *Journal of Personality and Social Psychology* 58, 6: 1062–72.
Baumgardner, A. M., Kaufman, C. M., and Levy, P. E. (1989) "Regulating Affect

Interpersonally: When Low Esteem Leads to Greater Enhancement," *Journal of Personality and Social Psychology* 56, 6: 907–21.

Belk, R. W. (1983) "Worldly Possessions: Issues and Criticisms," in R. P. Bagozzi and A. M. Tybout (eds) *Advances in Consumer Research*, Vol. 10, Ann Arbor, MI: Association for Consumer Research, 514–19.

—— (1984a) "Cultural and Historical Differences in Concepts of Self and Their Effects on Attitudes Toward Having and Giving," in T. C. Kinnear (ed.) *Advances in Consumer Research*, Vol. 11, Provo, UT: Association for Consumer Research, 754–60.

—— (1984b) "Three Scales to Measure Constructs Related to Materialism: Reliability, Validity, and Relationships to Measures of Happiness," in T. C. Kinnear (ed.) *Advances in Consumer Research*, Vol. 11, Provo, UT: Association for Consumer Research, 291–97.

—— (1988) "Possessions and the Extended Self," *Journal of Consumer Research* 15, 2: 139–68.

Bem, D. J. (1972) "Self-Perception Theory," in L. Berkowitz (ed.) *Advances in Experimental and Social Psychology*, Vol. 6, New York: Academic Press, 1–62.

Boorstin, D. J. (1973) *The Americans: The Democratic Experience*, New York: Random House.

Braun, O. L. and Wicklund, R. A. (1989) "Psychological Antecedents of Conspicuous Consumption," *Journal of Economic Psychology* 10, 2: 161–87.

Bredemeier, H. C. and Toby, J. (1960) *Social Problems in America: Costs and Casualties in an Acquisitive Society*, New York: Wiley.

Briggs, S. R. and Cheek. J. M. (1988) "On the Nature of Self-Monitoring: Problems With Assessment, Problems With Validity," *Journal of Personality and Social Psychology* 54, 4: 663–78.

Brown, J. D. and Mankowski. T. A. (1993) "Self-Esteem, Mood, and Self-Evaluations: Changes in Mood and the Way You See You," *Journal of Personality and Social Psychology* 64, 3: 421–30.

Brown, J. D. and Smart, S. A. (1991) "The Self and Social Conduct: Linking Self-Representations to Prosocial Behavior," *Journal of Personality and Social Psychology* 60, 3: 368–75.

Campbell, J. D. (1990) "Self-Esteem and Clarity of the Self-Concept," *Journal of Personality and Social Psychology* 59, 3: 538–49.

Chatterjee, A. and Hunt, J. M. (1996) "Self-Monitoring as a Personality Correlate of Materialism: An Investigation of Related Cognitive Orientation," *Psychological Reports* 79, 2: 523–8.

Cherulnik, P. D. and Bayless, J. K. (1986) "Person Perception in Environmental Context: The Influence of Residential Settings on Impressions of Their Occupants," *Journal of Social Psychology* 126, 5: 667–73.

Cooley, C. H. (1902) *Human Nature and the Social Order*, New York: Scribners.

Csikszentmihalyi, M. and Rochberg-Halton, E. (1981) *The Meaning of Things: Domestic Symbols and the Self*, Cambridge: Cambridge University Press.

Dittmar, H. (1992) *The Social Psychology of Material Possessions: To Have Is To Be*, New York: St. Martin's Press.

Dittmar, H. and Pepper, L. (1994) "To Have Is to Be: Materialism and Person Perception in Working-Class and Middle-Class British Adolescents," *Journal of Economic Psychology* 15, 2: 233–51.

Douglas, M. and Isherwood, B. (1979) *The World of Goods*, New York: Basic Books.

Erikson, E. (1959) "Identity and the Life Cycle," *Psychological Issues* 1, 1: 1–171.

Fazio, R. H. (1987) "Self-Perception Theory: A Current Perspective," in M. P. Zanna, J. M. Olson and C. P. Herman (eds) *Social Influence: The Ontario Symposium*, Vol. 5, Hillsdale, NJ: Lawrence Erlbaum, 129–50.

Felson, R. B. (1989) "Parents and the Reflected Appraisal Process: A Longitudinal Analysis," *Journal of Personality and Social Psychology* 56, 2: 965–71.

Form, W. H. and Stone, G. P. (1957) "Urbanism, Anonymity, and Status Symbolism," *American Journal of Sociology* 62, 5: 504–14.

Fournier, S. and Richins, M. L. (1991) "Some Theoretical and Popular Notions Concerning Materialism," *Journal of Social Behavior and Personality* 6, 6: 403–14.

Fox, R. W. and Lears, T. J. J. (1983) *The Culture of Consumption: Critical Essays in American History, 1880–1980*, New York: Pantheon.

Grubb, E. L. and Grathwohl, H. L. (1967) "Consumer Self-Concept, Symbolism and Market Behavior: A Theoretical Approach," *Journal of Marketing* 31, 4: 22–7.

Holman, R. H. (1981), "Apparel as Communication," in E. C. Hirschman and M. B. Holbrook (eds) *Symbolic Consumer Behavior*, Ann Arbor, MI: Association for Consumer Research, 7–15.

Hunt, J. M., Kernan, J. B., and Mitchell, D. J. (1996) "Materialism as Social Cognition: People, Possessions, and Perception," *Journal of Consumer Psychology* 5, 1: 65–83.

Hyatt, E. M. (1992) "Consumer Stereotyping: The Cognitive Bases of the Social Symbolism of Products," in J. F. Sherry, Jr., and B. Sternthal (eds) *Advances in Consumer Research*, Vol. 19, Provo, UT: Association for Consumer Research, 299–303.

Kenny, D. A. and DePaulo, B. M. (1993) "Do People Know How Others View Them? An Empirical and Theoretical Account," *Psychological Bulletin* 114, 1: 145–61.

Keshen, R. (1996) *Reasonable Self-Esteem*, Montreal: McGill-Queen's University Press.

LaBarbera, P. A. (1988) "The Nouveaux Riches: Conspicuous Consumption and the Issue of Self-Fulfillment," in E. Hirschman and J. N. Sheth (eds) *Research in Consumer Behavior*, Vol. 3, Greenwich, CT: JAI Press, 179–210.

Lasch, C. (1979) *The Culture of Narcissism*, New York: W. W. Norton.

Leary, M. R., and Kowalsky, R. M. (1990) "Impression Management: Literature Review and Two-Component Model," *Psychological Bulletin* 107, 1: 34–47.

Mason, R. S. (1981) *Conspicuous Consumption: A Study of Exceptional Consumer Behavior*, Westmead, England: Gower Publishing Company.

McAlexander, J. H., Schouten, J. W., and Roberts, S. D. (1993) "Consumer Behavior and Divorce," in J. A. Costa and R. W. Belk (eds) *Research in Consumer Behavior*, Vol. 6, Greenwich, CT: JAI Press, 153–84.

McCracken, G. (1986) "Culture and Consumption: A Theoretical Account of the Structure and Movement of the Cultural Meaning of Consumer Goods," *Journal of Consumer Research* 13, 1: 71–84.

Mead, G. H. (1934) *Mind, Self, and Society*, Chicago: University of Chicago Press.

Mick, D. G. (1986) "Consumer Research and Semiotics: Exploring the Morphology of Signs, Symbols, and Significance," *Journal of Consumer Research* 13, 2: 196–213.

National Center for Education Statistics (1988) *Youth Indicators 1988*, Washington, D.C.: US Department of Education.

Netemeyer, R. G., Burton, S., and Lichtenstein, D. R. (1995), "Trait Aspects of Vanity: Measurement and Relevance to Consumer Behavior," *Journal of Consumer Research* 21, 1: 612–26.

Noble, C. H. and Walker, B. A. (1997) "Exploring the Relationships among Liminal Transitions, Symbolic Consumption, and the Extended Self," *Psychology & Marketing* 14, 1: 29–47.

Pelham, B. W. and Swann, W. B., Jr. (1989) "From Self-Conceptions to Self-Worth: On the Sources and Structure of Global Self-Esteem," *Journal of Personality and Social Psychology* 57, 4: 672–80.

Richins, M. L. (1994a) "Special Possessions and the Expression of Material Values," *Journal of Consumer Research* 21, 3: 522–33.

Richins, M. L. (1994b), "Valuing Things: The Public and Private Meanings of Possessions," *Journal of Consumer Research* 21, 3: 504–21.

Richins, M. L. and Dawson, S. (1992) "A Consumer Values Orientation for Materialism and Its Measurement: Scale Development and Validation," *Journal of Consumer Research* 19, 3: 303–16.

Riesman, D. (1950), *The Lonely Crowd: A Study of the Changing American Character*, New Haven, CT: Yale University Press.

Riesman, D. (1980) "Egocentrism: Is the American Character Changing?," *Encounter* 55, 2: 19–28.

Rindfleisch, A., Burroughs, J. E., and Denton, F. (1997) "Family Structure, Materialism, and Compulsive Consumption," *Journal of Consumer Research* 23, 1: 312–25.

Rochberg-Halton, E. (1984) "Object Relations, Role Models, and Cultivation of the Self," *Environment and Behavior* 16, 3: 335–68.

Rosenberg, M. (1965) *Society and the Adolescent Self Image*, Princeton, NJ: Princeton University Press.

Sartre, J-.P. (1953/1966) *Being and Nothingness: An Essay on Phenomenological Ontology*, New York: Washington Square Press.

Scheier, M. F. and Carver, C. S. (1985) "The Self-Consciousness Scale: A Revised Version for Use with General Populations," *Journal of Applied Social Psychology* 15, 8: 687–99.

Schlenker, B. R. (1986) "Self-Identification: Toward an Integration of the Private and Public Self," in R. F. Baumeister (ed.) *Public Self and Private Self*, New York: Springer-Verlag, 21–62.

Schroeder, J. E. (1991) "Psychological Undercurrents of Materialism," paper presented at the 1991 Association for Consumer Research conference, Chicago, Ill.

Schroeder, J. E. and Dugal, S. S. (1995) "Psychological Correlates of the Materialism Construct," *Journal of Social Behavior and Personality* 10, 1: 243–53

Sennett, R. (1977) *The Fall of Public Man*, New York: Knopf.

Sirgy, M. J. (1982) "Self-Concept in Consumer Behavior: A Critical Review," *Journal of Consumer Research* 9, 3: 287–300.

Snyder, M. (1987) *Public Appearances/Private Realities: The Psychology of Self-Monitoring*, San Francisco: Freeman.

Snyder, M. and Gangestad, S. (1986) "On the Nature of Self-Monitoring: Matters of Assessment, Matters of Validity," *Journal of Personality and Social Psychology* 51, 1: 125–39.

Solomon, M. R. (1983) "The Role of Products as Social Stimuli: A Symbolic Interactionism Perspective," *Journal of Consumer Research* 10, 3: 319–29.

Solomon, M. R. and Anand, P. (1985) "Ritual Costumes and Status Transition: The Female Business Suit as Totemic Emblem," in E. C. Hirschman and M. Holbrook (eds) *Advances in Consumer Research*, Vol. 12, Provo, UT: Association for Consumer Research, 315–18.

Swann, W. B., Jr. (1987) "Identity Negotiation: Where Two Roads Meet," *Journal of Personality and Social Psychology* 53, 6: 1038–51.

Veblen, T. (1899/1953) *The Theory of the Leisure Class: An Economic Study in the Evolution of Institutions*, New York: The American Library.

Wachtel, P. L. (1983) *The Poverty of Affluence: A Psychological Portrait of the American Way of Life*, New York: Free Press.

Wicklund, R. A. and Gollwitzer, P. M. (1982) *Symbolic Self-Completion*, Hillsdale, NJ: Lawrence Erlbaum.

Wulf, S. (1996) "Triumph of Hated Snowboarders," *Time* 147, 5: 69.

# 5 The dangers and opportunities of playful consumption

*Kent Grayson*

A bar owner's business was doing poorly. Desperate for patrons, the owner put a sign in the bar's window with the following challenge: "Eat 50 Eggs in 15 Minutes and Drink Free for a Month." Within days, consumers from all over town were visiting the bar to cheer for contestants and enjoy the spectacle. Some contestants tried to eat the 50 eggs boiled, others attempted scrambled, and some even tried to drink them raw from an enormous pitcher. But none could win the prize. One evening a stranger entered the now bustling bar. "Does it matter what kind of eggs?" the stranger asked. "Nope," said the owner proudly, "we've had everything from fried to poached." "Excellent," said the now smiling stranger, who pulled out a jar of caviar and, with one large spoonful, was the toast of the bar for a month.

The "stranger" in the above story is an archetypal figure who has been depicted in stories and jokes for centuries. Known to folklore scholars as "the Trickster," this character appears in different guises throughout the world and goes by names as diverse as Loki, Coyote, Hermes, and the Monkey King (Radin 1956; Pelton 1980; Roberts 1989; Hynes 1993; Smith 1997). Although different Trickster stories have different characters and plots, they all often illustrate the important but sometimes subtle difference between playing *by* the rules and playing *with* the rules. At the start of the above story, the bar's consumers are willing to play by the explicit and implied rules set up by the bar owner, resulting in not only value to them but also more business for the bar owner. But at the end of the story, the stranger plays with one of the implied rules (the rule that "eggs" means chicken eggs), thus enjoying a different kind of value from the interaction – one that is not as conducive to the bar owner's business. Trickster stories emphasize that although play is often associated with fun, teamwork, and cooperation, it has an equally strong association with trouble-making, mischief, and deception.

Researchers – myself included – have found the concept of play to be as elusive as any Trickster (Deighton and Grayson 1995; Grayson and Deighton 1995). Play has attracted the attention of anthropologists, sociologists, psychologists, literary theorists, performance theorists, and even neurophysiologists. Their efforts have produced a wide and disparate body of scholarship on play that, in the words of Bende and Grastyán (1992: 271), would be "discouraging" and "hopeless" to review thoroughly. In the face of this ever-expanding literature, Schechner (1993: 24) goes so far as to suggest an academic moratorium on defining play, pointing to Victor Turner's assertion that play is "categorically uncategorizable." But just as Tom Sawyer (Mark Twain's Trickster) made painting a fence seem irresistible to his friends, play has a way of making itself seem irresistible to academics. Even Schechner (ibid.), after suggesting his moratorium, presents six "templates" against which play should be measured. And despite my growing appreciation for the ineffability of play, I nonetheless try in this chapter to explain its relevance to marketers and consumers.

## Play and Holbrook's typology

The challenge (and perhaps therefore the attraction) of studying play is that the word can be used in so many different ways. Playing a role is different from playing a piano. Playing around is different from playing to win. Playing along with someone is different from playing into their hands. Despite these multiple uses of the word, Huizinga (1950) argues that there is an essential similarity between these seemingly different types of play. In his influential book on play, he discerns a common play element in almost every human activity – from law, gambling, and war, to poetry, mythology, and philosophy. Applied to marketing, this observation points to the useful conclusion that, given the right perspective on the part of the consumer, nearly every product or service might be sold or consumed as play. This is Holbrook's (1994) stance regarding not just play, but also all other types of consumer value. Anything – a silk tie, for example – can be valued for its efficiency, its morality, its esthetics, or, indeed, its playfulness.

How can such diverse market offerings as amusement parks, legal services, tennis clubs, and television dramas each offer playful consumer value? Holbrook (ibid.) answers this question by defining playful value as that which is intrinsically motivating, self-oriented, and active. The consumption of something like an amusement park easily fits this tri-dimensional definition of play, but even consuming something such as legal services can be playful. For example, a defendant in a legal trial might inherently enjoy participating in trial strategy discussions, learning to play the appropriate courtroom role, or meeting the challenge of being questioned by the prosecution. When a client is actively participating in the activity for its own sake, this is playful consumption.

Despite the many differences among published definitions of play, there is fairly consistent agreement among scholars about the three dimensions that Holbrook uses to define play. For instance, most scholars agree that an activity is not play unless it is pursued for its own sake (Rainwater 1922; Mitchell and Mason 1937: 13; Huizinga 1950: 13; Fink 1968: 20; Garvey 1977: 2; Monighan-Nourot *et al.* 1987: 16; Holt 1995). The enjoyment derived from play is not described by researchers as that which comes from helping others or making others feel good, but as a self-oriented reward such as "fun" (Huizinga ibid.: 7), "happiness" (Fink ibid.), or "joy" (Lieberman 1977: 19). Lastly, play is commonly characterized as requiring active engagement – although scholars have tended to focus on the mental, rather than physical, engagement of the player (Huizinga ibid.: 13; Goffman 1961: 38; Garvey ibid.: 5; Monighan-Nourot *et al.* ibid.: 15). Moving a chess piece takes much less physical activity than tackling a quarterback, but both activities can provide comparable amounts of playful value.

Accepting this basic definition, it might initially seem that a marketer should always encourage consumer play. After all, what negative consequences could come from providing consumers with the opportunity to engage in a self-oriented, intrinsically rewarding activity? Answering this question requires a deeper understanding of the different types of play that consumers might enjoy. While Holbrook's (1994) typology is useful in distinguishing play from other types of value, it does not (nor does it aim to) distinguish between different types of play. The next section does this by relying on an additional definitional dimension of play: the relationship of the activity to the social rules of the situation.

## The importance of social rules in defining play

A number of social scientists have observed that a prerequisite for everyday social relations is a shared understanding or consensus among interactants about the rules governing the interaction. Goffman (1959) calls this a "definition of the situation." His concept is similar to James's (1890) "subuniverse of reality;" Wittgenstein's (1953) "language game" (see also Lyotard 1979); and Schutz and Luckmann's (1973) "finite province of meaning." Each of these terms refers to the perception that social life is subdivided into different spheres, each of which is governed by different rules. Interactants sometimes disagree about the rules governing a situation (Grayson 1998), but what is remarkable about everyday interaction is that – by attending to cues in the environment and to nonverbal signals sent by the other interactants – even a group of complete strangers can achieve a "working consensus" about the rules without having to address them explicitly in the interaction (Goffman 1959: 9–10). This consensus occurs despite the fact that, in any given day, interactants move through successive situational definitions (Schutz and Luckmann 1973: 24) and often operate at the intersection of several definitions (Lyotard 1979: 15; Wittgenstein 1953: 11–12).

For example, consider the multiple situational definitions faced by a man visiting a hospital. He will move from interacting with a front-desk clerk to a receptionist, to a nurse, and finally to a doctor – and each of these interactions carries with it a different situational definition. Furthermore, when participating in these interactions, the customer must not only meet the situational rules imposed on him because he is a patient, but also those imposed because he is a man, a husband, a father, etc. At the same time, all of these interactions will share some similar rules that fall under the situational heading of "visiting a hospital" and visiting a hospital will share some rules that apply to all service situations. In almost every social situation we are faced with a similarly complex set of expectations. But thanks to our exposure to countless social encounters during our lives, we gain an instinctual appreciation for the most appropriate behaviors in different situations, and can therefore operate successfully in them.

The expected sets of behaviors associated with each definition of the situation are called "roles" (Goffman 1959, 1961; Zurcher 1983, Solomon *et al.* 1985). Role expectations are sets of beliefs and subjective probabilities that interactants have about the appropriate conduct for individuals occupying a particular position within a given situation (Sarbin and Allen 1968: 498). They are the rules that different individuals must follow given a particular definition of a situation. Not everyone's role in a given situation will be the same. In the hospital example above, the role expectations for patient, nurse, doctor, etc. are different. Thus, many situations comprise a "role set" (Merton 1957), which is a group of complementary roles that are required for a situation to unfold successfully. The concept of a role set implies that once a particular role in a situation is defined, this has implications for the other roles that are also expected in the situation.

However, unlike theatrical roles, social roles do not rigidly routinize expectations but instead help interactants to balance between the conflicting requirements of routinization and contextualization in social interaction. As Athay and Darley explain:

> Roles "structure" interaction in the sense of imposing normative limits on the possibilities of variation, but they do not determine particular courses of action in the sense of laying down exact prescriptions of what to do when. The limitations they impose on thought and action are exceedingly strong ones, to the point that actors normally find it very difficult to see themselves as deviating. But the boundaries are so formulated as to incorporate a high degree of indeterminacy, permitting enormously varying patterns of action to count as instantiations of the role-specified behaviors.
>
> (1982: 76)

Thus, role expectations include certain very specific role-forbidden and role-required behaviors; and at the same time leave open a range of role-possible actions from which consumers may choose (see also Sarbin and Allen 1968: 503; and Secord 1982: 35). For example, when an individual is empathetically counselling a friend about a serious personal problem, a cough is likely to be viewed by both parties as role-possible – not something that is required or forbidden by the role, but certainly something that is allowed. On the other hand, a yawn is likely to be viewed as role forbidden because it carries the possibility of communicating boredom. Thus, the counsellor may try to stifle a yawn more than she would try to stifle a cough – or may try to yawn at a time when the friend does not see it. A yawn is role-possible only if the counsellor can show how the behavior does not conflict with role expectations, for example by explaining that she is tired because she was up all night worrying about the friend's problem.

My brief summary of role theory provides a foundation for presenting the central assertion of this chapter:

*Play is always enacted in relation to a definition of a situation. It involves either following or deviating from the situation's role expectations (or a combination of both).*

Indeed, not every instance of following or deviating from social expectations will be playful. As emphasized earlier, whether or not an activity is playful depends on whether or not the activity is considered by the individual to be intrinsically motivated, self-oriented, and active. This means that play is not dependent on the activity *per se*, but on the person's attitude toward the activity. Even an everyday chore can be thought of as play and even a game of hopscotch can be considered not-play. As Mitchell and Mason assert:

> There is no particular activity, be it baseball, fishing, playing with dolls, that is always necessarily play; neither can an activity be mentioned that may not under some conditions be play. When one runs a foot race, drives a car, rows a boat, or reads a book, it may be play or not, depending on the way he thinks and feels about it.
>
> (1924: 88)

Thus, accepting that the focus of this chapter is on intrinsically motivated, self-oriented activities, these can be distinguished from one another on a continuum that ranges from following situational rules to applying new rules (and applying new rules often means breaking old ones). The continuum from rule-following to rule-breaking is an important element of Caillois's (1979) typology of play, which I adapt to a role-theory perspective in the remainder of this section.

### From ludus to paida: a continuum of play

At the rule-following end of the continuum is what Caillois (ibid.) calls *ludus*, which is the Latin word for play or game. Ludus involves playfully following arbitrary, imperative, and purposely limiting conventions (Caillois ibid.: 13). For example, a basketball player might at some point in the game want to tuck the ball under her arm and make a run for the basket. However, the arbitrary, imperative, and limiting convention of having to dribble or pass the ball is part of the social definition of basketball. While basketball is a good prototypical example of ludus, the conventions of almost every social situation are not theoretically different from basketball's conventions. Consider, for example, shopping at a retail store. A buyer who walks into a store knowing what he wants may wish to pay at the register before taking his merchandise from the shelf. However, in most retail stores, the arbitrary, imperative, and limiting conventions of shopping require the buyer to bring the merchandise to the register in order to pay for it. This role expectation may be so familiar to us that it seems like the "logical" way to do things, but retail shopping really doesn't have to be done that way. For example, the Argos chain of stores in the United Kingdom requires consumers to pick an item out of a catalogue and pay for it at the cash register before having it handed to them at a delivery desk.

My point is not only that explicit rules govern most social interactions, but also that following these rules can be, and often is, intrinsically motivating. This motivation comes from the sheer enjoyment of having and using an "interaction competency" (Athay and Darley 1982). Not having the right competency to operate in a social situation can be awkward and unpleasant. For example, those who travel to a foreign country sometimes find that because they do not know the appropriate social rules, even mundane activities such as shopping can be difficult. However, once a consumer has gained competence in shopping at a foreign marketplace, he or she may enjoy intrinsic value simply by operating according to the rules of the situation. This is the same kind of reward that one gets from being able to step confidently into a pick-up basketball game, interact successfully in a foreign language, or participate appropriately in a religious ceremony. Each of these activities may provide additional types of value, but this does not negate their potential for ludic value, which is the enjoyment of successfully following the rules.

On the other hand, the existence of expectations does not mean that they will be met. Nothing physical keeps a basketball player from running with the ball or a retail shopper from trying to pay for items before bringing them to the register. However, because these behaviors are not part of the situation's role expectations, they are at best role irrelevant and at worst rule forbidden, in which case a referee or store manager is likely to intervene. When these role-breaking behaviors are intrinsically motivated and self-oriented, they fall toward the other end of Caillois's (1979) play continuum, which is anchored by *paida*. In its purest form, paida (which is the demotic Greek word for child) is characterized by free improvisation, carefree gaiety, and uncontrolled fantasy (Caillois ibid.: 13), all three of which involve behaving without regard for role expectations. Such behaviors can certainly be done for extrinsic reasons such as annoying teammates or speeding up the shopping process. But they are playful when they are performed simply for the fun of it.

Before moving on to examine ludus and paida in more detail, it is useful to note that Caillois (ibid.) is not the only researcher to use rules as a way of distinguishing between different types of play. For example, Garvey (1977) contrasts "play" with "games," describing the former as "spontaneous and voluntary" (p. 5) and the latter as requiring "acceptance of and adherence to a particular set of rules" (p. 104). Similarly, Goffman (1974: 57) argues that objects in play are "quite temporary, never fully established," whereas in games they are "institutionalized – stabilized as it were – just as the arena of action is fixed by the formal rules of activity." Still other scholars have referred to the rule dimension of play, but have focused more on paida than on ludus. For example, play is described as an activity that "permits freedom of action [and] diversion from routines" (Caplan and Caplan 1973), provides "freedom from external rules" (Monighan-Nourot *et al.* 1987: 18) and is "determined at a given time by the somatic structure and the social attitudes of the agent" (Rainwater 1922: 217).

## Seven ways in which 'X' can play with 'Y'

Caillois's continuum emphasizes that play is not a unitary phenomenon but instead comes in many guises. This section and the next more closely examine the different types of play. My purpose in presenting a detailed typology of play is twofold. First, I wish to emphasize that although playful activities share some common attributes, the concept of play actually encompasses an extremely wide range of very different activities. Second, as I will show in a later section, marketers and consumers will react differently to different types of playful activity, and so it is important to determine which type of play is being enacted in a consumption situation.

Although accounts of marginalized consumers (e.g., Eisen 1988) have shown that people do not need a marketer's intervention in order to play, the focus of this chapter is on playful value that involves a marketer's products, services, or representatives. This kind of playful value can come from three types of interactions. A consumer may, with the help of the marketer, play with another consumer. Alternatively, a consumer may play with the marketer. Lastly, a marketer may play with the consumer. To capture these different types of play interactions, Figure 5.1 outlines four different kinds of ludus and three different kinds of paida. As the figure indicates, all of the definitions assume that an individual (X) is directly or indirectly playing with someone else (Y). It is against Y's definition of the situation that X's play is defined. Y may also be playing in relation to X's definition of the situation, but the focus remains on X's actions, not Y's. This figure facilitates an analysis of how a consumer might play with another consumer or with a marketer; and how a marketer might play with a consumer. However, to simplify my exposition, X will be regarded in this section as a consumer and Y as a marketer.

In the lower portion of the figure, four types of ludus are described. At the very bottom is "competition," an activity in which the consumer competently fulfills the marketer's role expectations and in which these expectations include adopting goals that conflict with the marketer. For example, the goal of consumers at an auction is to pay as little as possible, but the goal of the auctioneer is to achieve the highest prices. And yet participating in an auction can provide considerable playful value for some consumers (see also Schindler 1995). The next type of play is "participation," which is similar to competition except that the consumer and marketer have complementary goals within the activity. Many tropical vacation-resort communities create environments in which consumers may playfully participate. When, at these resorts, a consumer steps into a pair of water skis, attends a dance aerobics class, or joins a hike in the mountains, both consumer and marketer have similar goals for the activity.

With both competition and participation, the consumer is competently and fully meeting role expectations. The next two types of ludus, "initiation" and "imitation," are those for which the consumer meets only a subset of the role expectations. Consumers undergoing initiation would like to fulfill all of the role expectations, but cannot do so because they do not yet have the competence

| | |
|---|---|
| **Paida** | X performs behaviors that conflict wtih Y's definition of the situation, but X keeps this conflict hidden from Y *(Deception)* |
| | X performs behaviors that conflict with Y's definition of the situation, and X does not keep this conflict hidden from Y *(Subversion)* |
| | X performs situationally relevant behaviors that are not included in Y's definition of the situation, but that also do not conflict with that definition *(Innovation)* |
| **Ludus** | X fulfills a subset of role expectations dictated by Y's definition of the situation for the purpose of referring to this role *(Imitation)* |
| | X fulfills a subset of role expectations dictated by Y's definition of the situation for the purpose of gaining a role competence *(Initiation)* |
| | X completely fulfills role expectations dictated by Y's definition of the situation and, within the situation, X's goals are complementary with Y's *(Participation)* |
| | X completely fulfills role expectations dictated by Y' definition of the situation and, within the situation, X's goals conflict with Y's *(Completion)* |

*Figure 5.1* Seven ways in which 'X' can play with 'Y'
*Note*:  * refers to intrinsically motivating, self-oriented, active consumption

or status. For example, when consumers embark on a path toward consumer socialization (Moschis 1985), they are engaging in initiation. In contrast, consumers engaging in "imitation" are not striving to play the role competently, but instead want to refer to the role for rhetorical or representational purposes. For instance, consumers are imitating when they wear a style of clothing worn by a prominent company spokesperson.

Moving to the upper portion of Figure 5.1, three types of paida are described. Each of these involves the consumer performing behaviors that, according to the marketer's definition of the situation, are role-possible or role-forbidden. First, there is "innovation," in which the consumer's behaviors are situationally relevant, not included in the marketer's definition of the situation, but not conflicting with this definition either. For example, a hotel customer who makes his hotel bed and cleans his own hotel bathroom is performing situationally relevant, but not role-forbidden behavior. It is situationally relevant, because it affects the way in which the housekeeper will fulfill his or her role expectations.

However, if the customer is doing these activities just for the enjoyment of doing them, his behavior is not likely to be seen as conflicting with the marketer's definition of the situation and therefore counts as an innovation.

In contrast, for the remaining two types of paida, the consumer's behaviors do conflict with the marketer's definition of the situation. If the consumer does not seek to hide this conflict, the activity is "subversion." Some music celebrities are notorious for breaking hotel role expectations by making considerable noise and damaging fixtures – behavior that they frequently display proudly. On the other hand, if the consumer does hide this conflict from the marketer, the activity is "deception." A consumer who gains playful value from stealing bathrobes or towels from a hotel room will not do so in view of the marketer.

In fact, there is a type of ludic play, which Schechner (1993: 36–9) calls "dark play," that depends on being deceptive. Dark play keeps the role conflict hidden but requires the active involvement of others who believe there is no role conflict. For example, pranks and practical jokes require "nonplayers" whose reactions are "a big part of what gives dark play its kick" (ibid.: 38). Although Biesty (1986) points out that dark play is often implemented to achieve extrinsic goals like status in a peer group, this does not preclude the possibility that dark play may also be intrinsically enjoyable to some. At the same time, Biesty's point highlights the fact that an individual can engage in what looks like playful activity, but which is not really intrinsically motivating. This behavior can be called "false play" (Huizinga 1950: 208). For example, a clown at a circus may appear to be playfully engaging with children, but may view this activity only as extrinsically motivated – that is, a way to earn a living.

A last type of play should be mentioned, which is raised in Geertz's (1976) oft-cited anthropological study of a Balinese cockfight. Geertz revives Jeremy Bentham's (1802) concept of "deep play" to describe playful-seeming activities where the stakes on both sides are actually very serious. Although a Balinese cockfight might appear to be playful competition, important issues of status and considerable sums of money are generally at stake. This is parallel to Turner's (1982) observation that although some tribal rituals may seem to involve participants who break rules for the transcendent experience of doing so, these participants are actually enacting required behaviors which help to maintain very important relations and functions in the community at large.

In sum, with dark play, X is playing with Y but appears not to be. With false play, X appears to be playing with Y but is not intrinsically motivated by the activity and so is not really playing. And with deep play, both X and Y appear to be playing with one another but the stakes are so high that they are both extrinsically motivated by the activity. Of these, only dark play can be truly playful because it is the only type that can have a strong intrinsic motivation.

## Further contextualizing the different types of play

Although the typology in Figure 5.1 presents seven clear categories of play, few playful activities will be wholly defined by any one of these categories. The playful value enjoyed by a consumer at a golfing range, for example, may move in sequence from participation (hitting the ball normally) to initiation (trying out a new swing learned from a golf video), to innovation (hitting the ball with the wrong side of the club), etc. Furthermore, what is experienced by the consumer as one type of play may from a marketer's perspective be another kind. For instance, one of the implicit role expectations for extended service encounters like white-water rafting is that the relationships between consumers and marketers become more "boundary open," providing scope for a wider range of role-possible behaviors (Price *et al.* 1995: 88–9). Consumers may see these boundary-open behaviors as innovative because they appear to break the role expectations implicit in service encounters. However, from the perspective of the marketer's definition of the situation, these behaviors amount to participation because they fit right into the role expectation for consumers in these encounters.

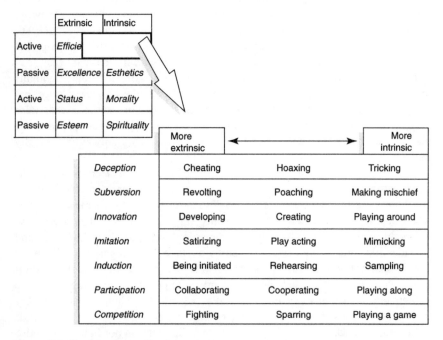

*Figure 5.2* Playful consumption in context

Each of the seven definitions of play in Figure 5.1 also inherently includes a continuum of playful activity that ranges from more intrinsic to more extrinsic. These continua are illustrated in Figure 5.2, which further contextualizes different types of play in relation to one another and further emphasizes that play exists on a continuum rather than within a strictly bounded category (see also Goffman 1974: 48–82). In the figure, each of the seven types of play is represented by a row. The three words in each row are situated according to how intrinsically or extrinsically motivated they tend to be.

## More intrinsically motivated activities

Listed in the column on the right (under the "more intrinsic" heading) are activities that, because of their strong intrinsic motivation, are the most playful. Thus, the words in this column were chosen to capture the most playful aspects of the seven types. For example, the most playful type of subversion is "making mischief," a phrase that is evocative of the kind of intrinsic motivation that is sometimes associated with clearly breaking the rules. As another example, the most playful type of innovation is "playing around," which reflects the fun of performing new behaviors that do not necessarily conflict with the definition of the situation – or "playing along" which is the fun of following the rules. Similarly, "mimicking," "sampling," "tricking," and "playing a game" all refer respectively to intrinsically motivated imitation, initiation, deception and competition.

## More extrinsically motivated activities

In contrast, the activities in the column on the left under the "more extrinsic" heading can be so extrinsically motivated that they should not even be categorized as play. For example, "developing" and "collaborating" are words usually used in relation to a project with an extrinsic purpose. And "satirizing" usually means imitating someone for the extrinsic purpose of causing discomfort or making a critical point. "Competing," "cheating," and "revolting" are also activities that are generally associated with attaining a specific goal rather than experiencing enjoyment of a particular activity for its own sake.

## Activities that combine motivations

In the middle of the figure is a column of activities that combine both intrinsic and extrinsic motivations. A "hoax," for example, is often used to refer to a pre-posterous type of deception motivated in part by a mischievous intent. And "sparring" is a type of competition whose consequences are not wholly serious and whose motivations are therefore less extrinsic. "Poaching" is a term coined by de Certeau (1984) to refer primarily to consumer adaptation of products, ideas, and texts to serve their own needs. One example is the way in which native South Americans adapted the rituals of Spanish colonizers to serve their own belief systems (ibid.: xiii). Although the natives were extrinsically motivated because of the Spanish imperative that the rituals be adopted, they were also intrinsically motivated to make the rituals work for them.

## The dangers and opportunities of paidic consumption

Looking at the different types of play listed in Figure 5.1, it becomes easy to see why play – paidic play in particular – may not always be a desirable value for a marketer to foster. To examine more closely the potentially negative impact of rule-breaking playful value, consider consumer behavior on the "Splash Mountain" ride at the Disneyland amusement park in Los Angeles. At the top of one of the steepest hills on the ride, Disney has placed a digital camera that takes pictures of consumers just as they start to hurtle downward. These pictures are made available as souvenirs for consumers at the end of the ride. Knowing this, some mischievous female consumers bare their breasts on the ride just at the point where the photo is taken. The resulting photographs typically are intercepted and destroyed by Disneyland employees who screen the photos before they are made available to the public. However, some of the pictures make it through the screen and are bought by consumers. And several photos have made their way to a web site called "Flash Mountain."

When a consumer's behavior conflicts with a marketer's expectations, the marketer is threatened in four related ways. First, the exchange between the marketer and the rule-breaker becomes more uncertain for both parties. In the Flash Mountain example, the rule-breakers are never sure whether their photo will be screened out or made available at the end of the ride. And Disney management is never sure which Splash Mountain consumers are using the ride for paidic playful value. When consumers are not sure whether or not their hopes for a product or service will be met, and when marketers are not sure how consumers will behave, the likelihood of consumer satisfaction diminishes, as does the potential for a profitable business.

Secondly, when a consumer engages in paidic consumption, the nature of the relationship between the marketer and the rule-breaker changes. Because successful exchange relationships generally depend on each party's fulfillment of role expectations, marketing exchange often requires that each party trust the other to meet these obligations (e.g., Morgan and Hunt 1994). But in the Flash Mountain example, the roller-coaster flashers gain value not by playing by the rules of the ride, but by playing with these rules. Rather than enjoying the kind of wholesome fun that Disney tends to encourage and expect at Disneyland, these consumers enjoy a more illicit value. Because this is not behavior that Disney wants to invite (or perhaps even allow) at the park, it undermines the trust that the company may have in these consumers and therefore changes the nature of the relationship between the company and these consumers.

Thirdly, rule-breaking consumers may affect the relationship that the marketer has with other consumers. For example, Disney's brand image among its core consumers may be negatively affected by its association with the Flash Mountain web site. In the feedback section of the site, one consumer (who appears to believe that the site is sponsored by Disney) commented that:

> I don't agree that this should be posted anywhere on the Internet. It is very degrading to women, not to mention the fact that Disneyland could easily have a lawsuit on their hands as a result of this. Please take this off the Internet! If I had kids, I would not take them to Disneyland for any reason.

Questions also arise regarding the potential negative effect that flashers may have on other consumers riding on Splash Mountain. Although some may accept this behavior with equanimity or even enthusiasm, others – particularly parents of small children – may be angry that the flashers' behavior clearly breaks with the family-entertainment expectations set up by Disney.

A final problem with consumers who break the rules is that they may encourage others to similarly flout marketers' expectations, with potentially exacerbated consequences. For example, the Flash Mountain web site encourages consumers to send their own photos in for publication on the site. One consumer on the website's feedback section expressed her intention to get a photo with everyone on the ride flashing the camera. For Disney, one or two flashers is a minor nuisance, while whole carloads of flashing consumers may require changes in policy or in the management of the ride.

## *Marketer response options*

When consumers engage in role-forbidden behavior, the marketer has two potential response options (aside from ignoring it). First, the marketer may maintain the current definition of the situation and therefore re-assert or re-clarify the role expectation in an attempt to keep the behavior from happening again. Secondly, the marketer may change the definition of the situation to allow the behavior as role possible or role-required in future interactions.

The first option – reasserting role expectations – usually means attempting to assert greater control over those who break the expectations. For example, when free "fanzines" about the popular Star Wars series of films were developed, Lucasfilm (the owner of the Star Wars brand) sought to control these publications, seeing them as rivals to their official fan organization. And when some of these fanzines depicted the Star Wars characters in situations that diverted from what were perceived to be the films' "family values," Lucas threatened to sue (Jenkins 1992: 31). Similarly, the management of Oasis, one of the United Kingdom's most successful rock groups in the 1990s, sent a formal warning to dozens of unofficial free Oasis web sites threatening to take legal action unless they stopped making unauthorized use of photographs, lyrics, video clips, and music samples (Rawsthorn 1997). And Disney has responded to roller-coaster flashers by tightening security procedures and adding more staff to screen photos and to monitor the ride more closely (CNN 1997).

While there is a potential cost associated with allowing consumers to engage in role-forbidden behavior, there are also potential costs to reasserting role expectations. These involve not only legal and administrative costs, but also the danger that mischievous behavior might turn into revolutionary behavior. Activities done primarily for the fun of it might turn into activities with an extrinsic motivation such as forcing a company to change its definition of the situation. For example, in response to the Oasis management's actions mentioned above, a new web site called Oasis Webmasters for Internet Freedom was launched to orchestrate a protest campaign and to advise other sites not to comply (Rawsthorn 1997). The negative impact and cost of this more extrinsically motivated behavior may be greater than that of the original more intrinsically motivated behavior.

The second option available in response to a rule-breaking consumer is for the marketer to redefine the behavior as rule-possible or even rule-required. For instance, ski resorts for many years did not allow consumers to use snowboards – initially because they were thought to be dangerous, but eventually because the culture associated with the sport did not fit within the situational definition of many ski resorts (Harverson 1997; Weatley 1997). However, the growing popularity of the sport eventually convinced many marketers that snowboarding was a creative innovation, not a threatening subversion. By 1998, snowboarding had become mainstream enough to be included as an event in the Winter Olympic Games as an officially role-possible activity. This meant that those associated with the games, from reporters to judges, had to include a number of new role-possible behaviors in their role expectations for Olympic competitors, including certain clothing styles and even the use of marijuana (Wilbon 1998).

Snowboarding is a good example of how paidic activity can be the source of new ideas for the marketer, even if the behavior first seems to conflict with the marketer's definition of the situation. Lessons learned by snowboarders and snowboard manufacturers have even encouraged innovation in the manufacturing of standard snow skis (Houlder 1997). The idea that play can be the source of innovation is at heart of Victor Turner's (1982) concept of "liminoid" activities, which are marginalized but playful rule-breaking behaviors that often provide a spark for changes in the mainstream culture. For instance, Disney now operates entertainment areas for adults, including "Pleasure Island" at Walt Disney World in Orlando and "Disney Village" at Disneyland Paris. One can imagine that the idea for these entertainment areas came from Disney's encounters with more "adult" behaviors (like those on Splash Mountain) at their family-oriented parks. At the adult-oriented parks, behaviors that are generally role-forbidden at other Disney parks (such as drinking considerable amounts of alcohol) are role-possible. For consumers, this removes the sheer fun of breaking the rules but also diminishes the uncertainty of whether or not their behavior will be sanctioned.

To summarize, encouraging paidic consumer value can be dangerous for a marketer because this kind of consumer play increases the uncertainty of the consumption situation. But it can also offer opportunities for the marketer, not only because it can provide a unique type of value for consumers but also because it can be a source of new ideas for additional kinds of value. Therefore, marketers who encourage paida must have a greater-than-average tolerance for unexpected and even unwanted consumer behavior. For example, on one of its web sites, the Shell company has a section dedicated to "sensitive subjects" where consumers may participate in a "speaker's corner" by posting their messages. To the company's credit, a considerable amount of behavior that other marketers might sanction is allowed in the Shell speaker's corner, including criticizing the company's environmental policies and political activities, complaining about company service, and posting satirical cartoons about the company.

Nonetheless, every marketer draws the line somewhere, and certain playful behaviors are not encouraged on the Shell site. Consider the exchange reproduced below, which is taken verbatim from the web site (with e-mail addresses removed), regarding a conflict between Shell and Greenpeace, the environmental advocacy group. It begins with one consumer (Claus O-J) advising Shell to simply ignore Greenpeace:

Date:       12 Mar.1997 (Wed) – 21:56
Author:     Claus O-J
Message:    Dump that thing, and forget about Greenpeace stupid advices. They
            don't know what to do anyway, except from making money.

Date:       15 Mar.1997 (Fri) – 22:21
Author:     Shell
Message:    Your right!!

Date:       18 Mar.1997 (Tue) – 10:01
Author:     WEBMASTER
Message:    Please note that this posting was not made by anybody from the Shell
            organisation. Could I ask that people wishing to use these forums use
            at least credible pseudonyms and not a name like the one used here.
            Thanks, Simon May.

The context and content of the second message suggest that the author was at least partially motivated by the intrinsic rewards of playfully thumbing one's nose at a large multi-national petroleum company – a role behavior that the Shell webmaster did not wish to include in his definition of a participant in the speaker's corner.

Having addressed the ways in which rule-breaking consumers may threaten the relationship between a marketer and a consumer, it is useful to note that marketers can encourage consumers to break rules set by *other* marketers, thus insulating themselves from some of the potentially negative results of paida. For example, a margarine manufacturer might encourage consumers to "counterbrand" (Chang 1997) its product by putting it in a butter tub – just for the fun of seeing whether or not other family members notice the difference. While butter manufacturers probably would prefer not to have their brands exposed to the potential of being associated with margarine taste, the margarine manufacturer may potentially benefit by encouraging this playful activity.

As another example, consider Howies, a London-based manufacturer whose line of clothing includes T-shirts specifically designed to set off security alarm systems when entering or leaving stores. Its "Shoplifter" T-shirt sold out completely last year, and the company has therefore manufactured a larger number of the new design this year (*Time Out* 1998). While these T-shirts are likely to cause consternation among some retailers, the negative impact of this paidic consumer behavior is unlikely to directly affect the manufacturer. However, there is still the potential that some retailers (or other stakeholders) will not find these articles of clothing playful at all, and may press to outlaw such clothing or pursue other sanctions against Howies. This potential consequence of the Shoplifter T-shirt raises the issue of how a particular playful behavior is defined, which is the topic of the following section.

## The importance of defining playful activity

The previous section illustrated that marketers who wish to offer playful value to consumers must make some important decisions about the extent to which this value will be paidic or ludic. In this section, I will consider whether the finer distinctions offered in Figures 5.1 and 5.2 are useful from a managerial or research perspective. In other words, while there is value in distinguishing between ludus and paida, is there any value in distinguishing between competition and participation or between sparring and cooperating?

To answer this question, let us consider how one might categorize the actions of the stranger in the story told at the outset of this chapter. Looking at Figure 5.1, it could be argued that the stranger in the story was engaging in *innovative* behavior. The use of fish eggs was not included in the bar owner's definition of the situation, but neither was it explicitly forbidden. Or maybe the stranger was being *deceptive* – why else were the fish eggs kept hidden until after the bartender had agreed that the kind of eggs did not matter? Furthermore, turning to Figure 5.2, there is the further question of whether the stranger's activities were extrinsically or intrinsically motivated. On one hand, perhaps the stranger was extrinsically motivated by the desire to drink free for a month or to make the bar owner look silly. On the other hand, perhaps the stranger was intrinsically motivated by the sheer enjoyment of playing around or making mischief.

These questions bring us back to the Mitchell and Mason (1934: 88) quotation cited earlier, which asserted that play depends on the way in which the player feels about the activity. Thus, deciding what kind of play the stranger was enacting is simply a matter of asking the stranger. However, while this view emphasizes the importance of human perception in making judgments about social actions, it suggests that a definition of social behavior can be made unilaterally. This may be true for the examples they cite, such as rowing a boat or reading a book, which are not social interactions. However, for more social playful activities, a mutual consensus about roles and situational definitions is an important pre-requisite for smooth social interaction. In other words, the meaning of a consumption situation is rarely decided by one person and is instead a negotiation between marketer, consumer, and the broader social reality in which the consumption takes place (Deighton and Grayson 1995). For instance, what if the stranger felt that the introduction of fish eggs was a fun way to be innovative (playing around) while the bar owner felt that it was a deceptive way to get free drinks for a month (cheating)? Despite the stranger's belief that the activity was playful, dissensus about the stranger's role could result in a conflict with serious outcomes for either or both parties.

Turning back to the real-world Flash Mountain example, a male consumer claimed on the website that, having flashed his genitals on the ride, he found

Disney security waiting for him at the end of the ride and faced legal proceedings that resulted in eight hours of required community service. The consumer may have thought that he was simply playing around like the female consumers on the ride – or perhaps even playing the game according to the pre-established rules. However, Disney's definition of the consumer's behavior as subversive (and, apparently, the broader social reality's similar determination) meant that the consumer did not on the whole enjoy value from the exchange.

Thus, it is in many cases extremely important for marketers and consumers to distinguish among the finer types of playful activity. This is because once a role definition has been decided for one party, this implies certain role expectations from the other. A marketer may be expected to tolerate a little playing around on the part of consumers, but is usually expected to prohibit fighting or cheating. Because of the interactivity and interdependence inherent in social encounters, the marketer's ability to respond in a particular way depends on the way in which a consumer's actions are defined.

## Conclusion: the marketer as trickster

This chapter has emphasized that although play is often thought to be inherently enjoyable it is actually an exceedingly complex concept with sometimes para-doxical qualities. Play can be harmlessly pleasant or threateningly subversive, which means that there are at least two general types of playful consumer value: one in which consumers follow the rules expected by the marketer, and one in which they break the rules. Although rule-breaking consumer behavior offers extra challenges for marketers, it also offers an opportunity to provide unique consumer value and a greater potential for discovering potential consumer innovation. That said, it is sometimes difficult for consumers and marketers to agree whether or not a particular activity is rule-following or rule-breaking, and furthermore whether the activity is innovative, deceptive, etc. The definition of a given behavior is important because it has consequences for all exchange partners and for the outcome of the exchange.

Because the purpose of this chapter has been to address *consumer* value, the possibility that a *marketer* might also enjoy playful value has been addressed only briefly. However, at least since the story of Genesis was written, marketers and salespeople have been notorious for playing with the rules of consumption by playing around, making mischief, or engaging in trickery. Although marketing is often (extrinsically) motivated by profit, marketers and salespeople are often depicted as those who not only profit from playing with consumers but also simply enjoy doing so. Because of this, marketers have been described as modern-day incarnations of the Trickster archetype mentioned at the outset of this chapter (Lenz 1985: 1; Shorris 1994: 42). Given marketing's longstanding association with exchange (Bagozzi 1974; Kotler 1972), it is no surprise that change and exchange have historically been the Trickster's central areas of influence (Wadlington 1975: 6).

However, the basic principles and observations outlined in this chapter apply equally well to playful marketers as to playful consumers. Consider the example of Tango, a well-established range of fruit-flavored carbonated soft drinks that historically has been sold in the United Kingdom using hilariously unorthodox advertisements. In 1994, the company ran an uncharacteristically straightforward advertisement in which the company's marketing director warned that some supermarkets and convenience stores were selling an unauthorized noncarbonated version of the company's beverage. Customers were told that if they saw this beverage on sale they should call a toll-free number to report the rogue distributor. On the first evening the commercial ran, a reported thirty thousand customers called the number and were told by a recorded message that they had been "Tango-ed" as part of a promotion for the company's new non-carbonated beverage called "Still Tango." Callers were also told that if they left their name and address they could receive a coupon for the new product (Summers 1994).

As with any paidic playfulness, the Tango advertising campaign raised some dangers for the company's relationships with its consumers. For example, it is likely that the advertisements changed the nature of the trust existing between Tango and its consumers – at least to the extent that these consumers will have heightened suspicion when viewing future Tango advertisements. In fact, the advertisement generated a larger-than-average number of complaints to the Independent Television Commission (ITC), which monitors deceptive and offensive television advertising in the UK. Furthermore, the advertisements also had a more general impact on consumers and members of the marketing community, many of whom raised concerns about whether or not Tango had exploited the credibility and authority of advertising media by playing with the rules of public service announcements and product recalls (Murphy 1994).

Thus, the company found itself in the position of a Splash Mountain flasher arguing over whether or not an activity was playful and, if so, what kind of play the activity represented. In its defense, the company explained that its target market was "advertising-aware" young adults who enjoyed Tango's "tongue-in-cheek" approach. In essence their argument was that, to Tango's target audience, the advertisements were simply an example of playing around. The ITC disagreed and asked that the advertisements be taken off the air, defining the advertisements as at best trickery and at worst a hoax: "If this was not quite setting off the fire alarm for a laugh," the Commission said in its decision, "it was certainly ringing door bells and running away."

Whether from the perspective of a marketer or a consumer, there are no easy solutions when it comes to defining play. It comes in many guises – and in each of its guises can be viewed in divergent ways by different consumers or marketers. However, even if a marketer wished to avoid playful value entirely, it is doubtful that this could be accomplished. As many scholars (e.g., Huizinga 1950; Eisen 1988) argue, human beings have an inherent desire to play – that is, to busy themselves with the workings of social rules and to find enjoyment by following or breaking these rules. This suggests that, no matter what the consumption situation, there will always be a consumer writing a rogue e-mail message, using a product in an unconventional way, or pulling a jar of caviar from a coat pocket.

## Acknowledgments

The author thanks Lysa Miller for her contribution to the concepts of the paper, and John Deighton for his encouragement of this work in its early stages.

## References

Athay, M. and Darley, J. (1982) "Social Roles as Interaction Competencies," in W. Ickes and E. S. Knowles (eds) *Personality, Roles and Social Behavior*, New York: Springer Verlag, 55–83.

Bagozzi, R. P. (1974) "Marketing as an Organized Behavioral System of Exchange," *Journal of Marketing* 38 (October): 77–81.

Bende, I. and Grastyán, E. (1992) "A Neurophysical Theory of Play," in G. C. Cupchik and J. László (eds) *Emerging Visions of the Aesthetic Process: Psychology, Semiology, and Philosophy*, Cambridge: Cambridge University Press, 271–85.

Bentham, J. (1802) *The Theory of Legislation*, London: Kegan Paul.

Biesty, P. (1986) "If It's Fun, Is It Play? A Meadian Analysis," in B. Mergen (ed.) *Cultural Dimensions of Play, Games, and Sport*, Champaign, IL: Human Kinetics, 61–72.

Caillois, R. (1979) *Man, Play and Games*, New York: Free Press.

Caplan, F. and Caplan, T. (1973) *The Power of Play*, New York: Anchor Press/Doubleday.

de Certeau, M. (1984) *The Practice of Everyday Life*, S. F. Rendall (trans) Berkeley, CA: University of California Press.

Chang, J. E. (1997) "Brand Essence in the Household: A Symbolic Interactionist Perspective," Northwestern University Working Paper.

CNN (1997) "Exhibitionists Given New Meaning to 'Thrill' Ride," *CNN Interactive*, 31 May, http://www.cnn.com.

Deighton, J. and Grayson, K. (1995) "Marketing and Seduction: Building Exchange Relationships by Managing Social Consensus," *Journal of Consumer Research* 21 (March): 660–76.

Eisen, G. (1988) *Children and Play in the Holocaust: Games among the Shadows*, Amherst, MA: The University of Massachusetts Press.

Fink, E. (1968) "The Oasis of Happiness: Toward an Otology of Play," in J. Ehrmann (ed.) *Game, Play, Literature*, Boston, MA: Beacon Press, 19–30.

Garvey, C. (1977) *Play*, Cambridge, MA: Harvard University Press.

Geertz, C. (1976) "Deep Play: A Description of a Balinese Cockfight," in J. S. Bruner, A. Jolly and K. Sylva (eds) *Play – Its Role in Development and Evolution*, New York: Basic Books, 656–74.

Goffman, E. (1959) *The Presentation of Self in Everyday Life*, Woodstock, NY: Overlook Press.

—— (1962) *Encounters: Two Studies in the Sociology of Interaction*, Indianapolis, IN: Bobbs Merrill.

—— (1974) *Frame Analysis*, Boston, MA: Northeastern University Press.

Grayson, K. (1998) "Commercial Activity at Home: Managing the Private Servicescape," in J. Sherry (ed.) *Servicescapes*, Chicago, IL: NTC Business Books.

Grayson, K. and J. Deighton (1995) "Playing and the Locus of Rules," in F. R. Kardes and M. Sujan (eds) *Advances in Consumer Research* 22, 241–2.

Harverson, P. (1997) "Back to the Pratfalls: Snowboarding," *The Financial Times* 15 October: 17.

Holbrook, M. (1994) "Axiology, Aesthetics, and Apparel: Some Reflections on the Old School Tie," in M. R. DeLong and A. M. Fiore (eds) *Aesthetics of Textiles and Clothing: Advancing Multi-Disciplinary Perspectives*, ITAA Special Publication 7, Monument, CO: Internationl Textile and Apparel Association.

Holt, D. (1995) "How Consumers Consume: A Typology of Consumption Practices," *Journal of Consumer Research* 22 (June): 1–16.

Houlder, V. (1997) "Slippery Customers," *The Financial Times* 27 January: 18.

Huizinga, J. (1950) *Homo Ludens: A Study of the Play Element in Culture*, Boston, MA: The Beacon Press.

Hynes, W. J. (1993) "Inconclusive Conclusions: Tricksters – Metaplayers and Revealers," in W. J. Hynes and W. G. Doty (eds) *Mythical Trickster Figures*, Tuscaloosa, AL: University of Alabama Press, 202–17.

James, W. (1890) "The Perception of Reality," *Principles of Psychology*, Volume 2, New York: Dover Publications, 283–324.

Jenkins, H. (1992) *Textual Poachers: Television Fans and Participatory Culture*, New York: Routledge.

Kotler, P. (1972) "A Generic Concept of Marketing," *Journal of Marketing* 36 (April): 46–54.

Lenz, W. E. (1985) *Fast Talk and Flush Times: The Confidence Man as a Literary Convention*, Columbia, MO: University of Missouri Press.

Lieberman, N. J. (1977) *Playfulness: Its Relation to Imagination and Creativity*, New York: Academic Press.

Lyotard, J.-F. (1985) *The Postmodern Condition: A Report on Knowledge*, Geoff Bennington and Brian Massumi (trans.) Minneapolis, MN: University of Minnesota Press.

Merton, R. K. (1957) "The Role Set: Problems in Sociological Theory," *British Journal of Sociology* 8: 106–20.

Mitchell, E. D. and Mason, B. S. (1934) *The Theory of Play*, New York: A. S. Barnes.

Monighan-Nourot, P., Scales, B., Van Hoorn, J., and Almy, M. (1987) *Looking at Children's Play: A Bridge Between Theory and Practice*, New York: Teachers College Press.

Morgan, R. M. and Hunt, S. D. (1994) "The Commitment-Trust Theory of Marketing," *Journal of Marketing* 58 (July): 20–38.

Moschis, G. P. (1985) "The Role of Family Communication in Consumer Socialization of Children and Adolescents," *Journal of Consumer Research* 11 (March): 898–913.

Murphy, C. (1994) "When the Teasers Become Unbearable," *Marketing Week* 17 (15 July): 21.

Pelton, R. D. (1980) *The Trickster in West Africa: A Study of Mythic Irony and Sacred Delight*, Berkeley, CA: University of California Press.

Price, L. L., Arnould, E. J., and Tierney, P. (1995) "Going to Extremes: Managing Service Encounters and Assessing Provider Performance," *Journal of Marketing* 59 (April): 83–97.

Radin, P. (1956) *The Trickster: A Study in American Indian Mythology*, New York: Schocken.

Rahner, H. (1965) *Man at Play*, New York: Herder and Herder

Rainwater, C. E. (1922) *The Play Movement in the United States*, Chicago, IL: University of Chicago Press.

Rawsthorn, A. (1997) "Oasis May Act over Internet Breaches," *The Financial Times* June 5: 14.

Roberts, J. W. (1989) *From Trickster to Badman: The Black Folk Hero in Slavery and Freedom*, Philadelphia, PA: University of Pennsylvania Press.

Sarbin, T. R. and Allen, V. L. (1968) "Role Theory," in G. Lindzey and E. Aronson (eds) *The Handbook of Social Psychology*, Reading, MA: Addison Wesley, 488–567.

Schechner, R. (1993) *The Future of Ritual: Writings on Culture and Performance*, New York: Routledge.

Schindler, R. M. (1995) " 'Guess What I Paid For This' and Other Games Bargain Hunters Play," in F. R. Kardes and M. Sujan (eds) *Advances in Consumer Research* 22: 241–2.

Schutz, A. and Luckmann, T. (1973) *Structures of the Life-World*, R. M. Zaner and H. T. Englehardt, Jr. (trans.) Evanston, IL: Northwestern University Press.

Secord, P. F. (1982) "The Origin and Maintenance of Social Roles: The Case of Sex Roles," in W. Ickes and E. S. Knowles (eds) *Personality, Roles and Social Behavior*, New York: Springer Verglag, 33–53.

Shorris, E. (1994) *A Nation of Salesmen: The Tyranny of the Market and the Subversion of Culture*, New York: Avon Books.

Smith, J. R. (1997) *Writing Tricksters: Mythic Gambols in American Ethnic Literature*, Berkeley, CA: University of California Press.

Solomon, M. R., Surprenant, C., Czepiel, J. A., and E. G. Gutman (1985) "A Role Theory Perspective on Dyadic Interactions: The Service Encounter," *Journal of Marketing* 49 (Winter): 99–111.

Summers, D. (1994) "Britvic Censured over TV Advert," *Financial Times* 7 July: 11.

*Time Out* (1998) "Trends," *Time Out* (March 4–11): 6.

Turner, V. (1982) "Liminal to Liminoid in Play, Flow, and Ritual," in *From Ritual to Theatre: The Human Seriousness of Play*, New York: Performing Arts Journal Publications, 20–60.

Wadlington, W. (1975) *The Confidence Game in American Literature*, Princeton, NJ: Princeton University Press.

Weatley, K. (1997) "The New Generation Game: Skiing," *The Financial Times* 15 November, 12.

Wilbon, M. (1998) "US Snowboarders Toss Out the Script," *The Washington Post* 8 February, A01.

Wittgenstein, L. (1953) *Philosophical Invstigations*, New York: Macmillan.

Zurcher, L. A (1983) *Social Roles*, Beverly Hills, CA: Sage.

# 6 Aesthetic value

## Beauty in art and fashion

*Janet Wagner*

## Introduction

Consumer researchers have an approach-avoidance relationship with aesthetic value. In their private lives, they embrace aesthetic value because beauty in the products they buy, the homes they live in, and the public spaces they frequent brings them pleasure and personal enrichment. But in their professional lives, they avoid research on aesthetic value. One reason for this may be that beauty is viewed as an abstruse concept, difficult to define and operationalize. The purpose of this chapter is to encourage more research on aesthetic value by exploring the nature of beauty. In the process, it will be shown that aesthetic value is as amenable to scientific inquiry as quality, status, esteem, or any other category of consumer value.

In this chapter, the many linkages between the concept of aesthetic value, as defined by philosophers, and the consumer decision-making framework, as derived from psychology and economics, will be highlighted. A review of the concept of value, as defined in the theory of axiology, will be presented first, as background. Although philosophers are inclined to take descriptive approaches, with little regard for empirical relationships, axiological theory is helpful in understanding aesthetic value because it clarifies the meaning of value as a generic term. A detailed analysis of aesthetic value will follow, with a critique of the position of beauty in the Consumer-Value Typology, described in the Introduction (Holbrook 1994a; 1994b). Next, research on aesthetic value in fashion goods will be reviewed. Although research on fashion is highly specialized, it represents one of the more extensive bodies of literature on aesthetic value and serves to demonstrate the potential for more generalized research on beauty .

## Axiology and consumer value

A basic assumption of axiology is that value is an interactive experience, requiring both an object and a subject to perceive it. In the context of consumer value, this means that the subject interacts with the object by using or experiencing it in some way. Value is an intangible, derived from the tangible characteristics of an object, that is influenced by characteristics of the subject, including his or her personal values. Ultimately, value pervades the entire experience of processing information about an object, including perception, evaluation, and preference formation. Because value is so pervasive in the consumption experience, the concept has multiple meanings, causing confusion among marketing researchers and resulting in indiscriminate use of the term by marketing practitioners.

In the following discussion, concepts of value from axiological theory will be reviewed, as they pertain to the Consumer-Value Typology. The purpose of this discussion is to provide background for an analysis of aesthetic value, a critique of the position of aesthetic value in the typology, and a review of research on aesthetic value in the consumption of fashion goods. To structure the freestanding concepts of axiology, the discussion is organized on the assumption that value links the consumer to an object via the processing of information. Under this assumption, value is realized in personal norms, perception, evaluation, and judgment. As suggested by the typology, value can occur in any domain of consumer behavior, economic, social, artistic, or spiritual.

## *Value in personal norms*

A value is a personal norm – a belief about what is needed, wanted, or ought to be, which serves as a guide to consumers in making decisions. Motivational systems are organized in such a way that consumers' values "match" their needs. Values create a readiness to respond to an appropriate object and trigger the perception of value (Edwards 1967; Handy 1969). By this reckoning, convenience is a value held by consumers who need to save time; status is a value of consumers who need to impress others; and beauty is a value of consumers who need personal enrichment.

## *Value in perception*

Value is also the perception of a need-satisfying capability in an object. In this guise, value has a "parasitical" existence; it depends on an object as its "value carrier." According to Frondizi (1971), value is part of a three-level hierarchy of qualities. In the first level are primary qualities: the physical materials of which the object is composed or constructed. Secondary qualities are sensory features – such as size, shape, or texture – which are detected by sight, hearing, taste, smell, or touch. In the third level is value, a tertiary quality, which is an intangible property perceived by the subject to provide worth by meeting his or her needs. The perception of value is a gestalt, derived from the processing of information on the configuration of primary and secondary qualities. For example, convenience is a gestalt derived from perceiving a microwave; success is a gestalt derived from perception of a luxury car; and beauty is a gestalt derived from perception of an Impressionist painting or a piano concerto.

## *Value in evaluation and judgment*

The process of evaluation is an act of reflecting upon the gestalt of the value object and comparing it to an ideal or to other value objects in the consumer's experience. Such an evaluation has three dimensions – polarity, valence, and hierarchy. Although polarity implies a positive or negative evaluation, value is usually positive in that it results in pleasure. Valence is the intensity of the pleasure experienced in value. Intensity varies within and across categories of value. The consumer may be satisfied by efficiency, delighted by status, or enraptured by beauty. The hierarchy of value is revealed in a preference judgment: when confronted with two value qualities, the consumer will prefer the more highly rated of the two (Frondizi 1971).

## Aesthetic value

Aesthetics, like the term "value," has multiple meanings. It is a subdiscipline of philosophy, a concept within axiology, and a synonym for style. While aesthetics traces its roots to Plato's idea of beauty and Aristotle's notion of the gestalt, it was not recognized as a division of philosophy until the eighteenth century. In aesthetics, the focus of discourse is art and the aesthetic experience. Central issues include what makes the aesthetic experience different from other domains of value, how the aesthetic qualities of objects differ from nonaesthetic qualities, and how to define beauty. In axiology, the term "qualities" is used to refer to features, properties, characteristics, or attributes of objects. This usage is not to be confused with "quality," which is a synonym for excellence in the Consumer-Value Typology.

As a concept, the term "aesthetic" is used to refer to a category of value. One unique aspect of aesthetic value is that it is closely identified with the fine arts – painting, sculpture, architecture, music, dance, and poetry. However, among twentieth-century philosophers (e.g., Santayana 1955; Mothersill 1984; Shusterman 1997) analysis of aesthetic value has been extended to include the applied arts – everyday objects such as appliances, cars, furniture, computers, and clothing – purchased and used by consumers, for which aesthetic aspects are becoming more important as differentiating factors. Aesthetic value shares two assumptions with other categories of value: first, it involves interaction between an object and a subject; and second, it encompasses the entire experience of perceiving, evaluating, and judging an object, in this case an art object.

The aesthetic experience has been described as immediate, dynamic, unified, meaningful, pleasant, and vividly felt, emerging from the perception of an aesthetic object. The aesthetic experience differs from other types of value in that it is disinterested, detached, and distanced from practical concerns (Burchert 1996). Like other types of value, the aesthetic experience is affected by characteristics of the object, characteristics of the subject, and the context in which the experience occurs (Mothersill 1984; Hermeren 1988). Characteristics of the object are its aesthetic qualities, the ultimate of which is beauty – a gestalt derived from a perception of design elements (as configured in the aesthetic object) and the meaning inferred from the associations engendered. Characteristics of the subject include motives, taste, and experience. Contextual influences on the aesthetic experience are cultural and historical factors that shape stylistic preferences.

## The aesthetic object and aesthetic characteristics

The aesthetic object is broadly defined to include any artifact, person, event, or idea that attracts and sustains the interest of a subject (Osborne 1986) and is characterized by a set of aesthetic and nonaesthetic qualities (Sibley 1959; Hermeren 1988). For the purposes of this analysis, discussion will be limited to artifacts of visual art, in the fine and applied arts. The visual arts are familiar to most consumers, because we are exposed to them on a daily basis – in homes, in retail stores, and in public spaces. In the everyday environment of the consumer, the visual arts are "axioforms" – objects conveying the aesthetic value of beauty (Fiebleman 1968).

To understand aesthetic value, it is necessary to distinguish between the aesthetic and nonaesthetic qualities of an object and to show how the two are related. In Frondizi's (1971) classic work on value, the qualities of an object are defined at three levels. The primary and secondary qualities are nonaesthetic – physical and sensory features of the object that exist with or without a subject to perceive them. In an art object, the tertiary qualities include aesthetic qualities, which contribute to the overall perception of beauty.

For consumer researchers, this scheme presents several difficulties. First, the status of the elements of design (color, line, shape, space, light) isn't clear. Are they really nonaesthetic qualities, as Frondizi seems to believe? Second, there is no mention at all of the principles of design (e.g., unity, harmony, balance), by which visual images are organized. Third, the relationship of aesthetic to non-aesthetic qualities is not obvious.

With respect to the latter issue, there is consensus among philosophers: the aesthetic qualities supervene on nonaesthetic qualities (Beardsley 1958; Sibley 1959; Kainz 1962; Burchert 1996). Thus, the perception of beauty depends on the primary and secondary qualities of the aesthetic object. Following Frondizi (1971), an art object derives its beauty from its materials and the elements of design. Thus, a Mondrian painting derives beauty from canvas and paint, a Brancusi sculpture from its polished steel, and an Eames chair from its curved wooden contours. All derive beauty from color, texture, line, shape, and light.

Hermeren (1988) focuses entirely on aesthetic properties (qualities), and in doing so, resolves the issues of how to classify the elements of design and where to position the principles of design in the hierarchy of value. Assuming that all aesthetic properties are perceptual, there are two basic categories: local and regional. The local properties (also called simple properties) of an aesthetic object are the elements of design. The regional properties (which are more complex) fall into two categories – structural and emergent properties. The structural properties of an aesthetic object are the principles of design, which are used to organize the local properties into a pleasing visual image. The emergent properties are of two types. Type 1 emergent properties depend on the local properties (elements of design); for example, warmth is a perception that "emerges" from the color orange; movement emerges from diagonal line; and etherealness emerges from light. Type 2 emergent properties depend on the structural properties (principles of design). Beauty of form, for example, emerges from perceived unity and harmony; beauty of expression emerges from variety, such as contrast in color, light, or line; the latter holds the attention of the consumer and makes the aesthetic object more interesting.

Goldman (1995) builds on Hermeren's scheme by further classifying aesthetic properties as non-evaluative or evaluative. There are two categories of non-evaluative properties – formal and expressive. The formal properties are the principles of design, which enable perception and cognition of the visual image. The expressive properties are associations the subject makes with previous objects and experiences, engaging the memory, imagination, and affective capacity. The expressive properties have an escapist character – they create value in the form of "distinct worlds," in which consumers can become involved, without incurring any of the costs of real encounters. The evaluative properties, which supervene on the nonevaluative properties, include three categories: pure properties, which include beauty and elegance; evocative properties, which include power or amusement; and emotive properties, which include joy and delight.

## *Characteristics of the subject*

For the aesthetic experience to occur, there must be a subject to perceive the beauty inherent in an aesthetic object. Characteristics of the subject that affect the aesthetic experience include motives, taste, and experience (Mothersill 1984; Goldman 1995).

*Motives* In Maslovian terms, beauty is an experience that represents a higher order need of the human motivational system. This view entails the belief that perceiving an aesthetic object is an intrinsically desirable, worthwhile, or important experience. Although beauty has no practical purpose, it is important because it meets a "a fundamental need of mind" (Santayana 1955). The nature of this need has been described as something akin to either self-actualization or cognitive complexity. Thus, beauty meets the consumer's need for self-realization (Puffer 1905), personal enrichment (Osborne 1986), or the mental processing of positive, unified, and complex visual images (Turner and Poppel 1988). According to Mothersill (1984, 1995), beauty caters to a need that motivates consumers to attend to, contemplate, and appreciate aesthetic objects.

*Taste* The ability to recognize or discern beauty is a characteristic of the consumer known as taste (Bell 1914; Santayana 1955) or aesthetic sensibility (Mothersill 1984). According to Sibley (1959), one way in which aesthetic qualities differ from nonaesthetic qualities is that taste is required to perceive them. The individual with taste recognizes (or values) beauty, allows it to capture his attention, and is surprised and delighted by it. The individual with taste is also able to interpret an image and associate it with other experiences, giving it meaning (Sibley 1959; Mothersill 1984; Goldman 1995). Good taste is not the same as popular taste, but coincides with the taste of experts over time and across cultures (Whewell 1995).

Taste is a study in nature and nurture. It is a natural endowment, which varies in degree from coarseness to refinement. However, it can also be cultivated, in that individuals learn over time the relationship between certain qualities of an object and the aesthetic experience.

*Experience* The aesthetic experience involves learning visual images and updating standards of beauty with exposure to new images over time (Eibl-Eibesfeldt 1988). This requires experience with, knowledge of, and involvement in a particular art form (Goldman 1995). Thus, experience in judging beauty in painting, for example, does not necessarily translate to expertise in judging beauty in sculpture, architecture or fashion – much less in literature or music. Knowledge of beauty, accumulated in the form of representations stored in memory, has been termed "funded perception" (Feldman 1972) or the "beholder's share" of the aesthetic experience (Gombrich 1958).

### Context of the aesthetic experience

The aesthetic experience is also context-dependent (Mothersill 1984). The aesthetic value of an object will vary by the organization of design elements within an art object, as well as by the surroundings in which the aesthetic judgment occurs. A curved line perceived as beautiful when juxtaposed with a straight line may not be perceived as beautiful when positioned next to a jagged line. Similarly, a vibrant red may be viewed as beautiful in the context of a black background, but not in the context of a lime green background. A variety of situational factors may come into play, including the social and cultural environment (Gombrich 1958; Mothersill 1984). In particular, style – a unique configuration of design elements – has been shown to vary by time, location, and subcultural grouping (e.g., the Bauhaus aesthetic, the Santa Fe aesthetic, the African-American aesthetic). Style itself is an aesthetic quality, because it conveys value through associations – memories that represent the "survival of experience."

## Components of the aesthetic experience

### Aesthetic attitude: contemplation and appreciation

According to Kainz (1962), aesthetic attitude is the "key" to the aesthetic experience – without aesthetic attitude, there can be no aesthetic experience. Aesthetic attitude presents itself in two guises – contemplation, which serves as a guide to perception; and appreciation, which is the process of evaluating the image perceived (Osborne 1986).

Contemplation is a passive state similar to need recognition, in which the consumer attends to an aesthetic object (Lewis 1946; Berenson 1954; Santayana 1955; Stolnitz 1960). To induce contemplation, an object must be attractive enough to sustain the interest of the consumer. In attending to the object, the consumer's attention is selective, concentrating on qualities that contribute to the aesthetic experience (Gombrich 1958). If the consumer recognizes aesthetic relevance – the ability to meet the consumer's need for beauty – the stage is set for apprehension. Further, contemplation is "disinterested" (Stolnitz 1960). That is, the consumer has no practical or utilitarian reason for attending to the object. Moreover, in contemplating an aesthetic object, the consumer has no interest in "possessing" it – using it to advance social or material goals (Santayana 1955). Rather, the consumer attends to the aesthetic object simply for the sake of the experience itself.

In its second guise, aesthetic attitude is appreciation – the active process of evaluation that follows apprehension of the object (Dewey 1934; Goodman 1968). In appreciation, the consumer compares the appearance of the object to an ideal and to other objects with which he has had experience. Appreciation of the aesthetic object is like other types of value, in that the positive is stressed; the aesthetic experience is valuable because it is liked (Kainz 1962). Of the categories of value, the aesthetic experience is believed to be among the most intense, verging on the spiritual. The intensity of the aesthetic experience may stem from its purity: the consumer enjoys the benefits without the risk or cost associated with practical experience (Goldman 1995).

## *Apprehension*

Apprehension is the perception of beauty – the essence of aesthetic value (Santayana 1955; Croce 1965; Mothersill 1984). What is perceived is derived from the configuration of aesthetic qualities – the elements of design, as organized by the principles of design – in a coherent visual image. For consumers with taste or aesthetic sensibility, the aesthetic qualities are selected for their aesthetic relevance or capacity to meet the need for beauty (Mothersill 1984). In apprehension, the aesthetic qualities are organized into a gestalt, setting the stage for appreciation.

There is consensus among philosophers that beauty indulges a need, met through the process of perception (Mothersill 1995). It also confers a positive value, linked to pleasure, and stems from a distinctive judgment, with no practical relevance.

The perception of beauty is a gestalt – a unified, coherent image (Kainz 1962). The process by which this image is generated has been the source of considerable debate across disciplines. Philosophers view the gestalt as an *apprehensio ipsa* (Mothersill 1984) – a flash of insight that is the product of intuition (Croce 1965). Recent work in neuroaesthetics suggests, however, that the processing of aesthetic information is like the processing of any other type of information – that is, the aesthetic qualities of an object are selected, organized, interpreted, and integrated into an image (Turner and Poppel 1988). The immediacy of the experience is a function of how experienced the consumer is in judging the type of object being contemplated.

*Formal and expressive beauty* Beauty is believed to have two dimensions. According to Croce (1965), the two dimensions are form and content. Form is an image, representing an idea, which elicits an emotional reaction. Content is the feeling engendered by understanding and interpreting the image. To Santayana (1955), the two dimensions are sensory beauty or "the object as presented" and expressive beauty or "the object as suggested."

Sensory beauty is formal beauty, based on perception of the elements of design, organized in an orderly, harmonious manner, consistent with the principles of design. In formal beauty, the sheer recognition of order is pleasing to consumers who have the taste to value it (Goldman 1995). Formal beauty sets the stage for appreciation, because it presents a coherent image, easy to understand and remember. The image can't be too plain, however. The design principle of "unity in variety" holds true: a certain amount of "controlled novelty" makes an image interesting and holds the observer's attention (Turner and Poppel 1988).

Expressive beauty is a quality of an object acquired through association – a model of some aspect of the human experience with which the consumer identifies and empathizes (Feldman 1972). In perceiving expressive beauty, the consumer not only identifies with the object, but also is reminded of other objects or events in his experience. Memories and feelings are evoked, giving the aesthetic experience meaning (Turner and Poppel 1988) and increasing the consumer's involvement with the visual image. According to Gombrich (1958), the real value of the visual image is its capacity to convey information that can't be communicated in any other way.

In the aesthetic experience, formal beauty and expressive beauty "fuse" (Dickie 1964) or are "synthesized" to produce the *apprehensio ipsa* or perception of the gestalt (Croce 1965). This is the aesthetic moment – the "fleeting instant when the spectator is at one with the work of art he is looking at" (Berenson 1954).

Formal and expressive beauty may interact. In particular, expressive beauty is thought to heighten the aesthetic value of objects with formal beauty, creating the perception of what Bell (1914) called "significant form." According to Goldman (1995: 346), the interaction of formal and expressive beauty makes for an "intensely meaningful and rich experience."

*Aesthetic autonomy* While many philosophers view beauty as distinct from other types of value (e.g., Kant 1928; Burke 1958; Croce 1965), others maintain that beauty melds with utility and spirituality (Santayana 1955; Mothersill 1984). The link between beauty and other types of value is pleasure. Beauty may interact with other types of value to heighten pleasure.

According to Santayana (1955), aesthetic value may "blend" with practical value. While the purest form of beauty is in the fine arts, consumers may also perceive beauty in the applied art objects that they consume. In *Kindergarten Chats*, the architect Louis Kahn wrote that "form follows function." This implies that, in the applied arts, significant form is one which presents an elegant solution to a practical problem – beauty interacts with utility to intensify the experience of pleasure. Thus, improving the design of an applied art object may heighten the perception of convenience or quality, intensifying the consumer's satisfaction. For example, the perception of beauty in an Eames chair (graceful contours) may interact with its practicality (comfort) to increase the consumer's pleasure from sitting in it.

Philosophers do not deal directly with the issues of either status or esteem in their discourse on beauty. However, if the notion of practical value can be extended to include social value, it seems reasonable that beauty may also interact with status or esteem to enhance pleasure. Thus, the beauty perceived in a luxury car may interact with its perceived status to intensify the pleasure experienced by the driver.

Beauty may also be linked to spirituality. Mothersill (1995: 48) writes, "physical beauty is a clue to and a reminder of the beauty that is higher but less obvious – namely, the beauty of the virtuous soul secure in its faith." The pleasure derived from spirituality is thought to be more intense than that of beauty. However, enhancing the design of religious art and artifacts may heighten the spiritual experience and interact with spirituality to create ecstasy.

## *Aesthetic pleasure*

While pleasure is derived from all value (Frondizi 1971), the pleasure derived from beauty has a unique combination of attributes. First, the pleasure of beauty is immediate; the extent to which the perceived aesthetic value of the object exceeds the expected aesthetic value takes the consumer by surprise. Second, the pleasure of beauty is intense – the delight or joy experienced in perceiving the object is enhanced by emotion. Third, the pleasure of beauty is complex, having both a sensory and a cognitive component (Levinson 1995; Mothersill 1984): the consumer finds delight in the configuration of the aesthetic (local and regional, formal and expressive) qualities. Finally, the pleasure of beauty is not just psychological, it may also involve an involuntary physical response (Berenson 1954; Feldman 1972; Eibl-Eibesfeldt 1988; Turner and Poppel 1988) – a flicker of the eye, a quickening of the pulse, a tightening of the stomach, or the onset of tears.

## Dimensions of aesthetic value

The Typology of Consumer Value is predicated on two assumptions, which are derived from axiological theory. First, the purpose of all value is to meet consumer needs; and second, each type of value meets a particular category of need. In the Typology of Consumer Value, the eight types of value are classified on three subject-centered dimensions: intrinsic/extrinsic, self-oriented/other-oriented, and active/reactive. Aesthetic value is classified as intrinsic, self-oriented, and reactive.

These three dimensions reflect three fundamental conceptual issues with respect to consumer value in general and aesthetic value in particular. The intrinsic/ extrinsic dimension focuses on the nature of the value provided – instrumental or terminal; the self-oriented/other-oriented dimension addresses the origin of the relevant need or want – the consumer or someone else; and the active/reactive dimension deals with the locus of the consumer's pleasure – the process or the outcome of value.

## *Intrinsic/extrinsic value*

The major distinction between intrinsic and extrinsic value involves the difference between a means to an end and an end in itself. Objects with extrinsic value meet instrumental needs; they are used for practical purposes – increasing convenience, improving quality, or cultivating status. Experiences with intrinsic value, on the other hand, meet terminal needs; they are consumed only for the pleasure derived from having fun, feeling virtuous, or rejoicing in spirituality.

The consensus of philosophers is that aesthetic value is a type of intrinsic value (Kant 1928; Santayana 1955; Beardsley 1958; 1982; Kainz 1962; Croce 1965). In his seminal work on beauty, Plato described beauty as "pure" intrinsic value, a notion consistent with aestheticians' view of aesthetic value as autonomous (Bullough 1912), disinterested (Stolnitz 1960), and divorced from practical concerns (Silvers 1996). By this line of reasoning, the only motive for consuming the aesthetic object is the pleasure of experiencing beauty.

Citing beauty as "the only motive" for consuming an aesthetic object is not to denigrate the role of aesthetic value in meeting human needs. Rather, it is important to recognize that, as a type of intrinsic value, aesthetic value meets a set of needs qualitatively different from the needs met by extrinsic categories such as efficiency, excellence, or status. Needs met by aesthetic value are of a higher order, including self-realization, personal enrichment, and cognitive complexity.

An additional need met by beauty is suggested by neuroaestheticians, who argue that beauty has "adaptive utility." As a gestalt, beauty enhances the ability of the consumer to retain information in memory (Eibl-Eibesfeldt 1988; Paul 1988; Turner and Poppel 1988). It seems unlikely, however, that adaptive utility is unique to beauty. In axiological theory, all value is conceptualized as a gestalt. By extension, all value should have adaptive utility.

## *Self-oriented/other-oriented value*

In the Typology of Consumer Value, aesthetic value is classified as self-oriented; that is, the consumer values beauty because it pleases him or her, and not for the sake of some "other" person. The positioning of aesthetic value on this dimension can be defined in terms of the notion, borrowed from neuroaestheticians, that beauty is "self-rewarding;" that is, the consumer is "rewarded by" (pleased by) activities that meet his or her needs (Eibl-Eibesfeldt 1988; Turner and Poppel 1988). In the case of aesthetic value, the consumer values beauty because it is a personally enriching experience that pleases him.

While defining aesthetic value as self-oriented is defensible, there is reason to doubt that there is any type of value that *isn't* self-oriented. The idea that any category of value is strictly "other-oriented" runs counter to a basic assumption of individual decision-making models in economics and psychology, which are the foundation of consumer-behavior theory. In such models, it is assumed that the goal of consumption is to satisfy the consumer's needs. This assumption implies that aesthetics and its "sister" categories of efficiency, excellence, and play, are not the only categories of self-oriented value. Ultimately, all categories of value are self-oriented. The consumer values objects (including aesthetic objects) because they meet his personal needs and please him. Among his needs may be the desire to please or to elicit the reaction of others.

Theoretical support for the self-orientation of all types of consumer value is available in economics and psychology. In the theory of social interaction, the economist Becker (1974; 1976) argues that, in addition to goods and services, the responses of others may enter the utility function and may thereby affect consumer satisfaction. Just as consumers need beauty, they need the approval of others. Thus, Becker's model implies that status (for example), which is now classified as other-oriented, might also be considered self-oriented, because the consumer is pleased by the admiration of others. Similarly, ethics might also be considered self-oriented, because the consumer is pleased by conforming to public standards of morality. The contribution of other persons to consumer satisfaction is also recognized in psychology. In the theory of reasoned action (Fishbein 1967), for example, consumers are motivated to comply by social norms, which represent the reactions of others to their behavior. Presumably, they derive satisfaction or pleasure from doing so.

The validity of the self–other dichotomy has also been indirectly, and perhaps inadvertently, challenged by the philosopher Osborne (1986), who identified three categories of "self-rewarding" value – basic, social and cultural. In Osborne's thinking, all categories of value are self-rewarding, because they satisfy needs. Thus, categories of other-oriented value – including status, esteem, ethics, and spirituality – are also self-oriented, simply by virtue of the fact that they meet consumer needs.

### Active/reactive dimension

There is ample support in the philosophy literature for classifying aesthetic value as reactive, based on the idea that the consumer responds to the aesthetic object with pleasure (Santayana 1955; Mothersill 1984; Levinson 1995). However, there is also support – in the philosophy and neuroaesthetics literature – for classifying aesthetic value as active, because the perception of beauty (like all perception) is an active process (Osborne 1986; Eibl-Eibesfeldt 1988). The crux of this issue is the nature of pleasure. If aesthetic value is active, then there is pleasure inherent in the processing of visual information. If aesthetic value is reactive, then pleasure is simply the outcome of the process.

Philosophers' take on the active/reactive dimension of value is instructive (e.g., Stolnitz 1960). The condition for assigning value to one dimension or another is "control" over the experience.

In active value, the consumer controls the experience by trying to meet some need. Active value can be narrowly construed to mean physical use of an object – using a microwave for efficiency or driving a car for status. However, as Holbrook (1994a, 1994b) indicates, active value can also be more broadly construed to mean mental manipulation of an object – the processing of information about it. By this definition, active value can be extended to include all of the categories of reactive value, including aesthetic value. In active value, the consumer enjoys the process of consuming (either physically or mentally) the object. For example, the consumer might derive pleasure from studying a sculpture, examining a painting, or stroking the velvet of a dress.

In reactive value – which includes play, ethics, aesthetics, and spirituality – the experience controls the consumer (figuratively speaking). For example, the consumer might be enthralled by a pitcher's performance during a no-hitter or inspired by a sermon on the second coming. In the case of aesthetic value, the consumer might be overcome by the beauty of Michelangelo's David or struck by the elegance of a Chanel suit. When the experience controls the consumer, he or she is mesmerized by the experience and becomes aware of its pleasure only in the outcome.

## Aesthetic value in fashion

To be aesthetically valuable, an image must be attractive to the consumer – that is, the beauty of the image must be compelling enough to attract and hold attention. While the focus of philosophical discourse on beauty has been the fine arts, the importance of attractiveness in the applied arts – the everyday objects purchased and used by consumers – has also been acknowledged. The fine arts are the domain in which "aesthetic feeling appears almost pure"; however, consumers also perceive beauty in their "houses, clothes, and friends" (Santayana 1955). Mothersill (1995: 45) notes that appearance is important to consumers and writes, "We care *a lot* about good appearance: to be beautiful, to have good-looking children, nice clothes, a fine house . . . perceptions of beauty are deeply intertwined in the complexities of our affective lives."

Some of the most comprehensive research on aesthetic value has been conducted in the field of textiles and clothing (with meaningful contributions from consumer researchers, such as Holbrook and Moore (1981)). The focus of this research has been the fashion object, as perceived by the consumer. Fashion is related to aesthetic value, because it involves changes in style, which are reflected in consumer preferences for particular design elements or configurations of design elements. While fashion may involve any type of value object – a good, a service, an event, or an idea – the classic example is clothing. In fact, the term "fashion" is often used synonymously with clothing.

As applied art, a fashion good combines beauty of form, perceived visually and tactilely, with beauty of expression. While the aesthetic function of a fashion object is to make the wearer more attractive or sometimes to be admired purely on its own terms, the most beautiful garments also perform utilitarian and social functions. Fabric, a two-dimensional material, is translated into a three-dimensional object that fits the body, allows movement, and protects the wearer. At the same time, the object promotes social acceptance by conveying information about the wearer. Consumers perceiving a fashion object make style-based inferences about the characteristics of the wearer, such as age, gender, status, and sexual availability.

Fashion objects differ from other axioforms, in that the "value carrier" is the clothed body. DeLong (1987) coined the term "Apparel-Body Construct (ABC)" to describe the resulting image. In research on the aesthetic value of fashion objects, subjects are usually presented with sketches or photographs of garments as they are worn. However, body type is held constant and facial features are removed, in order to focus on the aesthetic qualities of the garment itself.

### Aesthetic qualities of the fashion object

Sproles (1979) identified a set of "critical characteristics" (qualities) of fashion objects that may affect judgments of aesthetic value. As in fine art objects, the aesthetic qualities (local and regional) of fashion objects are assumed to supervene on the nonaesthetic qualities (fiber, fabric, finish).

Perhaps the most comprehensive treatment of the aesthetic qualities of fashion objects appears in the work of Davis (1987), who provides a detailed analysis of the elements and principles of design. In a fashion object, the elements of design (local qualities) include line, space, shape, form, light, color, texture, and pattern. Line, space, and shape are configured to create silhouette – a two-dimensional image. In contrast, form is the three-dimensional image of space enclosed by the surface of the garment, which is designed to fit (and presumably to flatter) the body. The principles of design (structural qualities) include synthesizing, directional, and highlighting principles. The synthesizing principles – the focus of philosophical discourse because of their contribution to the creation of the gestalt – are proportion, scale, balance, harmony, and unity. The directional principles, which guide the attention of the consumer to the focal point of the fashion object (e.g., face, midriff, ankle), include repetition, alternation, transition, and rhythm. The highlighting principles, which attract attention to the object, include contrast and emphasis.

Style, which is an emergent quality of the fashion object, has several meanings. It is often used as a synonym for silhouette or form, as in "the style of the dress is A-line." Style may also be used in reference to an individual's unique sense of beauty, as in "the Duchess of Windsor had style." Finally, style is often used to refer to a particular design element or configuration of design elements that is considered fashionable, as in "black is in style."

### Characteristics of the consumer

Fashion objects are similar to other aesthetic axioforms in that the primary motive for consumption is the need for beauty (Sproles 1985), as reflected in newness of style and attractiveness of appearance. Thus, aesthetic value in fashion objects appears to be intrinsic – consumers who appreciate fashion often do so for reasons that are not practical (Morganosky 1987).

Consumers of taste have the ability to perceive beauty and a heightened sense of what constitutes beauty (Sproles 1985). Taste in fashion objects has been termed "aesthetic sensitivity" or "style sensitivity." For example, Rudd and Tedrick (1994) compared the aesthetic sensitivity of homosexual and heterosexual males, defining aesthetic sensitivity as preference for innovative styling. Homosexual males were more likely than heterosexual males to show aesthetic sensitivity, thus defined, preferring innovative styling in a variety of categories, including casual pants, shirts, and shoes; dress pants, shirts, and jackets; and accessories, such as ties and socks. Homosexual males were also more likely to consider fragrance an element of the fashion image.

"Style sensitive" consumers are a small percentage of the population (about 20 percent) that derives aesthetic value primarily from the cut (silhouette and form) of fashion objects. Style sensitive consumers also appreciate quality (Gadel 1985). Here, aesthetic properties, such as style, supervene on nonaesthetic properties, such as fabric and construction. Consequently, excellence in execution of the fashion object contributes to its aesthetic value.

Taste in fashion objects can be cultivated by experience. To appreciate aesthetic value in fashion, new design elements and configurations must be continually learned. Consumers learn to recognize aesthetic value through repeated exposure to newness – observing other consumers, watching the media, and shopping in retail stores. A new fashion trend is established when a substantial proportion of consumers learns to evaluate a new style as beauty (Sproles 1981b). Consumers also learn to recognize aesthetic value by training in critical judgment. DeLong (1978) demonstrated the effect of training in aesthetic analysis on the evaluation of clothing. In a pretest, students were shown slides of clothed body forms and asked to evaluate the images. They were then trained in aesthetic analysis, shown the slides again, and asked to reevaluate them. Responses to the pretest ranged from entirely morphological (cognitive) to entirely axiological (evaluative), with the majority mixed. In morphological judgments, students focused on perceptions of formal beauty, explaining them in terms of the elements and principles of design. In axiological judgments, students focused on perceptions of expressive beauty, described them by the associations engendered by the visual image. The majority of judgments used some combination of the two focuses. After the training, the nature of the responses changed, becoming more morphological and less axiological.

## *Effect of context on aesthetic value in fashion*

One way in which consumers learn standards of beauty is through culture. Culture conditions beliefs about beauty, which vary from one society to another and from one historical period to the next. Each society has its own ideal of beauty, which changes over time. When philosophers argue that beauty is universal and timeless, they mean only that aesthetic qualities remain unchanged. What changes is consumer preferences for specific aesthetic properties, such as color, silhouette, or proportion. Thus, in the 1960s, the colors "in style" were psychedelic – hot pink, lime green, and electric blue. In the US in the 1990s, the fashion colors were neutrals – black, brown, and navy blue.

Fashion is a cultural norm – a standard of beauty to which consumers are expected to conform. Fashion affects (and reflects) preferences for aesthetic qualities, through short run and long run trends. Short run trends involve minor changes in aesthetic qualities, such as silhouette, proportion, and color. Long run trends involve major changes in preferences for silhouette and proportion. While tracking fashion trends is largely unscientific, there is research based on time-series analysis to document the direction and magnitude of change in consumer preferences for silhouette and proportion over time (Lowe and Lowe 1985).

Both cultures and subcultures have their own standards of attractiveness and interpretations of visual cues (Davis 1987). For example, Henderson (1994) surveyed female undergraduates on standards of attractiveness in style. Two groups were identified, one holding conventional standards of attractiveness in style, the other holding an "alternative" aesthetic. In the conventional standard, judgments of attractiveness were status-driven: students used brand name as a proxy for style. The alternative standard, on the other hand, was heavily influenced by postmodern aesthetic values. While the synthesizing principles of design still held in that the fashion object was expected to present a unified, coherent image, aesthetic value was derived from highlighting principles, particularly contrast. Judgments of attractiveness were driven by expression through contrast in line, shape, color, texture, and pattern, as well as by historical allusions, based on an incorporation of vintage clothes into the ensemble.

## *The aesthetic attitude: contemplating and evaluating the fashion object*

To capture and sustain the attention of the consumer (inducing contemplation), a new fashion object must show a sufficient (but not excessive) degree of novelty. In the design of fashion goods, color is the aesthetic quality used most often to attract attention and is often an important consideration in the aesthetic evaluation of a new style (Sproles 1981b).

Whether a consumer likes or dislikes a new style depends on how much it deviates from the ideal, as well as what is considered typical for its category (Sproles 1985). For example, DeLong, Minshall and Larntz (1986) studied the effect of evaluation (the affective component) and schema (the cognitive component) on preferences for new styles in sweaters. The basic schema for "sweater" was conceptualized in terms of aesthetic propoerties such as light vs. heavy, and thin vs. bulky. Subjects' preferences were dominated by affect, rather than cognition.

## The gestalt of the fashion object

As is true of all axioforms, beauty in fashion objects is perceived as a gestalt. Two research issues with respect to the fashion gestalt include, first, the nature of the hierarchy of value in aesthetic qualities, and, second, the role of interaction effects in perception of aesthetic value.

With respect to the hierarchy of value, one question is how beauty of form relates to beauty of expression. In a survey of aesthetic judgments among adult shoppers, Morganosky and Postelwait (1989) analysed the relative importance of form and expression. Subjects rated the appearance of two models – one male and one female. The results showed that, for both models, attractiveness of form was more important than expression. Similar results were reported by Bell (1991), to the effect that in men's clothing, formal (proper) garb is perceived to be more attractive than expressive (daring) attire. A second question regarding the hierarchy of value concerns the relative importance of the design elements (local qualities). Sproles (1981b) proposed that silhouette is dominant, a proposition confirmed in research on the aesthetic judgments of American consumers (Eckman and Wagner 1994) as well as in cross-cultural research comparing judgments of attractiveness by Chinese and American consumers (Wagner, Anderson, and Ettenson 1990). Indirect support for the dominance of silhouette also appears in the work of DeLong and Geum (1994), who studied perceptions of beauty in traditional dress among Korean women. Subjects were shown slides of six examples of traditional dress in three combinations of aesthetic qualities: first, a strictly traditional garment with traditional silhouette, color, and motifs; second, a slightly stylized garment with traditional silhouette and Westernized color and motifs; an third, a highly stylized garment with Westernized silhouette, color, and motifs. The strictly traditional and slightly stylized garments, both of which had the traditional Korean silhouette, were evaluated as more beautiful than the highly stylized garment. There was evidence of a monotonic effect between beauty and traditionalism, in that the garment evaluated as most beautiful was the slightly stylized one, which included a traditional silhouette but Westernized details. The garment evaluated as least beautiful was highly stylized with a Westernized silhouette and Westernized details.

From a theoretical standpoint, interactions among aesthetic qualities are to be expected. Indeed, interactions are fundamental to the concept of a gestalt and are inherent in some elements of design. For example, shape depends on the interaction of line and space. Among the first to demonstrate the role of interaction effects in aesthetic judgments of fashion objects were Holbrook and Moore (1981). In ensuing research, Winakor and Navarro (1987) analyzed the relative importance of overall style and light–dark shade on perceptions of attractiveness in women's attire. Subjects evaluated drawings of three types of garments (dress, skirted suit, jacket-and-pants), at three levels of style, in nine combinations of light and dark value. While style dominated aesthetic preferences, significant interactions were observed between style and shade. Wagner, Anderson, and Ettenson (1990) studied aesthetic judgments of women's suits among Chinese and American consumers. Subjects were shown slides of sketches, wherein suits were varied via different configurations of design elements. Support for the gestalt was evident – the total amount of variance explained by interaction effects was greater than the total reported for main effects. The most important inter-action was between silhouette and pattern. In a related study, Eckman and Wagner (1994) explored judgments of attractiveness of men's tailored clothing. Again, subjects were shown slides of sketches, with style systematically varied. And again, aesthetic judgments were dominated by gestalts – in this case, the interaction of proportion (a design principle) with pattern (a design element) – suggesting that the dimensions of a garment may reinforce or counter the effects of its fabric's design.

There is a large body of literature on the expressive aspects of the fashion object. From the appearance of a fashion object, consumers infer information on personality, self-esteem, status, prestige, group membership, and lifestyle (Holman and Wiener 1985; Sproles 1981a, 1985). In addition, there is abundant anecdotal information on the meanings consumers associate with specific elements of design, though there is little empirical evidence to substantiate such interpretations.

Davis (1987) reviewed meanings associated with specific elements of design. For example, line has directional associations: horizontal lines are perceived as restful, diagonal lines are perceived as active, and vertical lines are perceived as stable. Color has physical and psychological associations. Physical associations include temperature (warm or cool), motion (light advances toward and dark recedes away), and sound (loud or quiet). Psychological associations are emo-tional: red is perceived to be primitive or passionate; blue is perceived to be peaceful or serene. Associations with texture are derived from the surface of fabric: the nap of flannel suggests coziness and security; the smoothness of satin is reminiscent of elegance. In related research, DeLong (1983–84) explored how consumers associate aesthetic qualities with seasons of the year. The local quali-ties of color (dark and neutral), line (curved) and texture (rough) were associated with winter. The emergent qualities of attractive, pleasing, and elegant were associated with summer. In a study of traditional Korean dress, DeLong and Geum (1994) observed a number of culture-specific associations: red and green are associated with marriage, and white with mourning. Traditional garments in which the cuffs and the tie are rendered in the same pattern convey information on life-cycle stage – that the wearer is married and has a son.

## Fashion and the Typology of Consumer Value

As applied art objects, fashion goods represent a more complicated aesthetic than do fine art objects. In the fine arts, aesthetic value is "pure" intrinsic value; that is, the fine art object is consumed just for the sake of experiencing its beauty. In fashion, aesthetic value is derived not from beauty alone, but from a complex of values that includes extrinsic values, such as quality and status. Therefore, aesthetic value in fashion involves both intrinsic *and* extrinsic value.

Aesthetic value in fashion objects, like aesthetic value in fine art objects, is self-oriented. Consumers have the need to be attractive and to surround themselves with other people who are attractive. However, unlike aesthetic value in the fine arts, aesthetic value in fashion is also other-oriented. Attractiveness of appearance is a way of eliciting the reaction of others and facilitating social interaction. Thus, aesthetic value in fashion objects is both self-oriented *and* other-oriented.

The aesthetic value of fashion objects is an example of active value, because clothing is physically and mentally manipulated, in its everyday usage. Clothing is physically manipulated in the process of dressing to make consumers more attractive; it is also mentally manipulated because consumers process information about the attractiveness of the fashion objects they wear and see being worn by others. From the aesthetic qualities of a fashion object, valuable information is conveyed and processed about characteristics of the wearer, such as age, gender, status, and sexual availability. The aesthetic value of fashion objects is also an example of reactive value. Consumers react with pleasure to having their needs met. The aesthetic value of fashion objects provides the attractiveness consumers believe they need in themselves and others. When fashion objects offer elegance – simple, attractive solutions to utilitarian and social needs – consumers react with pleasure. Thus, aesthetic value in fashion is both active and reactive.

## Conclusion: aesthetic value and consumer research

In this chapter, linkages between the concept of aesthetic value and the consumer decision-making model have been highlighted. Aesthetic value appears to be a special type of consumer value, which occurs in its purest form in the fine arts through the experience of beauty. As an exemplar of applied art, fashion presents a more complicated type of beauty. In a fashion object, aesthetic value is derived from the consumer's perception of a form that not only is attractive, but that also meets a set of utilitarian and social needs.

Potential topics for future research on aesthetic value, in either the fine or applied arts, include the structure of the gestalt, the nature of significant form, and the process by which the visual image is updated to accommodate changes in preferences for style. The structure of the gestalt is a critical issue, because it represents the "ineffable" essence of aesthetic value. How are formal and expressive beauty related? How do the local and structural qualities of an aesthetic object interact to affect perceptions of beauty? What are the associations engendered by the elements and principles of design? Perceptions of significant form and preferences for style speak to the dynamics underlying fashion change in any art form, whether fine or applied. What are the aesthetic qualities of objects such as the Sistine ceiling (in the fine arts) or a Chanel suit (in the applied arts) that have enduring beauty? What is the process by which visual images are updated to accommodate stylistic change? How much change is too much?

In conclusion, aesthetic value is as amenable to research as any other category of consumer value. While consumer researchers have built impressive streams of research on other categories of value, such as quality, status, and esteem, they have virtually ignored aesthetic value. Given the role of beauty in enhancing and enriching the lives of consumers, aesthetic value emerges as a topic of compelling research interest.

# References

Beardsley, M. (1958) *Aesthetics: Problems in the Philosophy of Criticism*, New York: Harcourt, Brace.
—— (1982) "What is an Aesthetic Quality?" in M.J. Wreen and D. Callen (eds) *The Aesthetic Point of View*, Ithaca, NY: Cornell University Press: 93–110.
Becker, G. (1974) "A Theory of Social Interaction," *Journal of Political Economy* 82, November/December: 1063–93.
Becker, G. (1976) *The Economic Approach to Human Behavior*, Chicago, IL: The University of Chicago Press.
Bell, C. (1914) *Art*, New York: Capricorn Books.
Bell, E. (1991) "Adults' Perception of Male Garment Styles," *Clothing and Textiles Research Journal* 10, 1: 8–12.
Berenson, B. (1954) *Aesthetics and History*, Garden City, NY: Doubleday.
Bullough, E. (1912) "'Psychical Distance' as a Factor in Art and as an Aesthetic Principle," *British Journal of Psychology* 5: 87–98.
Burchert, D. M. (1996) *Encyclopedia of Philosophy Supplement*, New York: Simon and Schuster Macmillan.
Croce, B. (1965) *Guide to Aesthetics*, translated by P. Rommell, New York: Bobbs-Merrill.
Davis, M.L. (1987) *Visual Design in Dress*, Englewood Cliffs, NJ: Prentice-Hall, Inc.
DeLong, M.R. (1978) "Clothing and Aesthetics: Perception of Form," *Home Economics Research Journal* 47: 214–24.
—— (1983–84) "Cognitive Strategies to Describe Warm and Cool Appearances," *Clothing and Textiles Research Journal* 2, 1: 19–23.
—— (1987) *The Way We Look: A Framework for Visual Analysis of Dress*, Ames, IA: Iowa State University Press.
DeLong, M. R. and Geum, K. S. (1994), "A Systematic Analysis of the Aesthetic Experience of Korean Traditional Dress," in M.R. DeLong and A.M. Fiore (eds) *Aesthetics of Textiles and Clothing: Advancing Multi-Disciplinary Perspectives*, ITAA Special Publication #7, Monument, CO: International Textiles and Apparel Association, Inc.: 224–34.
DeLong, M., Kim, S., and Larntz, K. (1993) "Perceptions of Garment Proportions by Female Observers," *Perceptual and Motor Skills*, 76: 811–19.
DeLong, M. R., Minshall, B., and Larntz, K. (1986) "Use of Schema for Evaluating Consumer Response to an Apparel Product," *Clothing and Textiles Research Journal*, 5, 1: 17–26.
Dewey, J. (1934) *Art as Experience*, New York.
Dickie, G. (1964) "The Myth of the Aesthetic Attitude," *American Philosophical Quarterly*, 1, 1: 56–66.
Eckman, M., Damhorst, M. L., and Kadolph, S. J. (1990) "Toward a Model of the In-Store Purchase Decision Process: Consumer Use of Criteria for Evaluating Women's Apparel," *Clothing and Textiles Research Journal* 8, 2: 13–21.
Eckman, M. and Wagner, J. (1994) "Judging the Attractiveness of Product Design: The

Effect of Visual Attributes and Consumer Characteristics," in C.T. Allen and D.R. John (eds) *Advances in Consumer Research* Vol 21: 560–4.

Edwards, P. (1967) "Value and Valuation ," in P. Edwards (ed.) *The Encyclopedia of Philosophy*, NY: The Macmillan Company: 229–32.

Eibl-Eibesfeldt, I. (1988) "The Biological Foundation of Aesthetics," in I. Rentschler, B. Herzberger, and D. Epstein (eds) *Beauty and the Brain*, Birkhauser Verlag: Boston: 29–70.

Fiebleman, J. K. (1968) *Aesthetic Value*, New York: Humanities Press.

Feldman, E. B. (1972) *Varieties of Visual Experience* 2nd. ed., Englewood Cliffs, NY: Prentice-Hall, Inc.

Fishbein, M. (1967), "Attitudes and Prediction of Behavior," in Martin Fishbein (ed.) *Readings in Attitude Theory and Measurement*, New York: John Wiley.

Frondizi, R. (1971) *What is Value?* LaSalle, IL: Open Court Publishing Company.

Gadel, M. S. (1985) "Commentary: Style-Oriented Apparel Consumers," in M. R. Solomon (ed.), *The Psychology of Fashion*, Lexington, MA: Lexington Books: 155–7.

Goldman, A. H. (1995) "Aesthetic Properties," in D. Cooper (ed.) *A Companion to Aesthetics*, Malden, MA: Blackwell: 342–6.

Gombrich, E. H. (1958) "The Visual Image," *Scientific American* 199, September: 52–66.

Goodman, N. (1968) *Languages of Art*, New York: Bobbs-Merrill.

Handy, R. (1969) *Value Theory and the Behavioral Sciences*, Springfield, IL: Charles C. Thomas Publisher.

Henderson, B. E. (1994) "Teaching Aesthetics in a Post Modern Environment," in M. R. DeLong and A. M. Fiore (eds), *Advancing Multi-Disciplinary Perspectives*, ITAA Special Publication #7, Monument, CO: International Textiles and Apparel Association, Inc. 39–47.

Hermeren, G. (1988) *The Nature of Aesthetic Qualities*, Lund: Lund University Press.

Holbrook, M. B. (1994a) "Axiology, Aesthetics, and Apparel: Some Reflections on the Old School Tie," in M. R. DeLong and A. M. Fiore (eds) *Advancing Multi-Disciplinary Perspectives*, ITAA Special Publication #7, Monument, CO: International Textile and Apparel Association, Inc.: 131–41.

—— (1994b) "The Nature of Customer Value," in R. T. Rust. and R. L. Oliver (eds) *Service Quality*, London: Sage Publications: 21–71.

Holbrook, M. B. and Moore, W. L. (1981) "Feature Interactions in Consumer Judgments of Verbal Versus Pictorial Presentations," *Journal of Consumer Research*, 8, June: 103–13.

Holmna, R. H. and Wiener, S.E. (1985) "Fashionability and Clothing: A Values and Lifestyle Perspective," in M.R. Solomon (ed.) *The Psychology of Fashion*, New York: Lexington Books: 87–98.

Hume, D. (1965) *"Of the Standard of Taste" and Other Essays*, in J.W. Lenz (ed.) New York: Bobbs-Merrill.

Kainz, F. (1962) *Aesthetics the Science*, Detroit: Wayne State University Press.

Kant, I. (1928) *The Critique of Judgement*, Oxford: Oxford University Press.

Levinson, J. (1995) "Aesthetic Pleasure," in D. Cooper (ed.) *A Companion to Aesthetics*, Malden, MA: Blackwell: 330–5.

Lewis, C. I. (1946) *An Analysis of Knowledge and Valuation*, LaSalle: Open Court.

Lowe, E. D. and Lowe, J. W. G. (1985) "Quantitative Analysis of Women's Dress," in M.R. Solomon (ed.) *The Psychology of Fashion*, New York: Lexington Books: 193–206.

Morganosky, M. (1987) "Aesthetics, Function, and Fashion Consumer Values:

Relationships to Other Values and Demographics," *Clothing and Textiles Research Journal* 6, 1: 15–28.

Morganosky, M. A. and Postelwait, D. S. (1989) "Consumers' Evaluation of Apparel Form, Expression, and Aesthetic Quality," *Clothing and Textiles Research Journal* 7, 2: 11–15.

Mothersill, M. (1984) *Beauty Restored*, Oxford: Clarendon Press.

—— (1995) "Beauty," in D. Cooper (ed.) *A Companion to Aesthetics*, Malden, MA: Blackwell: 44–50.

Osborne, H. (1986) "Aesthetic Experience and Cultural Value," *The Journal of Aesthetics and Art Criticism*, 44, Summer: 331–7.

Paul, G. (1988) "Philosophical Theories of Beauty and Scientific Research on the Brain," in I. Rentschler, B. Herzberger, and D. Epstein (eds) *Beauty and the Brain*, Boston: Birhauser Verlig: 15–27.

Puffer, E. (1905) *The Psychology of Beauty*, New York: Houghton Mifflin.

Rudd, N. A. and Tedrick, L. S. (1994) "Male Appearance Aesthetics: Evidence to Target a Homosexual Market?" in M.R. DeLong and A.M. Fiore (eds) *Aesthetics of Textiles and Clothing: Advancing Multi-Disciplinary Perspectives*, ITAA Special Publication #7, Monument, CO: International Textiles and Apparel Association, Inc.: 224–34.

Santayana, G. (1955) *The Sense of Beauty*, New York: Dover Publications, Inc.

Shusterman, R. (1997) "The End of Aesthetic Experience," *The Journal of Aesthetics and Art Criticism* 55, Winter: 29–41.

Sibley, F. (1959) "Aesthetic Concepts," *Philosophical Review* 68: 421–9.

Silvers, A. (1996) "Aesthetic Autonomy," in D. Burchert (ed.) *Encyclopedia of Philosophy Supplement*, New York: Simon and Schuster Macmillan: 5–6.

Sproles, G. B. (1979) *Fashion: Consumer Behavior Toward Dress*, Minneapolis: Burgess Publishing Company.

—— (1981a) "Analyzing Fashion Life Cycles – Principles and Perspectives," *Journal of Marketing* 45, 3:116–24.

—— (1981b) "The Role of Aesthetics in Fashion-Oriented Consumer Behavior," in G. B. Sproles (ed.) *Perspectives of Fashion*, Minneapolis: Burgess Publishing Company: 124–7.

—— (1985) "Behavioral Science Theories of Fashion," in M. R. Solomon (ed.) *The Psychology of Fashion*, Lexington, MA: Lexington Books: 55–70.

Stolnitz, J. (1960) *Aesthetics and Philosophy of Art Criticism*, Boston, MA: Riverside.

Turner, F. and Poppel, E. (1988) "Metered Poetry, the Brain, and Time," in I. Rentschler, B. Herzberger, and D. Epstein (eds) *Beauty and the Brain*, Boston: Birhauser Verlag, 71–90.

Wagner, J., Anderson, C., and Ettenson, R. (1990) "Evaluating Attractiveness in Apparel Design: A Comparison of Chinese and American Consumers," in P.E. Horridge (ed.) ACPTC Proceedings, Monument, CO: Association of College Professors of Textiles and Clothing, Inc.: 97.

Whewell, D. A. (1995) "Taste," in D. Cooper (ed.), *A Companion to Aesthetics*, Malden, MA: Blackwell.

Winakor, G. and Navarro, R. (1987) "Effect of Achromatic Value of Stimulus on Responses to Women's Clothing Styles," *Clothing and Textiles Research Journal* 5, 2: 40–8.

# 7 Ethics and the Typology of Consumer Value[1]

*N. Craig Smith*

## Introduction

The Typology of Consumer Value posits that ethics (including justice, virtue, and morality) is one of eight kinds of value that may be attained in the consumption experience. This chapter examines ethics as a consumer value and its relationship to the other types of consumer value and to the framework as a whole. The merits of the typology of consumer value are highlighted and the role of ethics within the framework carefully delineated. In particular, the distinction is made between consumption experiences that have entirely altruistic motivations and those experiences that, in addition, have a less selfless aspect. Illustrations of ethics as a consumer value are provided, including the consumption of charity services and participation in consumer boycotts. Suggestions are made for research that may benefit from the integration provided by the framework.

The Typology of Consumer Value described in the Introduction (and Holbrook 1994a, 1994b), proposes ethics as one of eight kinds of value in the consumption experience. By way of illustration, Holbrook (1994b: 54) suggests that the consumption of charity services, such as donating one's blood to the Red Cross, provides this kind of consumer value; it "constitutes an ethically virtuous action if one pursues helping others purely for its own sake." As well as ethics (or morality), the typology proposes that efficiency, play, excellence, aesthetics, status (or politics), esteem, and spirituality are different kinds of value that consumers may attain through consumption. The different types of consumer value are categorized according to three dimensions; whether the value is extrinsic or intrinsic, self- or other-oriented, and active or reactive.

The purpose of this chapter is to examine ethics as a consumer value and its fit within the typology. First, I comment on the merits of the consumer value framework, confirming its "value" to consumer researchers. Second, I examine ethics as a consumer value, providing illustrations of when this type of value may be obtained. Next I examine the conceptualization of ethics within the framework and suggest an alternative conceptualization; I note that it is particularly important to differentiate between ethics and altruism. Finally, I conclude with some suggestions for future research.

## Holbrook's Typology of Consumer Value

Recognizing that exchange is central to the marketing concept and that marketing transactions involve exchanges of value, Holbrook (1994a: 134) highlights the importance of understanding the nature and types of value consumers obtain in the consumption experience. In other words, he asks: What form does the value take that consumers hope to receive when they hand over their hard-earned cash? Such a question clearly should be at the core of consumer research.

In providing an answer to this question, Holbrook (1994b: 26–39) identifies, or at least hypothesizes, four key characteristics of consumer value. He defines value as "an interactive relativistic preference experience" (1994b: 27). First, it is *interactive* because value can only be obtained through an interaction between the consumer and the product; while a product may have many qualities, they only come to represent consumer value when they are appreciated within the context of a consumption experience. With respect to art, for example, this suggests a distinction between artistic value and consumer value; a work of art appreciated by the artist alone may have artistic value but not consumer value (unless we regard the artist as the consumer of interest).

Second, value is *relativistic* because it can never be absolute when it is the result of consumers who differ amongst themselves and who make comparisons among alternative possible sources of value in a multitude of different situations. Fashion-clothing marketers know too well, for example, that consumer tastes differ and may change over time or in response to the arrival of new styles. Hence, the third characteristic that value is a judgment of *preference*.

Finally, value is found in the *experience* of consumption, rather than in the purchase of a product. Typically, the act of purchase is not an end in itself but only a means of obtaining experiences derived from the product. It is a marketing axiom that people do not buy products, they buy the services that products provide; as Levitt (1995: 13) put it: "People actually do not buy gasoline . . . what they buy is the right to continue driving their cars." However, we should also recognize that for some products and markets the act of purchase is a part of the consumption experience; I may choose to shop at an expensive delicatessen in preference to a conventional supermarket because this is more enjoyable. Arguably, this is part of the consumption experience derived from the goods purchased. Indeed, the shopping experience constitutes a form of consumption even when no purchases are made at all, as in "window shopping" or "just looking."

As well as fleshing out the nature of consumer value, Holbrook (1994b: 44–55) also proposes a framework or typology, classifying consumer value by three dimensions: 1) extrinsic versus intrinsic, 2) self- versus other-oriented, and 3) active versus reactive. (See Table 7.1 for a review of the complete typology in its most recent form.) Esteem, for example, is a value that might be obtained from owning a luxury automobile. It is extrinsic, because the esteem value is instrumentally derived rather than experienced through the act of consumption as an end in itself (compare with the intrinsic value of play). It is other-oriented,

*Table 7.1* Holbrook's Typology of Value in the consumption experience

|  |  | *Extrinsic* | *Intrinsic* |
|---|---|---|---|
| *Self-Oriented* | *Active* | EFFICIENCY (O/I, Convenience) | PLAY (Fun) |
|  | *Reactive* | EXCELLENCE (Quality) | AESTHETICS (Beauty) |
| *Other-Oriented* | *Active* | STATUS (Success, Impression Management) | ETHICS (Justice, Virtue, Morality) |
|  | *Reactive* | ESTEEM (Reputation, Materialism, Possessions) | SPIRITUALITY (Faith, Ecstasy, Sacredness) |

because the esteem value is derived from the reaction of others to the consumer's ownership of the car, rather than from his or her own reaction to it (compare with the self-oriented value of excellence that might be derived from a consumer's appreciation of product quality). It is reactive, because the esteem value comes from what the car does for the consumer rather than what he or she does to or with it (compare with the active value of efficiency resulting from the functional use of a product).

Types of value are not mutually exclusive. It follows from the earlier discussion of the nature of consumer value that a luxury automobile may provide different types of value to different consumers. For another consumer, the same luxury automobile may provide the extrinsic, self-oriented, and reactive value of excellence. Indeed, for any given consumer, the same luxury automobile may provide a combination of values, perhaps play and excellence in addition to esteem. As Holbrook (1994a: 138) notes: "*Any* or *all* of the value types distinguished earlier may and often do *occur simultaneously* to *varying degrees* in any given consumption experience." Accordingly, as further discussed below, the framework suggests that ethics is a value that consumers may attain *in addition* to other types of value.

Holbrook's conception of the nature and types of consumer value is a useful contribution to consumer research and marketing practice. Its merits for consumer researchers may be found in the recognition or assertion that: 1) consumer value lies in the consumption experience, not the product; 2) different types of value may be obtained; 3) these types of value may occur simultaneously and to varying degrees in any consumption experience; 4) there is an interrelationship between the different types of value that arise in consumption; and 5) the types of value may be subject to a higher order classification (such as the dimensions proposed in Holbrook's typology). Marketing managers would likely find Holbrook's conception of consumer value and the typology both accessible and intuitively appealing. It provides scope for improved understanding of the benefits sought by consumers and hence broadens the opportunities for increased consumer satisfaction. More specifically, it might suggest alternative approaches to organizing data in marketing research, concept testing in new product development, and message strategy in advertising.

However, this is not to suggest that researchers or managers should embrace the framework in its entirety. The conception of consumer value, including the recognition that there are different types of value, is well-argued by Holbrook (1994a, 1994b). The detail within the framework is more subject to question. It is beyond the scope of this chapter to examine the dimensions of the typology and all the different types of value proposed. However, it can be noted that there is uncertainty about the antecedents and consequences of the dimensions. What is the theoretical basis for the three dimensions chosen? Holbrook (1994b: 39–44) briefly discusses the literature supporting the dimensions chosen, but not alternative dimensions. For example, perhaps there is an affective dimension of the consumption experience – whether the consumer has positive or negative feelings. Do positive or negative feelings influence the type of value consumers obtain? Is this adequately captured in the existing framework? Likewise, is there an economic dimension of value or a tangible/intangible or a physical/mental dimension? Moreover, Holbrook (1994a: 137) has noted the "disappearance of the self–other dichotomy" when faith becomes a state of ecstasy. Does this, too, speak to a need for alternative formulations of the consumer value framework?

The classification of the types of value identified also may be questioned. Perhaps, as indicated above, faith may be classified as self-oriented as well as or instead of other-oriented. Further, is the framework sufficiently inclusive, does it capture all key types of value in consumption? Holbrook (1994b: 58) is correct to observe that some types of value identified in the framework have received little attention from consumer researchers, including ethics or morality in consumption. Yet are some important types of value missing, such as the intellectual value that may be obtained from a subscription to a current affairs magazine or the purchase of an encyclopedia? Indeed, this line of analysis soon suggests that more careful limits may need to be imposed on the domain of the framework if it is to avoid the impossible task of attempting to include virtually all types of human behavior. Moreover, are those values that are included adequately delimited and accurately defined?

Concerns about the dimensions of the framework and the types of value identified are addressed throughout the chapters in this volume. The primary focus of the present chapter is on ethics as a type of consumer value and how it is classified within the framework.

## Ethics as a consumer value

Holbrook's (1994a: 139; 1994b: 45) typology (subsequently modified in this book's Introduction, as shown in Table 7.1) refers to "morality" and, parenthetically, to "virtue or ethical acts." Holbrook (1994a: 137) refers to a "pursuit" of morality (hence its classification as active on the active/reactive dimension) that aims at "virtue sought for its own sake as its own reward." He continues by referring to "deontological value" and the concept of duty or obligation to others. Noting that such obligations "often appear in the form of socially accepted rules of conduct or conventions that dictate proper behavior," Holbrook illustrates morality as a consumer value by reference to wearing a white dress at one's wedding or a tuxedo to the prom. He adds that ethics is viewed as intrinsically motivated (hence its classification as intrinsic on the extrinsic/intrinsic dimension). Aside from references to charitable contributions, other illustrations of morality as a consumer value in Holbrook (1994a) are somewhat whimsical ("Holbrookian"?) in keeping with the lighter tone of this paper.

Holbrook (1994b: 52–4) gives more detailed attention to moral philosophy, yet the essence of his perspective on ethics as a consumer value remains the same: "Ethical action involves doing something for the sake of others – with concern for how it will affect them or how they will react to it" (p. 52). The motivation for such action is intrinsic because "virtue is its own reward" (pp. 53, 54). More controversially, he suggests that "the moment we stop pursuing some ethical action as an end in itself and begin pursuing it as a means to some ulterior purpose, it stops being ethical and partakes of some other sort of value" (p. 53). This perspective on ethics requires some examination, as will follow below. In addition, the use of the terms "ethics", "virtue", "morality" and (in Table 7.1) "justice" interchangeably, is also problematic. Nonetheless, it is clear that Holbrook (1994b) is referring to ethics as a consumer value where it reflects doing good for its own sake and as a result of a sense of moral obligation or duty.

By way of illustration, Holbrook (1994b: 54) "defends" the consumption of charity services "on the moral grounds that it is 'right' to behave generously without offering any further reason or objective;" for example, donating money to the United Way, one's blood to the Red Cross, and one's time to a soup kitchen. However, such behaviors only constitute "an ethically virtuous action [i.e., ethics as a consumer value] if one pursues helping others purely for its own sake." Indeed, Holbrook (1994b: 54) rejects from this category those behaviors that have any self-interested motivations: "If, by contrast, one were to invoke the aim of benefiting from tax deductions, earning gratitude, or improving the neighborhood by reducing the number of street people, the relevant type of value would become political [or status, to use the subsequently revised term reflected in Table 7.1] rather than moral." As I explain in more detail below, this is a narrow perspective on ethical conduct, and I will argue in favor of a broader and more widely accepted view. Holbrook (1994b) raises a conundrum in moral philosophy that has troubled philosophers for centuries: Can an act ever be entirely without self-interest? Moreover, from an empirical standpoint, can we ever know? It is generally accepted that doing good has a multitude of motivations, some of which may be self-interested.

While it will be argued that the role of ethics in the typology of consumer value needs to be carefully delineated, Holbrook's notion of ethics as a consumer value is not in principle disputed. Indeed, I have elsewhere (Smith 1987a, 1987b, 1990; Burke, Milberg, and Smith 1993) examined "ethical purchase behavior", as Holbrook (1994b: 58) acknowledges. The consumption of charity services and (arguably) the wearing of appropriate attire in formal settings have been used to illustrate ethics as a consumer value. In the next section, ethics as a consumer value is further illustrated by consumer boycotts, providing an inductive basis for specifying the meaning of ethics as a consumer value.

## Boycotts as an illustration of ethics as a consumer value

Boycotts can take many forms and have been used for centuries (Smith 1990: 134–66). Early examples include boycotts of British goods by American colonists in the Revolutionary War, boycotts of slave-made goods by abolitionists, and going back to 1327, a boycott of the monks of Christ's Church by the citizens of Canterbury, England in an agreement not to "buy, sell or exchange drinks or victuals with the monastery" (Laidler 1968: 27–30). Laidler (ibid.: 27) defines boycotting as "an organized effort to withdraw and induce others to withdraw from social or business relations with another." More specifically, the consumer boycott may be defined as "the organized exercising of consumer sovereignty by abstaining from purchase of an offering in order to exert influence on a matter of concern to the consumer and over the institution making the offering" (Smith 1990: 140). It is clear from the instrumental purpose evident in these definitions that a consumer boycott often would not qualify as an "ethically virtuous action" under Holbrook's (1994b: 54) conception of ethics. Indeed, Smith (1990: 278–82) argues that consumer boycotts should be viewed as a tool for achieving the social control of business.[2]

However, Smith (1990: 8–9) suggests consumer boycotts (especially where organized by pressure groups) are only the most clearly identifiable and deliberate form of a broader phenomenon, described as ethical purchase behavior, which occurs "where people are influenced in purchase by ethical concerns" (ibid.: 8). The ethical content of participation in a consumer boycott and ethical purchase behavior generally, notwithstanding possible instrumental motivations, may be illustrated by research on specific boycotts. Consider the following examples (Smith 1990: 233–55):

- An editorial in the *Financial Times*, headed "Moral Pressure in the Market," attributed the withdrawal from South Africa by Barclays Bank to a consumer boycott and concluded that this was effective because of the ethical concern of consumers: "ordinary people, revolted by what they have learned about the [apartheid] system from the news media . . . have proved they can bring effective pressure to bear on commercial organizations. . . . Moral pressure of this kind – whether against apartheid, whaling, the fur trade, vivisection or even the defence industry – is an increasingly important fact of business life" (*Financial Times*, 25 November, 1986).
- The moral opprobrium associated with Nestlé's marketing of infant formula

in developing countries is well captured in this letter from a supporter of the consumer boycott of Nestlé: "My children love Nestlé Quik. My husband and I are virtually addicted to Nescafé. But we will no longer be buying these or your other products. We have learned about the suffering your advertising of infant formula causes . . . our outrage joins with that of many others and together we will boycott Nestlé products until you change" (Smith 1990: 249).

- Middle-class urban America supported the successful 1965–70 grape boycott because of concern about the treatment of farm workers and issues of poverty, pesticide misuse, and civil rights. In a union pamphlet entitled *Why We Boycott*, Cesar Chavez later wrote, "The boycott is the way we take our cause to the public. For surely if we cannot find *justice* in the courts of rural California, we will find support with our brothers and sisters throughout the nation" (emphasis added).

- During the boycott of Douwe Egberts coffee, over its sourcing of coffee from Angola (when Angola was seeking independence from Portugal), a Douwe Egberts sales director made the following comment on instructions given to the sales force (Hofstede 1980): "We told them that the company could not take a political position. On the other hand, they know that they should follow the consumer – the consumer is always right. This was OK as long as the consumer was only interested in the taste of coffee. Now, for the first time, the consumer expressed an opinion about something very different."

Smith (1990: 260) highlights the importance of moral outrage in consumer boycott effectiveness and success. He notes (1990: 258) that boycotts have expressive as well as instrumental functions: "The boycott is a moral act; an expression by the consumer of disapproval of the firm's activities and disassociation from them." This desire on the part of the consumer to have "clean hands" may mean that it is inappropriate to refer to objectives or effectiveness in reference to consumer participation in a boycott; no instrumental motivation may be present, at least for some consumers. This is illustrated by "many consumers' refusal to purchase South African goods, [because of] the wish to avoid tainted (and being tainted by) products of apartheid" (Smith 1990: 158).

More broadly, Smith (1990: 178) defines ethical purchase behavior as "an expression of the individual's moral judgment in his or her purchase behavior." While this definition may be flawed because it can be argued that moral judgment is almost always present in any human behavior – there is a moral burden as a consequence of the human condition – it recognizes the possibility of ethics as a consumer value. As well as abstaining from purchase for ethical reasons, in consumer boycotts or perhaps as a vegetarian, Smith (1990: 2–3) also recognizes more affirmative forms of ethical purchase behavior, where products of a particular supplier are sought, as in buying domestically produced goods because it is "the right thing to do." Also noteworthy here is the literature on socially responsible consumption (Smith 1990: 178–81). For example, Engel and Blackwell (1982: 610) refer to socially conscious consumers as "those persons who not only are concerned with their own personal satisfactions, but also buy with some consideration of the social and environmental well-being of others." More broadly still, in a variety of spheres, scholars such as Etzioni (1988: 51–66) have recognized the moral dimension of economics and have provided many examples of people apparently acting unselfishly in their economic behavior. In short, there is ample evidence in consumer boycotts and elsewhere to support a role for ethical concern in consumer behavior and the possibility of ethics as a consumer value.

## An alternative conceptualization of ethics as a consumer value

While ethical concerns may be recognized as an influence on purchase behavior, can ethics be viewed as a value sought by consumers? There is something troubling about the concept of ethics as a consumer value that can be obtained in marketplace exchanges. It might be argued that ethics is not appropriately conceived as one of a number of possible values consumers might seek, that it is in some way above consideration alongside quality or fun, or that it is beyond the reach of commercial transactions. (Similarly, one might argue that spirituality, at least in relation to religious behavior, is also above comparison with the more earthly types of value.) However, the apparent contradiction of a form of value obtained as ethics is largely dependent upon a conception of ethics as selfless behavior. If ethics is for its own sake – an end in and of itself – it is difficult to argue that this also can provide "value" to the consumer; clearly, value is not being sought. Holbrook (1994b: 22) refers to exchange by way of an explanation of consumer value, noting that exchange is a transaction involving two agents in which each agent gives up something of value in return for something of greater value. It would seem that if consumer value is a form of utility obtained by the consumer, then it cannot be obtained for selfless reasons. There is a way of resolving this issue. It requires a broader and more widely accepted perspective on ethics and an understanding of altruism. First, however, let us consider the multiple motivations for participation in a consumer boycott.

In choosing to boycott Barclays Bank, a consumer may have strongly believed that apartheid was wrong and that Barclays' presence as the largest bank in South Africa supported apartheid and was therefore wrong as a consequence. Participation in the boycott may have been motivated by: a) the belief that support of the boycott could help the people of South Africa by forcing Barclays' withdrawal and speeding the downfall of the apartheid regime, an instrumental motivation; b) a desire not be associated with a company that directly or indirectly benefits from apartheid, a "clean hands" motivation; or c) a reluctance to be seen patronizing the "apartheid bank," an avoidance of unseemly conspicuous consumption. Although instrumental, the first motivation could qualify as an ethically virtuous action under Holbrook's definition. The second motivation of a clean conscience may also qualify. The third motivation is more problematic, not wishing to be embarrassed or having to brave protesters when visiting a Barclays Bank outlet reflects self-interest. Given that it is conceivable that all three motivations might be present for any one consumer, would this mean that ethics is not a consumer value obtained in participation in the Barclays boycott? Likewise, a vegetarian may be concerned about the treatment of animals and dislike the taste of meat, or working in a soup kitchen may be motivated by a desire to help the homeless and to be seen as a caring individual. In short, there may be ethically virtuous (as defined by Holbrook) and less selfless motivations to some consumption experiences, and yet we might still wish to characterize the participants as consumers obtaining ethics as a consumer value.

The concept of altruism provides clarification here. Altruism may be defined (Becker and Becker 1992: 35) in terms of an action intentionally aimed at helping others and involving some other-directed motivation, a regard for the well-being of others for its own sake. In addition, some restrict the term to the placing of the interests of others ahead of those of oneself. Holbrook's conceptualization of ethics as a consumer value may more accurately be described as altruism. This presents three problems for consumer researchers attempting to use the typology: 1) truly altruistic acts are rare and some would say never occur or are impossible to identify with certainty; 2) altruism does not include many behaviors we might wish to characterize as ethical; and 3) a broader conceptualization of ethics as a consumer value that goes beyond altruism may violate the framework dimensions. The third problem – particularly in terms of whether ethics as a consumer value is other-oriented, self-oriented, or both – is addressed in the next section. Below, I argue against a narrow conceptualization of ethics (i.e., altruism) as a consumer value in favor of a broader view that can encompass the motivations described in consumer boycott participation and other consumption experiences where ethical concerns are involved but with self-interest present too.

Clearly, to advance this argument, ethics needs to be defined in a way that includes altruism yet also permits less selfless motivations. A consumption experience that provides value or utility because it is ethical is the result of a consumer judgment of how he or she ought to behave, in accord with moral principles or, more simply, a belief about what is the right or good thing to do. Clearly such value could not be obtained by unethical behaviors; for example, by drinking and driving when it is known that driving under the influence of alcohol is wrong because it impairs driving ability and may result in harm to others.

To differentiate between consumption behaviors that are not unethical in the sense of not being wrong and behaviors that deliberately seek to do good, we need to introduce the role of values. (It is also useful to thereby distinguish between moral values and consumer value.) An affirmative act of "goodness," promotes what may be conceived as the currency of ethics, namely fundamental human values such as rights, freedom, and well-being. These values are "what philosophers call 'prescriptive' or 'action guiding' because they provide standards for directing human choice" (Donaldson 1989: 11). Accordingly, ethics as a consumer value results from an affirmative act of goodness that promotes one or more moral values of the individual. Hence, I may participate in a consumer boycott to promote the welfare of blacks in apartheid South Africa, or contribute to a charity to prevent harm to children.

The reference to values is preferred to Holbrook's (1994b: 53) use of virtue ("regarded as pursuing the moral end just defined") in part because of the more specialized meaning of virtue found within virtue ethics. Holbrook's reference to justice (see Table 7.1) is also presumably in regard to a moral end that may be realized when ethics is a consumer value. In both cases, the realization of moral values may be considered to be more encompassing.

Unresolved, however, is whether such behaviors are truly selfless. As earlier discussed, the notion that a consumption experience may provide utility because it is ethical suggests the behavior is also self-interested. Ethical egoism is defined by Beauchamp (1982: 57) as "the theory that the only valid moral standard is the obligation to promote one's own well-being above everyone else's." Moral philosophers rarely advocate it. However, the arguments of psychological egoists have presented serious challenges to the concept of purely selfless behavior. Psychological egoism discounts as selfless even acts of great personal sacrifice (that would clearly be in keeping with the earlier more restricted definition of altruism). As Beauchamp explains (1982: 58): "The psychological egoist does not contend that people always behave in an *outwardly* selfish manner. No matter how self-sacrificing a person's behavior may be at times . . . the desire behind the action is always selfish; one is ultimately out for oneself – whether in the long or the short run." Philosophical interest in psychological egoism may be traced back to Plato. However, resolution of the issues it raises for philosophers may only lie in a greater understanding of the psychology of human motivation, including unconscious motives (Beauchamp 1982: 61–2). Nonetheless, it cannot be argued with any certainty that an affirmative act of goodness that promotes moral values of the individual is ever ultimately without self-interest.

Donaldson (1989: 10–11) notes that "values possess legitimacy beyond the boundaries of simple self-interest" and suggests the possible role of "enlightened self-interest". Hence, to conclude this initial conceptualization, ethics as a consumer value may be said to arise in a consumption experience when the individual engages in an affirmative act of goodness, promoting one or more moral values for the well-being of others and for reasons of enlightened self-interest.

## Ethics within the Typology of Consumer Value

The broader, alternative conceptualization of ethics as a consumer value (above) is more accommodating of a greater variety of consumption experiences that include ethical concern as a motivating factor, such as those "acts of charity" that Holbrook would exclude. However, this presents problems when we attempt to return to the framework. Holbrook (1994b: 53) acknowledges that "an ethical egoist . . . pursues a self-oriented perspective that is clearly inconsistent with the present typology." Yet a self-oriented perspective is conceivably a component within acts that are ostensibly or largely other-oriented. To maintain the integrity of the existing framework, it must be argued that only altruistic value is other-oriented (and active and intrinsic). Any self-interest in otherwise altruistic consumer experiences must be accounted for elsewhere in the framework. This suggests future research to consider the possibility of expanding the framework by sub-dividing ethics as a consumer value, differentiating between consumption experiences that have largely altruistic motivations and those experiences that, in addition, have a less selfless aspect. Alternatively, a more parsimonious typology might exclude the self/other-oriented dimension, especially if its antecedents are uncertain or if it proves problematic when other types of value are more closely examined.

These concerns about the fit of ethics within the typology should be seen as a call for fine-tuning and not dismissing of the framework. The framework has definite merit and highlights interesting conceptual and empirical issues. Indeed, the scope for future research using this typology is considerable, especially research that adopts an integrative approach to consumer value. By way of illustration, consider consumer trade-offs between different types of value such as play and ethics in the consumption of alcohol. (Here it is suggested that ethics is a value obtained by moderating consumption.) Research on play and ethics as potentially conflicting types of value obtained in the consumption of alcohol would inform understanding of consumer behavior and, from an industry standpoint, would indicate possible approaches to more socially responsible forms of advertising. It might also identify more effective public policy interventions.

Holbrook's perspective on the consumption experience improves our understanding of consumer behavior and points to hypotheses for consumer researchers both directly (in work to develop the framework) and indirectly (in studies across the field that might benefit from a more integrative framework). Indeed, the framework may even have the potential to serve as a paradigm for some consumer researchers.

## Notes

1 This chapter is adapted from Smith, N. C. (1996) "Ethics and the Typology of Customer Value," in *Advances in Consumer Research*, Vol. XXIII, J. G. Lynch and K. P. Corfman (eds), Provo, UT: Association for Consumer Research, 148–53.
2 With consumer boycott defined as "abstaining from purchase" one might be tempted to argue that there is no exchange and hence no consumer value obtained. This is disputed on two grounds: 1) there is still an experience related to the domain of human behavior broadly characterized by Holbrook as consumption, as in research on possessions (Belk 1991); and 2) a boycott typically involves abstaining from the purchase of a given supplier's product with a substitute purchased instead, as Holbrook notes, consumer value is a preference experience.

## References

Beauchamp, T. L. (1982) *Philosophical Ethics: An Introduction to Moral Philosophy*, New York: McGraw-Hill.

Becker, L. C. and Becker, C. C. (1992) *Encyclopedia of Ethics*, New York: Garland Publishing.

Belk, R. W. (1991) "Possessions and the Sense of Past," in R. W. Belk (ed.) *Highways and Buyways: Naturalistic Research from the Consumer Behavior Odyssey*, Provo, UT: Association for Consumer Research, 114–30.

Burke, S. J., Milberg, S. J., and Smith, N. C. (1993) "The Role of Ethical Concerns in Consumer Purchase Behavior: Understanding Alternative Processes," in *Advances in Consumer Research*, Vol. XX, L. McAlister and M. L. Rothschild (eds), Provo, UT: Association for Consumer Research, 119–22.

Donaldson, T. (1989) *The Ethics of International Business*, New York: Oxford University Press.

Engel, J. F. and Blackwell, R. D. (1982) *Consumer Behavior*, New York: The Dryden Press.

Etzioni, A. (1988) *The Moral Dimension: Toward a New Economics*, New York: Free Press.

Hofstede, G. (1980) "Angola Coffee – or the Confrontation of an Organization with Changing Values in Its Environment," *Organization Studies* 1:1.

Holbrook, M. B. (1994a) "Axiology, Aesthetics, and Apparel: Some Reflections on the Old School Tie," in M. R. DeLong and A. M. Fiore (eds) *Aesthetics of Textiles and Clothing: Advancing Multi-Disciplinary Perspectives*, Monument, CO: International Textile and Apparel Association, 131–41.

—— (1994b) "The Nature of Consumer Value: An Axiology of Services in the Consumption Experience," in R. T. Rust and R. L. Oliver (eds) *Service Quality: New Directions in Theory and Practice*, Thousand Oaks, CA: Sage, 21–71.

Laidler, H. W. (1968) *Boycotts and the Labor Struggle: Economic and Legal Aspects*, New York: Russell and Russell (reissued, first published 1913).

Levitt, T. (1995) "Marketing Myopia" in B. M. Enis, K. K. Cox, and M. P. Mokwa (eds) *Marketing Classics*, Englewood Cliffs, NJ: Prentice Hall, 3–21 (first published in *Harvard Business Review*, July–August 1960).

Smith, N. C. (1987a) "Ethical Purchase Behavior," in *Understanding Economic Behavior*, Vol. III. Proceedings of the International Association for Research in Economic Psychology, Aarhus, Denmark: Aarhus School of Business, 949–64.

—— (1987b) "Consumer Boycotts and Consumer Sovereignty," *European Journal of Marketing* 21: 5, 7–19.

—— (1990) *Morality and the Market: Consumer Pressure for Corporate Accountability*, London: Routledge.

# 8 Devaluing value

## The apophatic ethic and the spirit of postmodern consumption

*Stephen Brown*

Where to start? It is with some fear and not a little trembling that I open a new file on consumer value, even though I'm writing this longhand and only pretending to compose direct to screen like every self-respecting scholar nowadays. Jeez, they're at it everywhere, aren't they? – in restaurants, on trains, in airport departure lounges and even on trans-Atlantic flights, seemingly oblivious to the damage that their digital prestidigitation may be doing to the navigational equipment or the fact that all 400 of us may plunge screaming to our doom because some bloody economist, ethnographer or Goddam marketing researcher can't wait to download their earth-shattering thoughts onto a notebook, powerbook, laptop, palmtop or the latest Wild Bill Gatesian gizmo that enables them to write and surf the net simultaneously whilst cruising at an altitude of 35,000 feet. What a postmodern way to go. Word (for Windows) and the World (Wide Web) finally collide. *Il n'y a pas de hors Microsoft.*[1]

(You may laugh, but did you hear the one about the guy who plugged his laptop into a socket on a 747 – the ones used by ground staff to vacuum clean the planes between flights – instantaneously blew the mighty Boeing's electrical circuits and caused the fully-laden Behemoth to plummet 12,000 feet before the back-up systems kicked in? No? Not surprising, because I just made it up. And you wonder where all those urban myths come from.)

My fear and trembling, it must be stressed, are not simply the result of some post-Freudian cyber-thanatic aerophobia, albeit I keep having this weird dream about a (computer) mouse and a terrified jumbo jet. Nor are they due to the fact that this chapter is dreadfully late, appallingly late, inexcusably late, give-me-an-epidural-for-the-labour-pains late (perhaps I should have used my time over the Atlantic more productively than musing on metal fatigue and PowerPoint precipitated death dives). In this regard, please spare a thought for our good shepherd, the editor, who can't concoct some suitably uplifting concluding remarks until all his errant literary lambs are safely gathered in. I'm the Brown sheep – the test tube scrapings – of this carefully selected, painstakingly cloned, kinda pretty if you're that way inclined flock of value-added marketing Marinos. Having, on occasion, found an editorial baton in my own academic knapsack, I know only too well the frustrations of coping with laggardly contributors, on the one hand, and a looming MS deadline, on the other. What's more, when these learned sluggards completely ignore the manuscript preparation guidelines (as they always do); proceed to engage with issues that have nothing whatsoever to do with the overarching theme of the volume (if they think they'll get away with it); and, as often as not, simply write about whatever happens to take their fancy (goodness, they'll be writing about not writing next), then editorial meltdown is not only inevitable but imminent. I've been there, done that and bear the scars for souvenirs.

My textual anxieties, rather, are attributable to a problem I have with the concept of consumer value in general and the grandly, some would say grandiosely, named Typology of Consumer Value in particular. Now, I don't know about you, but whenever I come across a Capitalized Concept I go all weak at the knees, as my manifold intellectual insecurities manifest themselves. I have this overwhelming urge to abase myself before it, to kiss the hem of its gown, to retreat backwards from its presence, as one would with ostentatiously appellated potentates of legend – Lord High Executioner, Great Earth Mother, His Holiness the Capo de Cappuccino and what have you. Faced with this magnificent, munificent, magniloquent matrix, this Ur-matrix, this dominatrix matrix, this matrix maximus, this matrix *über alles*, I feel compelled to tug a forelock, to lower my voice, to refer to it at all times by its proper title, The Typology of Consumer Value (or The Typology of Value in the Consumption Experience), even though the TCV abbreviation is kinda cute. To risk anything else, surely, requires written permission – preferably in the applicant's blood or that of his first-born – which must be countersigned in triplicate by the commissioning editor (the Routledge Stasi rides again). What's more, I wouldn't dream of criticizing the concept or even mentioning the plural of value, lest I incur the wrath of our chapter wrangler, mixed metaphor minder and praetorian of professorial prolixity, Morris the Catachresis.

I suppose our scholarly sentinel will be somewhat surprised, not to say astonished, by such idiotic opening remarks. After all, he has repeatedly stressed his willingness to accept criticism, that the matrix is not set in stone, that it is simply a framework for discussion, that we contributors are not only free but *expected* to condemn his conceptualization. Frankly, one couldn't ask for anything more from an editor and, for a contributor then to respond with fear and trembling – like a rabbit transfixed in the Holbrookian headlights – hardly seems sensible. I mean, if you're not up to the task, why bother to contribute a chapter?[2]

To infer, furthermore, that the compiler is a closet authoritarian, when he is actually a pussycat personified, is almost as absurd as casting aspersions on Bill Clinton's monogamy, O.J. Simpson's innocence or Michael Jackson's parenting skills. Admittedly, it is arguable that exhibitions of academic self-abasement are singularly apt in a chapter that's supposed to be about *spirituality*, but that still doesn't excuse my unorthodox introductory remarks, flamboyant figures of speech and use of the first person singular in what purports to be a work of scholarship.

Pathetic I may be – the Marquis de Sad of marketing and consumer research (that's right no "e", they don't come much sadder than me) – but I'm not going to apologize for my anxieties, nor ask for editorial absolution. Holbrook, let's not forget, has frequently urged the marketing and consumer research community, and his copious catechumen, to adopt a capricious, creative, circuitous and, above all, self-centered approach to academic endeavor. His own publications are nothing if not egoistic, his alliterative abilities and aptitude for assonance are unequalled, and he is singular in his fondness for the first person, the all-seeing "I", the all-singing, all-dancing, all-for-one, one-for-all "I". The autobiographical "I". He may not like the fact that there are lots of little Holbrookites running around the marketing academy, trying to write creatively before they are properly house trained, but the occasional misbegotten manuscript is a small price to pay for the perpetuation of Morris's intellectual crusade.[3] Well, that's my excuse and I'm sticking to it.

However, lest you think that these textual deviations and exhibitions of ersatz self-abnegation are little more than postmodern narcissism run riot – can you just hold that mirror up a little? – let me make it clear that they do serve a purpose, that they are relevant to the Typology of Consumer Value, and that this chapter will deal with spirituality, the bottom right-hand cell of Morris's matrix. Before we do that, I suppose I ought to explain why I have such a problem with matrices per se and why The Typology of Value in the Consumption Experience gives me the stylistic shakes, caps notwithstanding. That's right, you guessed it, I'm a secret matrixomane, a backdoor boxaphile, a recovering typoloholic. I'm on the 2×2×2-step program and if I so much as glance at McDonald and Leppard's (1992) *Marketing by Matrix*, I'll be rolling in the modernist gutter before you can say BCG or TCV, come to think of it. Was it *that* obvious?

Now, don't get me wrong: as someone who has concocted one or two (by two) matrices in my time, I am well aware of the intoxicating appeal of the brutes. There's the sense of pixillated personal satisfaction, akin to completing a crossword or winning a game of naughts and crosses, that comes from their compilation. There's the inebriated feeling of spurious insightfulness that derives from imposing a coherent framework upon hitherto inchoate experience. There's the intemperate anticipation, unfailingly unrealized, that this will prove to be the contribution that catapults its creator into the pantheon of marketing immortals, the one reproduced in textbooks, lauded in lectures and, naturally, named after its suitably modest, painfully self-effacing, shy and retiring inventor (the Morris Minor Matrix, the Brown Box etc.).

At the same time, I know from painful personal experience that the two or three "key dimensions" are pretty arbitrary, having been whittled down from a much longer list of contenders and selected because they somehow seem to "work" better than the others (all of which have been tinkered with at length). The conceptual distinction between adjoining cells is often infinitesimal, though a resonant name can help disguise the fact (I name this cell "spirituality" and God bless all who flail in her). What's more, a great deal of shoehorning, massaging and general matrix manipulation is usually necessary to ensure that the field fits neatly into a multi-dimensional mould (it's a bit like packing a parachute, tucking a tent into its container or trying to close an overstuffed suitcase). And, when the framework is complete, there's the inevitable retrospective root through the literature in order to demonstrate its veracity, to find evidence to support the structure – gimcrack, jerry-built and decidedly rickety though it is. It pains me deeply to say this, but matrices are the apotheosis of the theory-ladenness of knowledge. They don't so much classify extant evidence as constitute what counts as evidence. They form not frame; they originate rather than organize; they are the iron cages of thought, the mind forg'd manacles of marketing. The "cells" are aptly named.

In fairness, matrices are rather less offensive than some of the other creations that swank on the cerebral catwalk of consumer research. You know the kind of thing I mean: time-warped boxes and arrows diagrams (seemingly written for Fortran, the Latin of the late-twentieth century); risible quasi-molecular, sub-sub-DNA structures (Crick and Watson knew my father); Great Pyramids of Geezer (constructed by middle-aged eight year olds, whose parents wouldn't buy them Lego for Christmas); or, increasingly, the clip-art sired, graphics-package promulgated monstrosities (bio-engineered from the cannibalized body parts of every other figure that has ever appeared in a marketing principles textbook).[4] Be that as it may, the matrix mongering of marketers and their consumer-orientated scions is one of the main reasons why the management sciences are held in such low esteem by the rest of the scholarly community (personally, I don't have a problem with the disdain of fellow academics – as I've never known anything else, it gets kinda reassuring after a while – but then again, I *am* convalescing from matrix cathexis).

The creators of matrices, to be sure, are well aware of the shortcomings of their conceptualizations, recognize that they are widely regarded as reductive and usually go to great pains to point out that their particular matrix is not meant to be rigid, that the categories are blurred, that the combination and recombination of cells is part of its inherent attraction. In practice, unfortunately, all these evasions, qualifications and circumlocutions go by the board or are completely ignored, especially if it is reproduced in a textbook-cum-anthology of some kind. The sad fact of the matter is that, for all their attractions (for the compiler at least), matrices are undeniably arbitrary, authoritarian, restrictive, repressive, mechanistic, methodical, utilitarian, unimaginative, inflexible, intolerable. They are redolent of the Kotlerite paradigm of analysis, planning, implementation and control. They are a monument to marketing in a non-monumental marketing milieu. They are the complete antithesis of the fluidity, flexibility, openness, ambiguity, multivocality, polysemousness of our postmodern, pre-millennial, neo-romantic times.

The Typology of Consumer Value suffers from all of these shortcomings and more besides. I'm sorry to have to say this – I'm mortified to have to say this – but I find it very difficult to accept several of the assertions that underpin the framework, although the fault is assuredly entirely mine. For instance, the basic rationale that marketing is about exchange and exchange is about value, therefore we need to know more about value, strikes me as somewhat dogmatic at best and decidedly disingenuous at worst (the marketing = exchange contention is questionable, for starters). The presupposition that value is comparative, insofar as the only valid utility assessments involve comparisons among objects within the same person, does not equate with everyday experience, or at least not mine. For Holbrook, it may not be legitimate to claim that I like Madonna more than he likes Madonna, but these are precisely the sorts of value judgments that we indulge in all the time ("I love you more than you love me"; "I'm cooler, smarter, sexier, better dressed, more with it or whatever, than the likes of you"; "I know more about values than you do, therefore my word on these matters is final"). To disallow such comparisons on the grounds of illogicality or invalidity is to erect self-supporting standards, standards which misappropriate the discourse of scientific rigour/validity/logic to render unquestionable a questionable distinction. Similarly, I simply cannot swallow Holbrook's pronouncement that value resides not in the product purchased but rather in the consumption experience derived therefrom. Yes, the consumption experience is very important, possibly of fundamental importance, but surely the product also has something to do with it, even if it's only as a cue, a trigger or an excuse for flights of hedonistic fantasy. Doubtless our avuncular editor will retort that I have misunderstood his position – after all, he argues elsewhere for an interactionist perspective, whereby value derives from some interplay between customer and product, subject and object – but, to my mind at least, this is the intellectual equivalent of having one's cake and eating it, of trying to get the best of both worlds, of living in a glass house and being encouraged to throw stones.

Worse still, the shortcomings of the Typology of Value in the Consumption Experience are reinforced by – or, rather, are the result of – the fact that it is Morris's matrix. No one but no one admires the work of Morris the Cat more than Stephen the Catastrophe, as I have elsewhere shown (Brown 1998a, 1999). Father forgive me for saying this, furthermore, but how on earth could Holbrook, one of the most prominent propagators of postmodern marketing, perhaps the finest literary stylist in our field and someone who has been a tireless champion of aesthetics, lyricism, scholarship, anti-utilitarianism and the transcendental power of great art, produce something as banal, banausic and, frankly, barbaric as The Typology of Consumer Value? This is the kind of thing we expect from managerially-oriented model-builders and analogous marketing Cro-Magnons, but not from Morris B. Holbrook. In fact, it almost beggars belief to think that Holbrook, of all people, could come up with a matrix, of all models, on the constituents of axiology, of all subjects. Surely if value is about anything, it is about beauty, wonder, sublimity, transcendence, ineffability, spirituality and so on (Gerber 1997; Magnell 1997). And we boil it down to a matrix? We can't put it into words but we can put it into a box. The greatest minds have wrestled with this intractable issue since time immemorial, or certainly since Pseudo-Longinus first explicated the sublime in the third century CE, but it takes late-twentieth-century marketing men to cut through the axiological crap. Thank God for good old-fashioned Anglo-American pragmatism, I say.

(Only joking, Morris. I'm a sucker for schemata as well, remember. Don't write nasty things about me in the next chapter. *Please.*)

What, then, is the value of the value matrix? Some may consider it efficient, many may deem it excellent, certain people may play with it, play politics with it or consider it a thing of beauty. Yet others may have their reputations enhanced because of it, become better scholarly citizens on account of its moral worth or even wholeheartedly express their faith in it (ecstatic outpourings of deeply felt emotion are perhaps too much to hope for). But I'm not one of them. I have mainlined on matrices in my time, I am familiar with the pleasures and pains of the matrix fix, I have cold-turkeyed in the 2×2 cell hell, take it from me, yet I still think the value matrix has devalued value. I believe Holbrook is trying to approach an inherently romantic issue from a neoclassical angle. However well intentioned, I feel that reductive typologies, classifications and frameworks only succeed in destroying the very thing they are trying to dissect. The butterfly of consumer value is killed in the very act of pinning it to the scholarly display board. The spirituality of consumption is not pigeonholeable, in my opinion, nor can it be captured in staid academese, the prosaic prose that passes for scholarship in our materialist and materialistic discipline. Hence my linguistic excesses, extravagances and effulgences.

The bottom line, I suppose, is that I find it very difficult to get excited about value or value judgments or whether they're valid or invalid values. Nor can I feign fascination for the purposes of this chapter. The whole issue makes me think of sad old men in anoraks – train-spotters, stamp collectors, jazz buffs – who have nothing better to do with themselves than compile lists of their all-time favorite Luc Besson movies (it's gotta be *Subway*, especially that scene where Isabelle Adjani makes her first appearance). As a wretch who sometimes subscribes, however erroneously, to the unprincipled principles of postmodernism, I just can't get enthused about these things and, as an advocate of "slacker scholarship", I'm not too enthusiastic about enthusiasm either (Brown 1998b). Anything not only goes, as far as I'm concerned, it's already outta sight, round the corner, over the horizon. Who cares whether Dylan's better than Keats, or the Beatles beat Beethoven hands down, or Coke is superior to Pepsi, or Nike negates Reebok? I suppose if I were going to get all pretentious about it – and I rarely pass an opportunity to parade my pretentiousness, as you've probably realized by now – I'd have to say that I'm with Nietzsche's "revaluation of all values" on this one, albeit I'm more of a devaluation of all values kinda guy. As Freddy makes clear, it is necessary not simply to replace one set of values with another – all values are ultimately arbitrary, not to say iniquitous – but also to question the value of the values we value, however unconsciously or inadvertently (Kaufmann 1974; Magnus and Higgins 1996).

In case you feel inclined to misconstrue my motives, let me emphasize that, while I refuse to endorse it unequivocally (or, rather, unequivocally refuse to endorse it), the Typology of Consumer Value is invaluable in another way. It's value, however, derives from its apophatic character. As everyone knows, apophasis is a theological term which refers to knowing God in terms of what (s)he is not (evil, cruel, spiteful, implacable or whatever), though it is also used as a technical term in Rhetoric for expressions which pretend not to say what is really being said. A typical example of this kind of thing – the kind of thing, incidentally, that gave Rhetoric a bad name – would be to start a chapter on, say, spirituality by self-consciously announcing what the chapter isn't about or, alternatively, throwing an arcane word – like, er, apophasis – into the argument and affecting to assume that everyone knows what it means. (Not that anyone would get away with such unscholarly behavior in a learned tome like this. Apophobia reigns in consumer research.)

Morris's value matrix, in short, is valuable because it makes us reflect on the valuelessness of matrices, on how much better off our field would be without them (or not, as the case may be), on the fact that marketing is afflicted by matrixmania (as far as other non-business disciplines are concerned), on their function as a sort of scholarly signature by which the output of our specialism is recognized (and woe betide anyone who tries to do anything different). More importantly perhaps, the Typology of Consumer Value itself is constructed on apophatic foundations. As Holbrook notes, the meaning of the various dimensions of value derive from what they are not: Quality is only understandable in terms of Beauty, Fun in terms of Morality and so on. True, these distinctions only serve to multiply the inherent definitional difficulties – what exactly do we mean by Beauty, Morality etc.? – and dialectical reasoning of this kind can hardly be described as novel. After all, the Structuralists, Marxists, Hegelians and God only knows who else got there before us (God did too, come to think of it, when he separated land and sea, light and darkness, male and female, something and nothing, good and evil). Be that as it may, apophatic thinking helps us organize our thoughts, not that most of our thoughts are worth organizing, not that organized thoughts are necessarily a good thing, not that good things are necessary, not that, not that, not that . . .

Enough, I hear you cry. No more. Engaging though your attempts to engage with your lack of engagement undoubtedly are, Stephen, and difficult though it is to stop you discussing the difficulties you have discussing what you are supposed to discuss, it's time to free the spirit. Instead of trying to raise our spirits with postmodern procrastination, prevarication, pedantry and peripherality, hit us with some real spirituality, the hard stuff, the marketing moonshine, the postmodern poteen that we know you have hidden under the Typology. Cut to the chaser.

Since you insist, let me confess that it is my belief that marketing and consumer behavior can be and often are profoundly spiritual, although I'm not going to pander to your modernist inclinations by trying to define precisely what I mean by spiritual. Such an ambition, after all, is not only unattainable but completely contrary to the spirit of our polyvalent, multi-vocal, logophobic postmodern times (hey, don't ask me what it means, you're the lexicologists around here). However, if forced under pain of excommunication, to spell out exactly what I understand by spirituality, I suppose I'd have to say that it has something to do with sacred things in general – as opposed to lay, temporal or material matters – and the experiential side of religiosity in particular (soul, sanctity, holiness, faith, belief, inspiration, immateriality, immortality, transcendence, saintliness, ecstasy etc.). If, indeed, I were the pretentious type, I could get all dewy-eyed and Hegelian about it – the self knowledge of Absolute Spirit (*Geist*) is arrived at only through the seriousness, the pain, the patience and the labour of the negative – but my heart isn't really in pseudo-philosophising at the moment, let alone my soul. It is sufficient to note that the spirit of spirituality seems to be very widespread at present, what with the latter-day emergence of New Religious Movements, many of which contain a strong ecstatic element, as well as the secular forms of spirituality that we find in New Ageism, UFOlogy, wicca and what have you (Cotton 1995). In this regard, the word also carries intriguing connotations of spiritualism, communicating with the dear departed via ouija boards, mediums, seances, crystal-balls and the like.

Of course, for many commentators, management science *per se* is a form of crystal-ball gazing. Micklethwait and Wooldridge (1996) describe its exponents as "witch doctors"; Sherden (1998) compares scenario planning to astrology; and several academic authorities have recently drawn attention to the essentially spiritual side of organisations (e.g., Firth and Campbell 1997; Pattison 1997). The marketing concept, moreover, is a form of quasi-religious dogma – an ideology possibly – and few would deny that the theological trope has provided rich pickings for a number of commentators. Kent (1996), for example, notes that the spirit of marketing scholarship is embedded in faith: faith in the efficacy of its preachings; faith in the catechisms of its teachings; faith in the textbooks of marketing doctrine; faith in the rituals of marketing planning, situation analyses, research reports, alliterative incantations, preferably beginning with "P"; and, not least, the magical power of matrix thinking (hey, who needs crystal therapy when you've got a $2\times2\times2$ typology?). Another academic apostate, who really ought to be burnt at the stake for such unregenerate blasphemy, has warned postmodern marketing backsliders that "in order to enter the land of marketing milk and honey, you must become a true believer, you must refuse to stray from the logical empiricist straight and narrow, you must resist the epistemological temptations that are placed in your path. Only then will the celestial city open its gates and permit you to enter. The eschaton of marketing orientation can be yours but only if you subscribe to the teachings of the prophets and the four commandments of analysis, planning, implementation and control" (Brown 1995: 163).

When it comes to consumer behavior, moreover, a strong spiritual element is discernible. For the purposes of discussion – yes, I too can play the reductionist card when it suits me – it may be useful to distinguish between consumer spirituality and spiritual consumption.[5] The former refers to religious or spiritual determinants of consumer behavior, whereas the latter pertains to the spiritual or religious character of consumption itself (Hirschman 1985). As a glance at almost any textbook on consumer research readily testifies, religious convictions are a significant influence on the buying behavior of certain consumer subcultures (e.g., Peter and Olson 1993; Solomon 1995). The acquisitional idiosyncrasies of Jews, WASPs, Mormons and evangelical Protestants, amongst others, have been studied in depth (Hirschman 1983, 1988; LaBarbara 1987; Belk 1994), as have the distinctive repertoires of consumption-related activities associated with significant religious occasions and locations such as Christmas, Easter, theological theme parks etc. (Hirschman and LaBarbara 1989; O'Guinn and Belk 1989; Belk 1993). In certain respects, however, the most interesting aspect of these activities pertains to what is proscribed rather than what is purchased. Thus, fascinating though it is to discover that Christian fundamentalists have an above average propensity to buy religious magazines, attend to religious broadcast media, participate in community-welfare organizations, indulge in good works and listen to country or gospel music, the really remarkable thing, for me at least, is their aversion to alcohol, drugs, sexual promiscuity and ostentation in apparel, their reluctance to listen to rock 'n' roll or death metal; and their preparedness to boycott stores that sell *Playboy*, the sponsors of *Saturday Night Live*, movies like Scorsese's *Last Temptation of Christ* and, famously, Procter & Gamble on account of its "Satanic" logo (*Economist* 1995; McDaniel and Burnett 1991; Weiss 1995). Indeed, as someone who was brought up in a washed-in-the-blood-of-the-lamb Protestant household, I was made constantly aware of what I couldn't or shouldn't do – go to the cinema, watch television or read newspapers on a Sunday, patronize retail outlets operated by the non-elect in general and Catholics in particular. Naturally I rebelled, but it has clearly stayed with me, somewhere in the depths of my unconscious. One of the first papers I ever wrote was about the impact of religion on Northern Ireland retailing and consumer behavior (Brown 1986).

Most people's purchasing activities, to be sure, are not determined by deeply held religious convictions, or at least not in today's decidedly secular – some would say degenerate – post-industrial, post-sacerdotal society. However, this does not mean to say that spirituality is absent from contemporary consumer behavior. On the contrary, consumption *itself* is increasingly imbued with a spiritual cast, as copious cultural commentators have recorded (Lasch 1979; Sherry 1987; Jhally 1989; Leiss, Kline, and Jhally 1990; Schudson 1993). The things once regarded as unalterably profane, unspeakably sinful, veritable one-way tickets to the gates of Gehenna – indulgence, extravagance, luxury, usury, hedonism, materialism, greed, covetousness, fashion consciousness and consumption in all its maleficent manifestations – are now deemed, if not quite next to Godliness, certainly within spitting distance of devotional. Shopping, in short, has become sanctified. Consumption is an act of consecration. St Michael is the patron saint of patronage behavior. Hallowed be thy brand name. So marked is this sacralization trajectory that the religious festivals of the twenty-first century are liable to comprise the Feast of the Seven-Eleven, Ronald McDonald's Thanksgiving, St Johnny Walker Day, the Dr Pepper Pentecost, Armani Ascension, Hilton Hanukkah, Rolex Ramadan and many more besides (see Belk 1996). Incredible, yes, but don't scoff too soon. Gucci, remember, moves in mysterious ways. And if Donna Karan's conceptions aren't immaculate, I don't know whose are.

Although the spiritual side of shopping, not to mention those cathedrals of consumption colloquially known as shopping malls, has attracted a considerable amount of academic attention, perhaps the fullest expression of this perspective has recently been articulated by Miller (1998). According to his modestly titled text, *A Theory of Shopping*, he argues that routine grocery shopping behavior is a kind of quasi-religious ritual, a form of familial and societal devotion – an act of unreciprocated love, no less – far removed from the base utilitarianism of economistic caprice. In an increasingly secular world, the romantic ideal of love serves as a substitute for religious observance. Passion has replaced piety, or rather compassion has replaced piety, since this romanticized religiosity is made manifest in everyday exhibitions of concern, care, sensitivity and dedication to the needs of others. Miller maintains, in fact, that shopping is akin to sacrifice, in so far as it is performed primarily to influence other people's behavior. Just as gods are petitioned to perform certain acts in return for votive offerings, so too the shopping ritual is performed to persuade people – those to whom the shopper is devoted – to behave in a certain manner, to prove worthy of the attentive treatment, to become deserving of what is being done for them. In short, to become better people ("eat up your greens," "you'll look good in this," "what about that weekend break in Paris?").

Miller's cosmological conception of consumption is indubitably on the wild and woolly side – he openly acknowledges that some might consider it "sanctimonious crap" (p. 62) – yet his emphasis on the spiritual side of shopping undoubtedly accords with my own admittedly amateurish research. For the past couple of years I have been asking final-year undergraduate students to write extended autobiographical essays about their shopping behavior. By inviting them, in effect, to reflect, ponder, mull over, cogitate, interrogate and observe their own actions, activities and proclivities as consumers – whether it be convenience shopping, comparison shopping, speciality shopping, Christmas shopping, shopping for gifts, hobbies, collections or whatever (it's entirely up to them) – I hope to gain a deeper understanding, or at least a different understanding, of the character of contemporary consumer behavior than is typically attainable from traditional qualitative methods like depth interviews and focus groups.[6]

Although this introspective research procedure is fairly routine in the humanities and certain social sciences, such as anthropology (Denzin (1997) has recently termed it 'mystories', albeit 'buystories' better describes what I've been trying to do), it has proven highly controversial in marketing and consumer research. This is hardly the place to make a case for the introspective method, nor to criticize the critics – Holbrook (1995, 1996) and Gould (1991, 1995) have proven more than adequate to the task. It is only necessary to note that while all techniques have shortcomings, the insights they provide help nullify any instrumental imperfections. Procedural propriety has its place, but so too does percipience, pertinence and perspicacity. Rejecting research on methodological grounds alone is the last resort of the reactionary (or, more usually, ex-radicals who are disturbed by subsequent demonstrations of the fact that their radicalism isn't that radical).

Methodological wrangles notwithstanding, the essays themselves are remarkably rich, evocative and, in many cases, exceptionally well written. Averaging approximately 2,000 words in length, they compare very favourably to the results of broadly analogous exercises undertaken by Rook (1987) and Hassay and Smith

(1996), which comprise 250 and 400 word *maxima*, respectively. On reading the one hundred plus accounts, moreover, one cannot help but be struck by the apparent "spirituality" of the reported consumption experiences. Again and again and again, the essayists comment on what can only be described as numinous aspects of shopping. For example:

> There it was, almost as if a light from Heaven was shining on it, my lime green shirt. Sizing wasn't a problem, they had everything. I immediately spotted a size 16 inch collar, this was what service was all about, meeting the demands of the consumer.
>
> (female, 20)

> Then like a vision from Heaven I see it, hanging high on a rail. The glow from its warm colour engulfs me. I bound over to where the burnt orange suit is hanging and search like a madwoman for my size. Yes, it's here. Happy dayz, I want to shout out loud. I hug the suit close to me, like a child with a teddy that someone is trying to take away
>
> (female, 20)

> On leaving the shopping centre we had to exit past River Island. I happened to glance at the window display and my attention was caught by a beautiful gleaming pair of shoes – which seemed literally to be crying out for me to buy them. Making my way over for a further investigation I knew that I was going to enter the store and try them on. . . . Standing in the queue satisfied that I had found something I liked and which fitted, I happened to glance around the rest of the outlet and to my shock and utter amazement were a number of suits neatly lined up against the wall, smiling at me. Hesitantly I made my way over; there it was, the perfect suit – similar to the one I had viewed earlier except this had a skirt to match! Lifting it gently from the rail, scared that I would find a flaw in the material or discover that it wouldn't fit, I was approached by an assistant who not only carried it into the changing area but brought the same suit in two different colours (was I dreaming?). Obviously not because, after trying on the suit and deciding that not only did it fit me perfectly but that green was the nicest color on me and that it matched with the new shoes I was also about to purchase, the assistant took the garments from me and to the cashier desk. Was it my imagination or had this girl a halo around her head? I don't know, but I followed her and paid for my purchases.
>
> (female, 21)

These ecstatic experiences, it must be stressed, are not confined to the product–purchaser dyad, significant though that is. On the contrary, broadly similar reactions are reported about individual retail stores, arresting window displays, vacant car parking spaces and promotional deals inscribed with those blessed words "sale", "free" or "reduced" (the "hallelujah", "hosanna" and "Jesus saves" of consumer society, surely). Analogous effects are also evident on encountering sales assistants of a pulchritudinous persuasion, although presenting personal magnetism as "spiritual" is stretching things somewhat. True, the mystical wings of many religious denominations, which tend to emphasize the union or coming together of believer and holy spirit, are often astonishingly sensuous (see Voaden 1995), but unless you have led a very sheltered life, you're unlikely to conclude that piety rather than priapism is the prime mover of this particular procurement episode.

> My attention was drawn towards this absolutely beautiful woman. Her hair, shape and posture, everything about this woman appealed to me. Being hypnotized by her presence I drifted over towards her, explaining with my tongue tied round my tonsils that I would like to see some suits. She gently pointed upstairs, indicating that it was not her department. Still fantasizing about this woman, I was promptly brought back to reality by a "45 stone" woman, carrying what must have been a month's shopping, as she was forced to thrust herself against me.
>
> (male, 22)

Indeed, it seems to me that the issue of labeling is all important. The way we frame and interpret our transcripts, the metaphors we bring to bear, the words we allocate or attribute to them help shape and determine what we actually find. Consider the following extracts:

> As I stepped into the shop I felt all the familiar symptoms take a grip of me. I felt so panicky, there was so much to look at. My eyes darted everywhere as I tried to take everything in, all at once. I was petrified in case in the split second that it took me to scan the shop that I would have missed my dream dress and that someone else would have bought it. My heart sunk and leapt with exhilaration all at once. Then I saw it. In that split second everything else in the world seemed to go out of focus. All I could see was that dress. Before I knew what was happening, I had unconsciously walked towards it. It was as if it contained a magnet. It was a rich chocolate brown colour with a luxurious velvet texture. I just knew that it would be perfect on. My heart stopped as I frantically scrambled inside for the price tag. It was meant for me.
>
> (female, 20)

> Dutifully, I browsed around to the clothes section and then my 'sensible' head started to grow weak as the most amazing jacket drew me like a magnet, like a fish to bait. My hands were trembling and knees weak as I made my way over to the object of my desire. It was mine! I had to have it! How did shopping for a birthday present eventually lead to this paralysing moment? It was versatile and could be co-ordinated with almost anything. Oh yes, I want it and God help anyone who stands in my way! Yes! I took deep breaths to

conquer hyper-ventilating and quickly searched for my size. They better have it! A size 10 red jacket soon replaced the worn-out black one on my back. My heart pounding (why did shopping always have this ridiculous effect on me?), I whisked the jacket to the counter and just like that, all in a turn of a card, my shopping trip was complete.

(female, 21)

The minute that I walked into that shop I was lost. I wandered around the shop in a daze, just glancing at everything because I knew that I couldn't afford to do anything else. Then I saw it. I walked over to it in a dream-like fashion, scared stiff of seeing it up close. My legs were like jelly as I approached it. Somewhere along the journey Rosaleen had joined me. "It's fabulous, just perfect for you," she gushed. As I stretched out my hand to hold the dress I thought I would faint. It was the most perfect dress in the whole world. It was scarlet red, the perfect color for Christmas. It had satin straps, a velvet bodice and then fell to the ground in layers of satin. It was even the right length. "I have to try it on," I whispered to Rosaleen. The next few minutes passed in a haze. The dress was perfect, but I couldn't get it, could I? I had already looked at the price tag on it. My mind started to work overtime, I knew that I couldn't let an opportunity like this pass me by. I would regret it for the rest of my life.

(female, 20)

Now, few would deny that some sort of ecstatic, emotionally charged experiences are taking place here. But how do we portray them? Are they examples of shopping spirituality? Well, it all depends on what we mean by, and how we define, "spirituality". Certainly a kind of quasi-mystical, extra-ordinary, super-natural coming together – a blissful blending of object and subject – seems to be occurring. If, as Belk, Wallendorf, and Sherry (1989) contend, the characteristic features of spirituality include: *hierophany*, where the sacred dramatically manifests itself; *kratophany*, a powerful sense of attraction-cum-repulsion; and *ecstasy*, a transcendent feeling of standing outside oneself, then such experiences can reasonably be described as spiritual.

At the same time, however, they can just as easily be described in erotic terms – erotic verging on the orgasmic, in point of fact. It certainly seems that way to me. But then, I have a dirty mind and am inclined to see sex everywhere, even in the ice cubes of advertisements for alcoholic beverages. (Hey, whaddya mean they're subliminal embeds? I'm *supposed* to feel that way? There *is* carnality in the cubes? You'll be telling me they put naked mud-wrestlers in the Rorschach ink blots next. Well, somebody did!) Doubtless there are many other ways of explicating these things – as play, aesthetics, (im)morality and so on – almost as many, in truth, as are found in The Typology of Consumer Value. And that's part of the problem I have with the matrix. Once you renege and begin to believe in the thing, you're on the slippery slope to positivism and, before you know it, you're dancing with the devils of analysis, planning, implementation and control, gamboling at the feet of the Goat of Marketing Mendes, taking an oath of fealty to Philip, the Prince of Marketing Darkness . . .

Naturally, we can't place too much reliance on the contents of a collection of autobiographical essays, however we define, delimit or defibrillate the categories. In this regard, of course, the essays merely reinforce points that have been made by several other consumer researchers, most notably Belk, Wallendorf, and Sherry (1989). In a landmark paper predicated on the findings of the Consumer Odyssey, a titanic scholarly voyage into the heartland of American consumption, they outlined the domains of sacred consumption (places, times, tangible things, intangibles, persons and experiences); noted the processes by which "ordinary" possessions become sacralized (ritual, pilgrimage, quintessence, gift-giving, collecting, inheritance and external sanction); and explained the ways in which sacredness was maintained and perpetuated (separation of sacred and profane, performance of sustaining rituals, continuation through inheritance and tangibilized contamination). Although not everyone is convinced by the appropriateness of the Odyssians' theological analogy (e.g., Holbrook 1995; McCreery 1995), it is difficult to gainsay their contention that "consumption involves more than the means by which people meet their everyday needs. Consumption can become a vehicle of transcendent experience; that is, consumer behavior exhibits certain aspects of the sacred" (Belk, Wallendorf, and Sherry 1989: 2)

If we accept that the spirit of consumption is abroad, then it seems reasonable to ask when and how this miracle transpired. After all, our insatiable desire to consume – exemplified, for many, by the mendacious money-grubbing antics of televangelists (Brown 1997) – is a comparatively recent phenomenon and by no means innate. On the contrary, "traditional" consumption is really quite fixed (a fixity reinforced, not to say rigidly policed, by the anti-materialistic ethos of an essentially clerical society), with only a finite number of needs to be filled. "Today, of course, matters seem to be reversed – the modern consumer considers with alarm anyone who does not want to consume more and more, who does not seem interested in new wants and desires" (Corrigan 1997: 10). Indeed, it is important to emphasize that almost every commentator on today's postmodern society stresses the overwhelming significance of consumption, the fact that people's identities are no longer defined by their occupations, social class, political affiliations and religious beliefs, but by their inventory of possessions, their repertoire of requisite brand names, their deck of credit cards, unshuffled or otherwise. It can, admittedly, be countered that this ostensible consuming mania is largely an artefact of the academic gaze. After ignoring consumption for decades, sociologists, anthropologists, cultural theorists and the like have finally acknowledged its place in the greater scheme of things, though some would say they're overcompensating (e.g., Gabriel and Lang 1995; Falk and Campbell 1997; Featherstone 1991). The notion of a pre-lapsarian consumer paradise, where sacred was sacred and profane profane, has also been convincingly refuted. As McDannell (1995) brilliantly demonstrates, consumption and Christianity have always been very closely related.

Be that as it may, it is not unreasonable to surmise that some kind of post-sacerdotal consumer revolution has transpired, that the traditional anti-consumption ethos of the church has been sacrificed on the alter of materialism. For example, I live in a community which remains deeply religious, to put it mildly, yet churches regularly hold services in the "nave" of our biggest shopping mall and the headquarters of the (declining) Presbyterian Church in Ireland has recently been converted into an upscale retailing development. Meanwhile, the (burgeoning) fundamentalist sects are literally awash in filthy lucre, as their ostentatious "megachurches", massive auditoria set in a sea of car-parking spaces, amply testify. God and Mammon may not be fornicating just yet, but they're undoubtedly at the heavy petting stage in my particular neck of the woods.

In our attempts to comprehend the advent of this credo of consumption, this belief in buying, these articles of acquisitional faith, perhaps the most significant contribution has come from sociologist Colin Campbell (1987), who contended that a "romantic ethic" stimulated the spirit of modern consumerism. Faced with the Weberian conundrum concerning the emergence of consumer society, at a time when the Puritan ethos of self-denial, dispassion, asceticism and the accumulation of capital was purportedly at its height, Campbell reported that Weber's Protestant ethic only really held sway until the end of the seventeenth century. Thereafter, thanks to the Neoplatonists' dilution of the austere Dissenting tradition; the emotional ecstasies that characterized the pre-romantic Age of Sensibility; and the Romantics' self-absorbed emphasis upon contemplation, longing, unrequited love, and the protean powers of the human imagination; a climate conducive to the advent of "modern autonomous imaginative hedonism" was created. According to Campbell, this desire for pleasure, as opposed to utilitarian need fulfilment, was driven by a disparity between idealized pre-experience expectations and the all too imperfect reality of actual consumption experiences themselves. This dialectic of imaginative anticipation and disappointing outcome generated a self-perpetuating desire for consuming experiences, an insatiable appetite for different, for new, for more, and more exciting, consumer behaviors. Consumption, in short, became an end in itself, an end expedited, exacerbated and exonerated by the romantic ethic.

Pathbreaking though it proved, Campbell's thesis is not without its critics. Holbrook (1993, 1996), for example, has challenged his representation of Romanticism – claiming that it ignores key elements in the Romantic Movement, most notably its medieval and oriental inclinations – though the romantic revolution was so disparate, and subject to *post hoc* reinterpretation, that de-emphasizing certain strands seems unavoidable, especially in a work which doesn't claim to offer a comprehensive account of Romanticism (Brown 1998c). More meaningfully perhaps, Campbell disregards (or, rather, considers but downplays) the pro-active part played by marketing-related institutions and developments – department stores, national brands, advertisements, magazines, gaslight, improved distribution networks – many of which date from the (late) romantic epoch (Fullerton 1985, 1988). Campbell's intimation that consumption experiences *always* prove disappointing is also questionable, because it is perfectly possible to exceed consumer expectations, as every exponent of services marketing can reliably attest. Once satisfaction is permitted, however, Campbell's thesis breaks down, since it is predicated on the assumption that consumers' pre-experience experiences, which are rehearsed and anticipated through day-dreaming, reverie and suchlike, are unfailingly superior to the "real thing". It is this disjunction between perfect image and imperfect reality that perpetuates the whole process and stimulates consumer desire for more (which are once again imaginatively prefigured and once again disappoint, thereby stimulating the desire for more and more and more).

While it may not explain everything, Campbell's romantic ethic helps us comprehend why today's postmodern consumers seem to be consumed with consumption, take pleasure from pleasure, desire to desire and find Heaven and Hell in a bar of chocolate (where sinful indulgence meets spiritual experience). Equally significant for his thesis, though less remarked upon, is the all-important part played by customer dissatisfaction. The consuming urge, for Campbell at least, is driven by disappointment, by failure, by frustration, rather than contentment, satiation and the blissed out transcendence of satisfying one's acquisitive inclinations. Now, I appreciate that I'm not exactly a leading academic authority on consumer research – ham-fisted dabbler perhaps – but it seems to me that the aversive, contra-spiritual side of consumption is of considerable conceptual consequence. Before we go any farther, however, let me make it clear that I'm not referring to the counter-spiritual components of the Typology of Consumer Value like utilitarianism, efficiency or convenience (i.e., the "opposite" cells of the matrix). I'm thinking, rather, of the apophatic aspects of transcendental consumer encounters – call it blasphemous buying, if you wish – such as the unremitting horror, the frustrations, the hellish, well-nigh purgatorial occurrences that are an integral but often overlooked part the shopping experience. For every manifestation of the Holy Spirit in Harrods or Hamleys, for every moment of extra-sensory bliss brought about by burying one's head in a bucket of Ben and Jerry's, there are encounters that only Mephistopheles himself and his mephitic marketing myrmidons could have concocted. Ironically, however, it is these abominable consumer experiences, these Stygian shopping torments, these infernal retailing regions, that render the pleasurable side of shopping so rapturous, exhilarating, joyous, spiritual – to some extent at least. An apophatic dialectic of good and evil, pleasure and pain, sacred and profane thus appears to obtain.

Once again, my students' introspective essays illustrate this kako-spiritual state of affairs. Shopping encounters are frequently described in hellish, nightmarish, soul-in-torment terms. Evil spirits, so it seems, are abroad in the retailing environment, whether it be with regard to the well-established fact that the "other" line always moves faster or the unhinged shopping cart that is plainly suffering from demonic possession or the puckish goods that prefer to hide themselves away, but only when you are specifically searching for them (at all other times they are irritatingly ubiquitous), or the shamans of the shopping center, who shake their cure-for-cancer collecting receptacles in the faces of credulous passers-by.

Miracles R Us. Then, of course, there's the evil eye – the baleful stare – employed by sales clerks to inform us that we are not welcome in, not worthy of, the hallowed halls of their blessed retail establishment. And if that doesn't work, they employ certain infallible spells and incantations, such as "can I help you?" or "are you looking for anything in particular?", that are guaranteed to exorcise the shopping spirit of even the most eager would-be purchaser. What's more, retailers actually have the postmodern gall to appropriate the spirit of Christmas for their decidedly desanctified ends, only to turn *that* into a well-nigh purgatorial experience. Eternity in the lake of fire seems like a bubble bath by comparison.

> We eventually get our trolley and it seems to be quite co-operative. As soon as we enter the supermarket, the trolley begins to squeak and yes, you've guessed it, the wheels have minds of their own, oblivious and uninterested in what way I may wish to go. Oh no, we've hired the trolley from Hell! As we stand and plan our route of attack, I receive a sharp dig in the ankles from a trolley being badly navigated by a granny with a semi-satanic grin on her face. "Sorry," she mutters, then off she shuffles. . . . The next stop is the meat counter. As we go towards our destination, the trolley from Hell seems to have its own ideas and veers off in the direction of the cereal display. Just missing by inches, we gently persuade the trolley to come round to our way of thinking by giving it a good hard kick. I do not know if this treatment did the trolley any good but it sure made me feel better.
>
> (female, 21)

> We went into the shop and proceeded up the stairs to the ladies' department. On the way up the stairs the sales assistants from the men's department stared at us as if we had horns. When we got upstairs we had a quick look around the rest of the stock and at the price tags, which were quite dear. We could not find the outfit that was displayed in the downstairs window, so we asked one of the two sales assistants to show it to us. She took a long hard look at us, she looked us up and down and then went to get the skirt and jumper. By this stage I felt like I was the lowest class that could be found and that I was dressed as a tramp, which I was not actually.
>
> (female, 22)

> Now I had a personal crusade to accomplish and God help the people who hold me back . . . outside I encountered one group of people whom I truly and wholeheartedly despise with every atom in my body. They will certainly ruin any chance of having a pleasant shopping experience. A guy was holding his arm aloft and preaching, no screaming, about how we had all lost the meaning of Christmas. I mean, how dare he tell me what to do and how to spend Christmas. If I want to squander my money and get drunk every night, it's my God given right. I don't come into town wearing a sandwich-board and shout my feelings and beliefs to the world, so why should he?
>
> (male, 22)

Noisome as the incubi and succubae of shopping undoubtedly are, there is one malefic occurrence that surpasses all other malefences in the hellfire-singed, brimstone-besmirched,  impale-my-nether-regions-upon-a-rusty-spike-until-the-end-of-time league. And that is *not getting what one's looking for* (no matter how inchoate or ill-formed the consuming impulse may be). In fact, it goes without saying that whenever merchandise is available, it always *but always* turns out to be the wrong colour, size, shade, fit, brand, model, specification, price or whatever. Fate intervenes to ensure that failure is ever-present, that dissatisfaction is guaranteed. Worse still, failure is agonizingly ever-present since the fit, colour, match or specification is *almost* but not quite right, every size is stocked *except* the one that is required, the *very last* item was sold only half-an-hour beforehand (and replenishment, naturally, will take several weeks), the goods *are* available in one's local branch (which was earlier bypassed in favour of the "better choice" at the main outlet) and, when a purchase is eventually made, the *exact same* merchandise is sure to be spotted in another shop, at a substantially lower price. It is no exaggeration to state that when consumer expectations are raised, only to be dashed against the rocks of stockouts, the anguish thereby engendered is truly satanic, chthonic, diabolical.

> Sinking my feet into the deep pile carpet I felt soothed by the gentle music. I walked to the ladieswear department and there it was, the dress of all dresses! A warm chiffon creation with layer upon layer of quality textile, flowing from a fitted satin bodice, soft to the touch and pleasing to the eye. Feeling euphoric, I sprinted to the first assistant that I could find and asked her to fetch my size. She apologetically informed me that "them dresses are out of stock, love." Gutted, I reluctantly returned the dress to its rail and meandered down the escalator to the Food Hall.
>
> (female, 22)

> After waiting patiently to cross at the traffic lights, I almost sprinted over and hailed the shop with adoration. Passing the fully glassed window that contained what looked like hundreds of shoes, my eyes for once could not see enough. I was almost pushing other so-called shoppers out of the way to determine whether or not the display contained the one and only thing I wanted. And there they were, gorgeously standing on a tall, almost regal platform, a pair of sleek, well cut, long, knee-length boots! My heart jumped, my stomach leapt and my eyes almost doubled in size. I bounced forward, almost knocking down a customer deeply engrossed in pair of shoes. When I reached my desired destination, I ran my hands up and down their tailored physique. I lifted them gently off the platform, eased the zip down, slid off my sandal and sock, and placed my foot into my dream boot. They looked fabulous. I slowly began zipping them up, but alas they stopped just above my ankle. The fat (or as I prefer to call it – large calves) was destroying and obviating my chances of success. It was looking at me almost saying "you haven't a hope in hell of getting this zip past me love" . . . I attempted to pull

up the zips on a number of different styles, but it was useless. I seriously wanted to take a bacon slicer to my legs and cut half of it away. So again I left the shop empty-handed.

(female, 21)

I had made it to the front of the queue and was facing an overly attractive girl who was about twenty or twenty-one years of age. The wait was worthwhile, I thought. I gave her the docket that I had carefully filled out and she proceeded to type the information into her little computer. Standing with £40 in my hand I prepared to pay for the product. The following conversation took place:

"I'm sorry sir, but there does not appear to be any of those products in stock at the present moment."

"You're kidding, aren't you?"

"I'm afraid not, but we can order you the product from another branch but it may not be here for Christmas. It is a Christmas present, isn't it?"

My initial thoughts of this girl being a goddess were ruined in a matter of seconds. This girl had suddenly turned from a romantically approachable girl into the wicked witch of the west. I followed the yellow brick road directly out of the store. The thought of nooses and razor blades clearly in my head.

(male, 21)

Indeed, if there is an absolutely inviolate law of the marketplace, it is that whenever one is flush with funds or looking for something in particular, there is nothing to be found, whereas the most wonderful merchandise – the perfect item – always materializes at the most inopportune moment, when the pocketbook is empty or there are other more pressing pecuniary demands to be met. God, so it seems, continues to conspire against our consuming passions, even if the church has lost its way.

When I am looking for something specific, like an outfit for a wedding, I can be sure that even if I spend all day, and look around every clothing outfit, I will never find just the right outfit that I am looking for, or if I do, it will not be available in my size.

(female, 20)

I wanted something new to wear, so I traipsed round every clothing shop I could find, but I could not find anything I liked that I could afford. That is just typical as whenever I have no money, I see plenty of things that I would love to have and when I do have money to spend, I cannot find anything at all. If I do see something I like and it is within my price range, it is sure not to be available in my size. I must be the unluckiest person in the world.

(female, 21)

It seems to me that every time I go shopping with a certain article in mind, I can never get what I am looking for, but when I have no money I see several things I like.

(female, 22)

The story of my life at present is "sorry but . . . we ran out of stock yesterday", "we don't seem to stock your size sir." But just why do they not have my size, or stock that particular item? Oh, but why?, tell me why? Is it not a simple request to have every item in every size, in every flavour, all of the time? And, when you finally make a decision "they" are all the time working and plotting against my choice. So one may ask, why decide at all? You know what they say about shopping; it's the pastime of the masses, everyone partakes in it to a greater or lesser extent. Children buy, teenagers buy, mothers buy, fathers buy, young and old buy, everyone buys. But why can't I?

(male, 21)

Well, no joy! I still hadn't spent a penny. I always find this. When I have no money I see lots of things that I would love to purchase and can't afford, and when I do intend to spend money nothing seems to appeal to me.

(female, 22)

What, then, are we to make of all these hateful fateful encounters and the abyssal anti-spiritual depths of the shopping experience generally? Well, rather than try to get too serious and scholarly about it – justifying my, er, methodology, defending the mode of exposition, summarizing the findings, such as they are – let me just conclude by suggesting that the nugatory side of shopping, the must-have-can't-have component of consumer behavior, the aptly named "sorrows" of consumption (Holbrook 1993), remains an enormously important yet somewhat neglected issue. Consumption may well be spiritual or magical, for some people at certain times, but for other people at different times, the spirits are evil and the magic is black. And, while this may seem like a comparatively trivial point, it has major implications for Campbell's much-vaunted "romantic ethic", his thesis that contemporary consumer behavior is driven by heightened pre-experience expectations and post-purchase disappointments. This may well be the case, but the evidence of my introspective essays suggests that consumer dejection, dis-satisfaction and disenchantment derives as much from the frustrations of *not* getting what they want as it does from the discontent that inevitably accompanies the attainment of our heart's desire. Failure, in fact, further stimulates consumer desire, heightens the anticipation and fuels the fantasy that, according to Campbell, eventually slams into the brick wall of unromantic everyday reality. What's more, since Campbell's thesis is premised on the questionable assumption that consumption experiences are always anti-climactic, introducing a double negative dimension creates a conceptual space for the admittedly paradoxical possibility of customer satisfaction, even if this is short lived. If, in addition,

Douglas's (1997) antithetical stance on shopper behavior – her eminently plausible thesis that consumers often don't know what they want but know what they don't want – is taken into account, then it can be contended, contra Campbell, that an apophatic ethic informs the spirit of postmodern consumption.

In this regard, of course, the apophatic ethic of shopper abjection is perfectly in keeping with the paradigmatic schema of religious belief (Hamilton 1995). Religious faith involves an ever-deepening, ever more intense cycle of spiritual agony and ecstasy. As doubts, anxieties, tests, torments, temptations and ordeals are overcome or obviated, the supplicant's convictions and commitment are augmented, heightened, enhanced, reinforced. Counterintuitive though this appears at first, religious beliefs are immeasurably strengthened by doubt, disappointment, despair and their associated trials and tribulations. The same is true of consumption; the same is true of life; the same is true of scholarship. As you've probably realized by now – no flies on you lot, that's for sure – this chapter has been included in *Consumer Value* solely on account of its apophatic spirit. It is badly written, abysmally assembled, egregiously unscholarly, totally incoherent. Good for nothing, in fact, except making the rest look learned. But, hey, if it weren't for the rotten apple how would you know the rest of the barrel was okay? Is it only by devaluing value that the value of value is eventually evaluated. And if you believe that, you really ought to get out more . . .

## Notes

1 Don't talk to me about incoming meteorites, alien invasions or the prophecies of Nostradamus. The world will end, not with a whisper, not with a bang, but with a crash – a cataclysmic crash of computer systems. Oh no, the millennium bug. We've had our (silicon) chips. Head for the cyber-hills. We need a virtual ark of some kind . . .

2 Ask a silly question. Because it's a publication, bozo! Don't you know, we academics would do anything for an another addition to our vitas – slice off extraneous bodily appendages, sell our spouses into bondage, pretend we know something about abstruse subjects like axiology. When Morris foolishly asked me to contribute to this text, I was under the impression that axiology had something to do with automobile maintenance (the science of subframes, perhaps?). What's more, when the abstract of this chapter went to outside review, one of the referees described it as "self-indulgent stupidity masquerading as cleverness." To be honest, I was really rather tickled by this remark, since I've never been accused of cleverness before. Stupidity? Yes, on countless occasions. Self-indulgence? I'd prefer not to discuss it, lest I'm accused of over-indulging in self-indulgence. And, while I appreciate that I'm merely masquerading as clever, at least it's a start, you must agree.

3 As the one and only Friedrich Nietzsche (1992: 4) puts it: "The man of knowledge must be able not only to love his enemies but also to hate his friends. One repays a teacher badly if one remains only a pupil. And why, then, should you not pluck at my laurels? You respect me; but how if one day your respect should tumble? Take care that a falling statue does not strike you dead!"

4 You know, they tell me that the geneticists of consumer research are working on a smart card which predicts your purchases for the next fifty years and correlates this against your projected income stream, inclusive of pensions, gratuities and consultancy fees you haven't told the taxman about, before deciding whether to accept payment, rescind your credit rating or dole out double cents-off coupons. You read it here first.

5 A similar distinction is made in an important paper by Hirschman (1985). She describes them as "the spirituality of products" and "ancestral traditions."
6 Questionnaire surveys? Sample surveys? Large-scale, positivistic, tick-box surveys? Is-that-an-attitude-statement-in-your-pocket-or-are-you-just-pleased-to-see-me surveys? I spit on such surveys, though I have difficulty expectorating after the first 200 or so!

# References

Belk, R. W. (1993) "Materialism and the making of the modern American Christmas," in D. Miller (ed.) *Unwrapping Christmas*, London: Routledge, 75–104.

—— (1994) "Battling worldliness in the new Zion: mercantilism versus homespun in 19th century Utah," *Journal of Macromarketing* 14, Spring: 9–22.

—— (1996) "Hyperreality and globalization: culture in the age of Ronald McDonald," *Journal of International Consumer Marketing* 8, 3/4: 23–37.

Belk, R. W., Wallendorf, M., and Sherry, J. F. (1989) "The sacred and profane in consumer behavior: theodicy on the Odyssey," *Journal of Consumer Research* 16, June: 1–38.

Brown, S. (1986) "The impact of religion on Northern Ireland retailing," *Retail and Distribution Management*, 14, 6: 7–11.

—— (1995) *Postmodern Marketing*, London: Routledge.

—— (1997) "Six sixty-six and all that (or, what the hell is marketing eschatology?)," *European Journal of Marketing* 31, 9/10: 639–53.

—— (1998a) *Postmodern Marketing Two: Telling Tales*, London: ITBP.

—— (1998b) "Unlucky for some: slacker scholarship and the well wrought turn," in B. B. Stern (ed.) *Representing Consumers*, London: Routledge.

—— (ed.) (1998c) *Romancing the Market*, London: Routledge.

—— (1999) "Marketing and literature: the anxiety of academic influence," *Journal of Marketing*, 63, January: in press.

Campbell, C. (1987) *The Romantic Ethic and the Spirit of Modern Consumerism*, Oxford: Blackwell.

Corrigan, P. (1997) *The Sociology of Consumption: An Introduction*, London: Sage.

Cotton, I. (1995) *The Hallelujah Revolution: The Rise of the New Christians*, London: Little Brown.

Denzin, N. K. (1997) *Interpretive Ethnography: Ethnographic Practices for the 21st Century*, Thousand Oaks: Sage.

Douglas, M. (1997) *Thought Styles: Critical Essays on Good Taste*, London: Sage.

*Economist* (1995) "America and religion – the counter-attack of God," *The Economist* 336, 7922: 19–21.

Falk, P. and Campbell C. (eds) (1997) *The Shopping Experience*, London: Sage.

Featherstone, M. (1991) *Consumer Culture and Postmodernism*, London: Sage.

Firth, D. and Campbell, H. (1997) *Sacred Business: Resurrecting the Spirit of Work*, Oxford: Capstone.

Fullerton, R. (1985) "Was there a 'production era' in marketing history? A multinational study," in S. C. Hollander and T. Nevett (eds) *Marketing in the Long Run*, East Lansing: Michigan State University, 388–400.

—— (1988), "How modern is modern marketing? Marketing's evolution and the myth of the 'production era'," *Journal of Marketing* 52, January: 108–25.

Gabriel Y. and Lang, T. (1995) *The Unmanageable Consumer: Contemporary Consumption and its Fragmentations*, London: Sage.

Gerber, W. (1997) *Anatomy of What we Value Most*, Atlanta: Rodopi.

Gould, S. J. (1991) "The self-manipulation of my pervasive, perceived vital energy through product use: an introspective-praxis perspective," *Journal of Consumer Research* 18, September: 194–207.

—— (1995) "Researcher introspection as a method in consumer research: applications, issues and implications," *Journal of Consumer Research* 21, March: 719–22.

Hamilton, M. B. (1995) *The Sociology of Religion*, London: Routledge.

Hassay, D. N. and Smith, M. C. (1996) "Fauna, foraging and shopping motives," in K. P. Corfman and J. G. Lynch (eds) *Advances in Consumer Research, Volume XXIII*, Provo: Association for Consumer Research, 510–15.

Hirschman, E. C. (1983) "Religious affiliation and consumption processes: an initial paradigm," in J. N. Sheth (ed.) *Research in Marketing, Vol. 6*, Greenwich: JAI Press, 131–70.

—— (1985) "Primitive aspects of consumption in modern American society," *Journal of Consumer Research* 12, September: 142–54.

—— (1988) "Upper class WASPs as consumers: a humanistic inquiry," in E. C. Hirschman and J. N. Sheth (eds) *Research in Consumer Behavior, Vol. 3*, Greenwich: JAI Press, 115–48.

Hirschman, E. C. and LaBarbara, P. A. (1989) "The meaning of Christmas," in E. C. Hirschman (ed.) *Interpretive Consumer Research*, Provo: Association for Consumer Research, 136–47.

Holbrook, M. B. (1993) "Romanticism and sentimentality in consumer behavior: a literary approach to the joys and sorrows of consumption," in M. B. Holbrook and E. C. Hirschman (eds) *The Semiotics of Consumption: Interpreting Symbolic Consumer Behavior in Popular Culture and Works of Art*, Berlin: Mouton de Gruyter, 151–228.

—— (1995) *Consumer Research: Introspective Essays on the Study of Consumption*, Thousand Oaks: Sage.

—— (1996) "Romanticism, introspection and the roots of experiential consumption: Morris the Epicurean," in R. W. Belk, N. Dholakia, and A. Venkatesh (eds) *Consumption and Marketing: Macro Dimensions*, Cincinnati: South-Western, 20–82.

Jhally, S. (1989) "Advertising as religion: the dialectic of technology and magic," in I. Angus and S. Jhally (eds) *Cultural Politics in Contemporary America*, New York: Routledge, 217–29.

Kaufmann, W. (1974) *Nietzsche: Philosopher, Psychologist, Antichrist*, Princeton: Princeton University Press.

Kent, R. (1996) "The Protestant ethic and the spirit of marketing," in S. Brown, J. Bell, and D. Carson (eds) *Marketing Apocalypse: Eschatology, Escapology and the Illusion of the End*, London: Routledge, 133–44.

LaBarbara, P. A. (1987) "Consumer behavior and born again Christianity," in J. N. Sheth and E. C. Hirschman (eds) *Research in Consumer Behavior, Vol. 2*, Greenwich: JAI Press, 193–222.

Lasch, C. (1979) *The Culture of Narcissism: American Life in an Age of Diminishing Expectations*, New York: Norton.

Leiss, W., Kline, S., and Jhally, S. (1990) *Social Communication in Advertising: Persons, Products and Images of Well-being*, Toronto: Methuen.

Magnell, T. (ed.) (1997) *Explorations of Value*, Atlanta: Rodopi.

Magnus, B. and Higgins, K. M. (1996) "Nietzsche's works and their themes," in B. Magnus and K. M. Higgins (eds) *The Cambridge Companion to Nietzsche*, Cambridge: Cambridge University Press, 21–68.

McCreery, J. (1995) "Malinowski, magic and advertising: on choosing metaphors," in J. F. Sherry (ed.) *Contemporary Marketing and Consumer Behavior: An Anthropological Sourcebook*, Thousand Oaks: Sage, 309–329.

McDaniel, S. W. and Burnett, J. J. (1991) "Targeting the evangelical market segment," *Journal of Advertising Research* 81, August–September: 26–33.

McDannell, C. (1995) *Material Christianity: Religion and Popular Culture in America*, New Haven: Yale University Press.

McDonald, M. H. B. and Leppard, J. W. (1992) *Marketing by Matrix*, Oxford: Butterworth-Heinemann.

Micklethwait, J. and Wooldridge, A. (1996) *The Witch Doctors: Making Sense of the Management Gurus*, New York: Times Books.

Miller, D. (1998) *A Theory of Shopping*, Oxford: Polity.

Nietzsche, F. (1992 [1888]) *Ecce Homo*, Harmondsworth: Penguin.

O'Guinn, T. C. and Belk, R. W. (1989) "Heaven on earth: consumption at Heritage Village, USA," *Journal of Consumer Research* 16, September: 227–38.

Pattison, S. (1997) *The Faith of the Managers: When Management Becomes Religion*, London: Cassell.

Peter, J. P. and Olsen, J. C. (1993) *Consumer Behavior and Marketing Strategy*, Homewood: Irwin.

Rook, D. W. (1987) "The buying impulse," *Journal of Consumer Research* 14, September: 189–99.

Schudson, M. (1993) *Advertising, the Uneasy Persuasion: Its Dubious Impact on American Society*, London: Routledge.

Sherden, W. A. (1998) *The Fortune Sellers: The Big Business of Buying and Selling Predictions*, New York: John Wiley.

Sherry, J. F. (1987) "Advertising as a cultural system," in J. Umiker-Sebeok (ed.) *Marketing and Semiotics: New Directions in the Study of Signs for Sale*, Berlin: de Gruyter, 285–306.

Solomon, M. R. (1995) *Consumer Behavior: Buying, Having, and Being*, Boston: Allyn and Bacon.

Voaden, R. (1995) "The language of love: medieval erotic vision and modern romance fiction," in L. Pearce and J. Stacey (eds) *Romance Revisited*, London: Lawrence and Wishart, 78–88.

Weiss, P. (1995) "Outcasts digging in for the Apocalypse," *Time*, Vol. 145, No. 17, pp. 34–5.

# Conclusions

*Morris B. Holbrook*

In reading the eight chapters on the various types of consumer value, I have responded with great admiration for the knowledge and scholarship that have gone into their preparation. Taken together, they add considerable depth to our understanding of the Typology of Consumer Value presented in the Introduction. They convey a more profound appreciation for each major type of value. Further, they raise some important questions that bear consideration in this concluding chapter. In addressing these issues, I shall organize my discussion as a progression from those that I believe prove least troublesome to those that I believe pose key conceptual problems or other difficulties still in need of more careful exploration in the future.

## The basic nature of value

Few of our contributors appear to hold serious reservations concerning the conceptualization of consumer value as *an interactive relativistic preference experience*. A partial exception appears in Chapter 8 when Brown – speaking on the issue of the relativity involved in comparisons among objects within a particular individual's preference ordering – demurs as follows:

> The presupposition that value is comparative, insofar as the only valid utility assessments involve comparisons among objects within the same person, does not equate with everyday experience. For Holbrook, it may not be legitimate to claim that I like Madonna more than he likes Madonna, but these are precisely the sorts of value judgments that we indulge in all the time.

Despite this heroic attempt to resurrect the generally discredited concept of cardinal utility (on which grounds, if pressed, I might indeed be willing to concede that almost everybody on the planet likes Madonna more than I do), it appears that Brown's heart is not really in it because he himself concedes that such an "indulgence" in interpersonal utility comparisons is "not . . . legitimate."

A more serious departure from the conceptualization of consumer value as an interactive relativistic preference experience appears in Chapter 6 when Wagner refers to the notion of "beauty inherent in an aesthetic object." This conception leans in the direction of treating beauty as an *objective property* of an object – as something located *in* the object and waiting to be perceived by a subject or lying *in* the product and waiting to be appreciated by a consumer: "Apprehension is the perception of beauty." The opposite extreme, of course, would involve *subjectivism* and would insist that "beauty is in the eye of the beholder." By contrast with either objectivism or subjectivism, I tend to regard the experience of beauty as involving an *interaction* between a subject and an object. In the Introduction, I presented my arguments for this view. However, I also acknowledged there that – like Wagner – many axiologists pursue an orientation oriented more toward the objectivist side of the subject–object interaction. Here, Wagner does *not* pursue an extreme form of objectivism. Rather she suggests that, whereas beauty itself may inhere in an object, "for the aesthetic experience to occur, there must be a subject to perceive the beauty inherent in an aesthetic object." Hence, I interpret her discussion of beauty as reflecting an objectivist leaning within a general agreement on the interactive nature of consumer value.

## The compresence of different types of value in a consumption experience

In one way or another, several chapters suggest or imply a criticism of the Typology of Consumer Value that, in my opinion, represents a basic logical error. Specifically, in Chapter 1, Leclerc and Schmitt suggest that, whereas the use of time relates to the value of efficiency in general and convenience in particular (that is to active, self-oriented, extrinsic value), it also relates to how the consumer might "react to wastes of time that are not under her control such as in the case of waiting lines" where "someone . . . does not have many options to act on" and to how "the queue constitutes a social system" so that "time is a consumer value that is . . . occasionally other-oriented." In other words, time-oriented value may contain a reactive component and may have implications for how we relate to others so as to involve other-oriented aspects.

Along similar lines, in Chapter 5, Grayson defines play as following rules, some of which are socially embedded so that playful activities may entail aspects of other-oriented value:

> Play could be placed on a continuum from solitary play . . . to social play. . . . However, this seemingly straightforward distinction obscures the important fact that play is always an interactive phenomenon. Even when a consumer enjoys playful value via the solitary use of a baseball, a doll, or a motorboat, that person is not only acting on the object, but is also reacting to a social definition of the object. . . . So although play is defined as an activity that focuses on self-oriented rewards, it inevitably involves a direct or indirect other-oriented focus in order to produce these rewards.

Further, Wagner in Chapter 6 suggests that aesthetic value based on the beauty of fashion also serves to accomplish extrinsic purposes related to self- and other-oriented value, as in the case of quality (reactive) and status (active): "In fashion, aesthetic value is derived not from beauty alone, but from a complex of values that includes extrinsic values such as quality and status." Wagner concludes that "therefore, aesthetic value in fashion involves both intrinsic *and* extrinsic value"; that "thus, aesthetic value in fashion objects is both self-oriented *and* other-oriented"; and that "thus, aesthetic value in fashion is both active *and* reactive."

And Smith in Chapter 7 notes that some forms of behavior deemed ethical – such as giving money to charity or engaging in a consumer boycott – may entail extrinsic other-oriented motivations so that "ethics" can, in this sense, also involve considerations of what I would call "status." For example, Smith suggests that a decision to boycott Barclays Bank may reflect a desire to "help the people of South Africa by forcing Barclays' withdrawal and speeding the downfall of the apartheid regime" (a clear case of active, other-oriented, intrinsic, and therefore ethical value) but may also evince "a reluctance to be seen patronizing the 'apartheid bank,' an avoidance of unseemly conspicuous consumption" (which he regards as a case of "self-interest," though I would have called it "extrinsic and other-oriented" in the service of active "status" or reactive "esteem"). Based on this, Smith worries that "there may be . . . less selfless motivations to some consumption experiences, and yet we might still wish to characterize the participants as consumers obtaining ethics as a customer value." Later, he repeats that "a self-oriented perspective is conceivably a component within acts that are ostensibly or largely other-oriented."

I believe that all such concerns involve a basic philosophical mistake. They boil down to a claim that some type of value is fostered by a given product or experience; that this product or experience also contributes to some other type of value; and that the two types of value are therefore somehow the same. In other words, they argue that $X \to Y$; that $Y \to Z$; so that, therefore, $Y = Z$. Stated in these terms, the argument entails an obvious fallacy. The more convoluted discussions that appear in some of the preceding chapters disguise this fallacy in part. But it lurks beneath the surface nonetheless.

Thus, using time efficiently contributes to convenience, a self-oriented value; time also involves other-related aspects of our social activities; but this does not mean that efficiency is other-oriented. Play undertaken for its own sake may or may not involve activities that follow rules; some rules or other aspects of playful activities contribute to other-oriented value; but this does not imply that play or fun is inherently other-oriented. Fashion may promote aesthetic value; fashion may also contribute to status; but this does not show that the aesthetic value of fashion involves status. Charitable donations or participation in boycotts may be ethical; they may also enhance one's prestige or standing in the community to produce value that is extrinsic and other-oriented in nature; but this does not demonstrate that ethical value involves status.

The root of the confusion just identified lies in an important consideration that I have repeatedly mentioned in my previous writings on the theme of consumer value (Holbrook 1986, 1994a, 1994b, 1994c, 1996; Holbrook and Corfman 1985). As Solomon points out near the end of Chapter 3, "The consumer-value typology forces us to realize how . . . the same product or experience can impart different types of value to different perceivers." Similarly, in Chapter 6, Smith reminds us that "different types of value may be obtained" and "these types of value may occur simultaneously and to varying degrees in any consumption experience." In general, then, *any given consumption experience can and generally does entail many or even all of the different types of consumer value identified by our typology.*

Philosophers refer to such a concept as involving *compresence* – in this case, a co-mingling of multiple types of value in any one consumption experience (Lee 1957: 190; Taylor 1961: 24; see also Eisert 1983; Hilliard 1950; Lewis 1946). Thus, a painting may be evaluated on both aesthetic and moral grounds, for both its pleasing appearance and its depiction of virtue (Morris 1964). A house may provide both beauty (as art) and quality (as shelter) (Perry 1954). Besides its obvious spiritual value, attending church may help to increase one's status in the community (Perry 1954; Rokeach 1973).

Further examples abound. Chewing gum can provide both fun (blowing bubbles) and beauty (a delicious taste); both efficiency (as a laxative that, quite literally, maximizes one's outputs from just one little input) and status (as a breath freshener that improves one's success with others); both esteem (conspicuously chewing an expensive imported brand) and virtue (using a sugarless version to avoid cavities). A paper clip can contribute to both efficiency (holding papers together) and aesthetics (its undulant shape). Voting for a particular political candidate might involve considerations of both ethics (scandals in the White House) and efficiency (lowering taxes). And owning a fine pedigreed cat might confer aspects of both excellence (the potential ability to catch mice even where mice do not exist) and status (impressing one's neighbors by parading a conspicuously expensive pet in front of them).

Because I have insisted on this point elsewhere, I shall just briefly summarize here by recalling one of my own favorite examples involving my "Old School Tie" (Holbrook 1994a). This tie is a navy blue rep cravat made of silk and featuring little silver-colored insignias of the Greek God Hermes (the official emblem of the school where I teach). Clearly, this mythically enriched piece of clothing provides *every relevant type of consumer value*:

*efficiency* by giving me an excuse for fastening the top button of my shirt so as to keep my neck warm;

*excellence* in the high-quality of its weaving and stitching (such that I could potentially tug at its seams without hurting it if I wanted to, which I don't);

*status* when worn to a cocktail party given by the Dean to impress him with my loyalty to the School in hopes of a generous salary increase;

*esteem* if hung (in)conspicuously in my closet to remind myself and the cleaning lady that I come from a "Good School";

*play* in the fun-loving manner in which I speak about this piece of apparel (especially my whimsically irreverent references to Hermes as not only the Greek God of Commerce but also the Hellenic Patron of Thieves);

*aesthetics*  in the subtle harmonization of the tie's blue-and-silver tones with the charcoal gray of my wool suite and the white expanse of my Oxford cloth shirt;

*ethics*  in the charitable contribution represented by paying the School's Alumni Office approximately four times what the tie is actually worth;

*spirituality*  in the deep Sense of the Academic Community that fills me with School Spirit as I proudly don this Sacred Garment when I visit the Hallowed Halls of Ivy.

In short, it appears clear that even so humble an object as a necktie can contribute to all eight types of consumer value. Equally clearly, this does not mean, in any sense, that efficiency is the same thing as esteem; that play involves status; that beauty is synonymous with quality; that ethics caters to status and esteem; or that any of the other confusions noted earlier have any logical validity whatsoever.

## The question of economic inputs into value

In defining the nature of consumer value as an interactive relativistic preference experience – where the relativism involved includes the concept of a comparison among competing sources of value – I have implicitly made room for the economist's view of value as a ratio of outputs to inputs or benefits to costs or rewards to price. Nonetheless, my own treatment of consumer value in the Intro- duction – as well as that in most of the chapters – implicitly regards consumer value as if it were a cost-free benefit that might be represented by an input- or price-independent preference function.

Possible problems with this conceptualization surface in the two cells in the upper left-hand corner of the Typology of Consumer Value. Specifically, in Chapter 1, Leclerc and Schmitt describe the value of time, which I had treated as an input into the experience of efficiency in general or convenience in particular. As long as the reader keeps in mind that an experience using excessive time tends to lose value – in other words, that a waste of time entails a loss in convenience or efficiency – the perspective adopted by Leclerc and Schmitt makes perfect sense. In the words of these authors, their research "is based on the assumption that consumers derive some '(dis)utility' for time saved (wasted)." Thus, "the value of using an object or a service consists of the time saved by means of this object or service."

Similarly, in connection with excellence as discussed in Chapter 2, Oliver devotes some attention to the economist's view of value as "an intra-product comparison such as when benefits are compared to costs"; as "comparisons of what is received to what is given . . . a function of rewards versus costs"; as a "ratio of what is received to its price"; or as "outcomes compared to sacrifices." Here, Oliver's treatment mirrors a common tendency to equate "customer value" with a balance between quality and price (Broydrick 1996: 110), a ratio of relative market-perceived quality to relative market-perceived price (Gale 1994: 19, 27), or a trade-off between positive and negative consequences (Woodruff and Gardial 1996: 57). Further, Oliver reflects linguistic habits embedded in our language or what he calls "the 'best buy' moniker." Typically, if we say that we got good "value" in stereo equipment, we mean that we bought (say) an amplifier for a lower-than-typical retail price. Better "value" in a new automobile would imply paying a smaller premium above the dealer's cost. At McDonald's or Burger King, a "value meal" provides more of the same lousy food (say, cola and fries plus a burger) for less money than the items would cost if purchased separately.

As long as one keeps such conventions in mind, little confusion will result. However, we should note that typically these conventions do not apply with respect to the other types of value represented by our classification scheme. For example, one does not account for status value according to a calculus based on prestige per dollar; indeed, more expensive consumption habits may actually increase rather than diminish the favorable social impression created, as in the flamboyant spending of money at a restaurant. Similarly, one does not address questions in aesthetics by speaking of beauty per hour; if one did, one would probably never get around to reading *Ulysses* or listening to Mahler. And, in the case of ethical value, one might appear stingy if one assessed the worth of donating blood to the Red Cross in terms of good will generated per drop expended.

## Fuzzy distinctions among different types of consumer value

A more serious flaw in the Typology of Consumer Value, implicit in several chapters, stems from a convention that I adopted in the Introduction when treating each of the typology's underlying dimensions as a simplifying dichotomy. At the time, I mentioned that each should more properly be regarded as a continuum of possibilities from one extreme to the other. Axiologists have agreed (Parker 1957: 93) and, indeed, have suggested the possibility of constructing a multidimensional value space based on a continuous representation of the relevant differentiating factors (Morris 1956: 6). In such a space, particular examples of experience-based value would occupy positions determined by the degrees to which they exemplified extrinsic versus intrinsic, self- versus other-oriented, and active versus reactive components. Clearly, many illustrative cases would occupy intermediate positions at the interior of such a space. These would constitute instances for which no simple dichotomy could capture the fuzzy, blurred, or gray areas of interest.

Nowhere in the Typology of Consumer Value is the demarcation between adjacent areas more problematic than for the two cells in the bottom left-hand corner – status and esteem. As noted earlier in the Introduction, the active nature of status and the reactive nature of esteem tend to blur together in ways that render the two hard to distinguish cleanly. Thus, if I park my Ferrari in the driveway, does that constitute an active impression-managing manipulation of my perceived prestige (status) or a reactive possessions-based reflection of my elite lifestyle (esteem)? Probably a little of each or something in between, one might conclude. Here, it is hard to think of aspects of reactive esteem that do not also involve some degree of active status manipulation. Hence – though the two phenomena are distinct conceptually – empirically and anecdotally, they tend to interpenetrate in ways that are difficult to unravel. For this reason, we find that Chapter 3 on status by Solomon and Chapter 4 on esteem by Richins tend to jostle together in ways that should prove challenging for the reader. As Solomon notes:

> Status . . . is contrasted in the typology with esteem, which Holbrook terms reactive in the sense that the mere possession of objects is sufficient to create a reputation. In this regard Holbrook's distinction may be a bit ambiguous . . . insofar as . . . the spectacle created by such a display often is artfully staged rather than accidental – active rather than reactive.

To this, Richins adds that "in empirical analysis it has been difficult to distinguish between active and reactive sources of value." In her Figure 4.1, she indicates this difficulty by drawing a dashed rather than solid line between the two lower left-hand cells representing status and esteem, respectively.

A further example of the confusion caused by fuzziness in the application of simplifying dichotomies appears in Chapter 6 when Wagner rightly notes that aesthetic and other forms of perception generally involve an active component of information processing wherein "the perception of beauty (like all perception) is an active process." Here, I believe that Wagner implicitly and correctly criticizes any sort of naive view of perception as passive in nature. I completely agree that perception is a process whereby we actively construct our apprehension of reality. This is precisely why I chose the word "reactive" to replace the word "passive" that I had misleadingly used in some previous versions of the typology. As I insist in the Introduction, consumer value is (re)*active* in that it entails an inter*action* between a subject (the consumer) and an object (the product). Hence, I would concur with Wagner that there exist different degrees of (re)activity; that these deserve representation via a continuum of possibilities; and that, only at one extreme degree, does reactivity verge on a condition of passivity such as that which might appear in the case of the proverbial couch potato for whom "the experience controls the consumer."

## Possible additional or alternative dimensions of value

Another possibility arises not so much from the likelihood that one or more of the proposed typology's value dimensions contains fuzzy or gray areas rather than a clean dichotomous distinction as from the possibility that we might better create a classification focused on additional or alternative dimensions of value. For example, in Chapter 6, Smith questions these aspects of "the detail within the framework" and their "theoretical basis" in general while raising questions in particular about possible "alternative dimensions" such as "an affective dimension," "an economic dimension," "a tangible/intangible . . . dimension," or "a physical/mental dimension." Similarly, in Chapter 8, Brown pronounces:

> I know from personal experience that the two or three "key dimensions" are pretty arbitrary, having been whittled down from a much longer list of

contenders and selected because they somehow seem to "work" better than the others (all of which have been tinkered with at length).

Actually, all these issues have been addressed in the Introduction and in my earlier contributions to the relevant discussions (cited earlier). In those contributions, I have tried to convey that the conceptualization represented by the value typology grew from an attempt to engage with the relevant axiological literature rather than from some effulgent effluence of my own fervid imagination. However, disputing this point, Brown implies that I must somehow have designed the typology first and then looked for conceptual support later:

> And, when the framework is complete, there's the inevitable retrospective root through the literature in order to demonstrate its veracity, to find evidence to support the structure, gimcrack, gerrybuilt, and decidedly rickety though it is.

So I take Smith (hesitantly) and Brown (vehemently) to imply that, having read the pertinent sources with care, they remain unconvinced on the merits of the dimensions chosen as a foundation for the typology. Essentially, this leaves the debate as a potentially fruitful topic for future research. In that direction, I should repeat that the present formulation does represent my best attempt to reflect a broad but poorly articulated and seldom synthesized consensus among axiologists. However, the ultimate validity of that consensus in the context of consumer research rests, in part, on the degree to which consumers appear willing, able, and/or inclined to use dimensions and categories of the sorts suggested to distinguish among the types of value of relevance in their lives. Reassurance that the present Typology of Consumer Value does capture distinctions of importance to real consumers comes from some recent empirical work by Mathwick, Malhotra, and Rigdon (1998; see also Holbrook and Corfman 1985). Focusing on just the top portion of the value typology (i.e., the self- as opposed to other-oriented types of value), these researchers pursue a rigorous approach to measurement and find support for the reliability and validity of a structural model based on our distinctions among efficiency, excellence, play, and aesthetics as key types of self-oriented consumer value. As these authors conclude, further research extending this work to incorporate such other-oriented types of value as status, esteem, ethics, and spirituality appears to represent a promising avenue for future exploration.

## The potential omission of key types of value

To me, a charge more troubling than the concern that one or more of the major value dimensions might not hold water is the possibility, raised by Smith in Chapter 6, that "some important types of value" are "missing." This suggests a potential flaw in the typology stemming from a lack of exhaustiveness. In this connection, Smith's example concerns "the intellectual value that may be obtained from a subscription to a current affairs magazine or the purchase of an encyclopedia."

Here, I would suggest that Smith has confused the conceptualization of key *types* of consumer value with the elaboration of *examples* intended to illustrate those types. As argued in the Introduction, efficiency or excellence are types of value, whereas convenience or quality are examples of those types. Similarly, play and aesthetics are types, while fun and beauty are examples. Obviously, as Richins indicates in Figure 4.1, there may well be many *other examples* of any given type.

Thus, following in a long line of psychological research on intrinsic value (Berlyne 1969; Deci 1975), I would argue that the satisfaction of intellectual curiosity often constitutes a form of playful value in that it is actively pursued and is prized as a self-oriented and self-justifying end in itself. To this, I would add that the purchase of an encyclopedia could, of course, also entail other types of value such as getting good grades in school (efficiency) or impressing one's friends (status). But neither of these examples could properly be called "intellectual" in the sense implied by a full-fledged conception of playfulness. On the other hand, certain aspects of intellectual value might be more reactive than active in nature and might therefore occupy a fuzzy region between play and aesthetics. This gray area conveys the sense in which intellectual satisfaction may consist of admiring some sort of conceptual achievement as a self-oriented experience valued for its own sake. Along these lines, mathematicians might refer to the proof of a theorem as "beautiful" – meaning that they admire its elegance as a source of self-oriented value appreciated as an end in itself.

## The paradox of altruism

Moving farther down the chain of problematicity, I come to a perplexing issue that I believe really does present some difficult questions worthy of further study. These appear in both Chapter 6 on aesthetics and Chapter 7 on ethics, in which both Wagner and Smith raise questions concerning the extent to which any type of value can ever be truly other- as opposed to self-oriented.

Pursuing a "decision-oriented model," Wagner finds "reason to doubt that there is any type of value that *isn't* self-oriented." She cites Gary Becker, Martin Fishbein, and Harold Osborne (a diverse lot if ever there was one) in support of the contention that "all categories of value are self-rewarding, because they satisfy needs." Thus, Wagner suggests that all value always ultimately constitutes a benefit to the self. If I do something for others, it is because it makes me feel good.

Similarly, Smith questions whether an act can ever be entirely without self-interest: "Truly altruistic acts are rare and some would say never occur or are impossible to identify with certainty."

In the philosophy of ethics, this insistence on the self-oriented nature of all value is called *ethical egoism*, as espoused by Epicurus, Hobbes, Nietzsche, and others (Frankena 1973). As Smith notes, a milder version known as *psychological egoism* holds that "it cannot be argued with certainty that an affirmative act of goodness that promotes moral values of the individual is ever ultimately without self-interest." These egoistic perspectives fly in the face of *ethical universalism*, which pursues the "greatest good of the greatest number" or "the greatest possible balance of good over evil . . . in the world as a whole," along the lines envisioned by Jeremy Bentham and John Stuart Mill (Frankena 1973: 34).

Clearly, egoism precludes whereas universalism embraces the possibility of true *altruism*, defined as an action that harms the self for the sake of helping others. Ultimately, ethical or psychological egoism raises profound questions about *why* one would engage in "altruistic" actions. If the answer is that they are, on balance, pleasing to the self, then they are not really "altruistic" in the purest sense.

One answer to this dilemma concerning the paradox of altruism emphasizes the intrinsically motivated nature of virtue or morality as "good in itself" (Frankena 1973: 89) or "its own reward" (Frankena 1973: 94) – something that ethical or psychological egoists appear to disregard. In a sense that parallels the argument for the intrinsic value of play, aesthetics, or spirituality, I engage in ethical actions to attain the relevant consumption experience valued for its own sake – that is, as a self-justifying or autotelic end in itself. Accordingly, to repeat, virtue is its own reward. It is *my* consumption experience, to be sure, but I value it for *its* own sake by virtue of the effect it has on *others*. Or, to put the point somewhat differently, "self-justifying" in the sense of "intrinsic" is *not* the same thing as "self-oriented" in the sense of "selfish." Hence, an action can be self-justifying and other-oriented rather than self-oriented at the same time. As indicated by the value typology, the two uses of the word "self" are orthogonal and should not in any sense be confounded.

To this, I would add that the important issue is not really whether any consumption experience is ever entirely selfless or other-oriented in the ethical sense just described, but rather whether different types of consumer value – including ethics as one potential type – involve different degrees of self- versus other-orientation. Here I believe the answer is that, demonstrably, they do. Thus, whether ethical value is ever one hundred percent other-oriented, it does appear that virtually all examples of what we would call ethical value (say, giving money to a beggar or eating dolphin-safe tuna) are more other-oriented than those that we might call efficiency (buying a stock for its low price-earnings ratio) or play (slapping a ball around a golf course).

## Lower and higher levels of value

Oliver concludes Chapter 2 by asking some probing questions about the relationship between value and satisfaction (cf. Woodruff and Gardial 1996: 86, 94). As shown in Figure 2.2, Oliver concludes in favor of a conceptualization that represents these concepts as "a constellation of consumption-related constructs." At the risk of oversimplification, I would describe his diagram as suggesting that Performance Outcomes and Sacrifices → Cost-Based Value → Satisfaction → Consumption Value → Value-Based Satisfaction → Extended Value.

In my view, Oliver's argument here could be reinterpreted as contributing a useful concept involving *levels* (l = 1, 2, 3 ,...) of value ($V_l$) and satisfaction ($S_l$)

in which $V_1 \rightarrow S_1$ at any given level but $S_1 \rightarrow V_{1+1}$ at the next highest level. In other words, the model suggests a chain of effects in which $V_1 \rightarrow S_1 \rightarrow V_2 \rightarrow S_2 \ldots$

In this spirit, as implied by Oliver's figure, one could envision a value-oriented hierarchy or an axiological "chain of being" that proceeds upward from the level of a product attribute to that of a product itself to that of a consumption experience to that of a lifestyle to that of the human condition (cf. Woodruff and Gardial 1996: 64, 70). Clearly, as Oliver notes, this conceptualization raises important questions that deserve exploration in future research.

## Soul searching in the service of solipsistic solecism

Finally, we come to a class of critique that poses true problems for the project at hand and on which I can profess to be something of an expert because I am fond of practising it myself, even though it appears most conspicuously in the present volume under the guise of Chapter 8 by Stephen Brown. Put simply, bent on matrixide, Brown objects to the idea of classificatory thinking in general and poses challenges to the Typology of Consumer Value as an example thereof in particular. This seems to be the essence of what he means when he says that "matrices are arbitrary, authoritarian, reductive, restrictive, repressive, mechanistic, methodical, utilitarian, unimaginative, inflexible, intolerant." (Notice his self-contradictory willingness to trap himself into a formulaic scheme: a–, a–, m–, m–, u–, u–, i–, i–. . . . ) To this Brown quickly adds that "matrices . . . are the complete antithesis of fluidity, flexibility, openness, ambiguity, multivocality, polysemousness of our postmodern, pre-millennial, neo-romantic times." (Here, but for an apparent lapse of attention, he could have completed another formulaic pattern: –ty, –ty, –ness, –ness, –ty, –ty. . . . ) Based on this, Brown can hardly believe that I could bring myself to produce "something as banal, banausic, and . . . barbaric as The Typology of Consumer Value." (Back in form, he executes another perfect formula: ban–, ban–, bar-bar. . . . ) So – abandoning his verbal play, getting ironic, and growing a bit cynical – Brown pronounces that "Morris's value matrix, in short, is valuable because it makes us reflect on the valuelessness of matrices, on how much better off our field would be without them."

In other words, when asked to organize his comments on spirituality into a framework that can simultaneously accommodate insights from at least seven other schools of thought, Brown tends to chafe at the bit a bit. He tends to resist the restrictions, constraints, constrictions, and restraints of what he perceives to be an oppressive authority threatening to squash his big ideas into narrow and confining little compartments. "Don't reign over me," he seems to say, "Don't rein me in; don't rain on my parade; rather rein-force the reins from which flow my wild rein-terpretations." In this, unlike our colleagues who obsess about "breaking out of the box" but usually only find ways of building bigger and better boxes to inhabit, Brown really does want to demolish the barriers that block, impede, confine, and otherwise limit our thinking. He wants those walls to come tumbling down. He sees himself as Joshua, remembered because he fit against, not because he fit in.

In these spirituality-related impulses toward *soul searching*, Chapter 8 mirrors my own frequently avowed fondness for subjective personal introspection or what many regard as *solipsism* in a manner that violates the structure on which the present volume is based in the direction of what some might label *solecism*. Toward this end, in a matrixidal mood, Brown assaults us with riotous and rebellious acts of textual terrorism that proceed to blur the boundaries and confound the categories I have so painstakingly constructed as the cornerstone for this volume on value. True, some of his righteous rhetoric may stem from nothing more insidious than an inveterate habit of reflexivity – as in his masterfully self-referential use of the word "catachresis" catachrestically. However, at bottom [sic (or, if you prefer, sick)] and as manifested in the passages already quoted, Brown's attack on the typology qua typology betrays his devotion to the Espisteme of the Moment in the shape of the Ethos of Postmodernism – that is the pomo penchant for polysemy, paradox, parody, pastiche, playfulness, pluralism, proliferation, promiscuity, panculturalism, and all the other proclivities of the poststructuralist posture.

Indeed, when one approaches the issue of using a typology as the framework to structure a book, the concept of *poststructuralism* more or less says it all. Who needs something as vulgar as an organizing scheme in the free-wheeling pomo-oriented age of poststructuralism? Why not just draw on one's endlessly fertile gift for humor and poke holes in the whole enterprise?

If we wonder where Brown acquired this iconoclastic, caste-castigating, castrating, Castroistic cast to his casuistry, he answers such questions in Chapter 8. Apparently, he grew up in a repressively "strict Protestant household" in which he was forbidden to go to the movies, watch TV, read the Sunday comics, or patronize establishments run by Catholics. In other words, while the rest of us were busy being children, poor little Stephen never got to see *Rebel Without a Cause*; never got to watch *The Twilight Zone*; never got to read "Li'l Abner," "Little Lulu," "Peanuts," or "Pogo"; never even got to eat at an Italian restaurant. Instead, culturally and indeed multi-culturally deprived to the core, he was force-fed a steady diet of Bible lessons, Bach chorales, Browning poems, and British cooking. Ugh! So, it turns out, Stephen now feels a strong need to rebel. Never having been able to be a child when he was young in years, Stephen needs to be a child now. From this sad story stem the explanations for, among other things, his recalcitrant nature and his comic genius.

Yes, I said "comic genius" because one would be hard-pressed to find a more reliably risible writer anywhere in our discipline . . . or beyond. But how, the reader might ask, can we be expected to treat in earnest the comedic gift of an inspired humorist who aims above all to be funny and *not* to be taken seriously? I would answer that we know of Brown's deeply dedicated commitment to such poststructuralist ideals by virtue of reading his excellent book entitled *Postmodern Marketing* (Brown 1995). Therein, we find the clues to his apparent affinity for paradox and self-parody.

As Brown notes in Chapter 8 – wherein he cheerfully confesses to his own classificatory temptations as "a secret matrixomane, a backdoor boxaphile, a recovering typoloholic" in need of "the 2×2×2-step program" – his work draws deeply on the postmodern aversion to logic chopping even while presenting innumerable illustrative matrices of his own design (Brown 1995: 14, 21, 28, 49, 51, 57, 61, 73, 120, 133, 155, 171). In this, Brown bravely demonstrates the paradoxical or even self-parodic (not to mention -parrotic, -paretic, and -pyretic) frame of mind in which a structural device on which he himself relies so enthusiastically in his own work could provoke such anathema from him in the present context!

But after all, what do you expect from a postmodernist? When pressed for a definition of that slippery concept, one of the prominent pomo prophets offered the following exegesis: "Simplifying to the extreme, I define *postmodern* as incredulity toward metanarratives" (Lyotard 1984: xxiv). How anyone could imagine that a three-word definition involving two words guaranteed to confound the typical reader – namely, "incredulity" and "metanarrative" – constitutes an extreme simplification, I cannot fathom. In essence, this grandiloquent guru appears to mean that postmodernists don't believe in any sort of universal truth.

But, as usual with nihilists, one must ask whether skeptics who proclaim the nonexistence of truth secretly commit the fallacy of believing their own convictions. Or just don't care. The latter stance seems to represent the self-proclaimed posture of Brown in Chapter 8: "The bottom line, I suppose, is that I find it very difficult to get excited about value or value judgments or whether they're valued on invalid lines. Nor can I feign fascination for the purposes of this chapter." Oh-Oh! Sounds like pomo promo to Mo Ho.

## Valediction

I hope that the reader who has persevered this far has been rewarded by a challenging introduction to the concepts and issues that surround the nature and types of consumer value. Recall that we defined consumer value as an interactive relativistic preference experience. With luck, the reader has interacted with the book in a way that has led toward the construction of meaning. Relativistically, I hope that the book will prove valuable by comparison with other less systematic and comprehensive volumes; that at least some readers will favor its approach; and that it will be found helpful in such contexts and situations as those presented by the problems of marketing management and the study of consumption experiences. Also recall that we distinguished between eight key types of consumer value. In this connection, I hope that the reader has found the book productive of insights given the money and time invested (efficiency in general and convenience in particular); that the book will linger on the shelf as a potential route to useful knowledge (excellence or quality); that readers will beneficially share their reactions with colleagues and friends (status or impression management); that they will view such ideas as a worthwhile part of their intellectual capital (esteem or reputation); that they have approached the book from the viewpoint of an argumentatively questioning perspective (play and fun); that they have found it well-constructed and pleasant to read (aesthetics and beauty); that they see no harm and even some good in it (ethics and morality); and that it has given them a sense of communion with that large and endlessly fascinating throng of humanity that we call consumers (spirituality or rapture).

# References

Berlyne, Daniel E. (1969) "Laughter, Humor, and Play," in G. Lindzey and E. Aronson (eds) *The Handbook of Social Psychology*, Vol. 3, Reading, MA: Addison-Wesley Publishing Company, 795–852.

Broydrick, Stephen C. (1996) *The 7 Universal Laws of Customer Value: How to Win Customers and Influence Markets*, Burr Ridge, IL: Irwin.

Deci, Edward L. (1975) *Intrinsic Motivation*, New York: Plenum Press.

Eisert, D. C. (1983) "Marriage and Parenting," in L. R. Kahle (ed.) *Social Values and Social Change*, New York: Praeger, 143–67.

Frankena, William K. (1973) *Ethics*, 2nd Ed., Englewood Cliffs, NJ: Prentice-Hall.

Gale, Bradley T. (1994) *Managing Customer Value: Creating Quality and Service That Customers Can See*, New York: The Free Press.

Hilliard, A. L. (1950) *The Forms of Value: The Extension of Hedonistic Axiology*, New York: Columbia University Press.

Holbrook, Morris B. (1986) "Emotion in the Consumption Experience: Toward a New Model of the Human Consumer," in R. A. Peterson, W. D. Hoyer, and W. R. Wilson (eds) *The Role of Affect in Consumer Behavior: Emerging Theories and Applications*, Lexington, MA: D. C. Heath and Company, 17–52.

—— (1994a) "Axiology, Aesthetics, and Apparel: Some Reflections on the Old School Tie," in M. R. DeLong and A. M. Fiore (eds) *Aesthetics of Textiles and Clothing: Advancing Multi-Disciplinary Perspectives*, ITAA Special Publication #7, Monument, CO 80132-1360: International Textile and Apparel Association, 131–41.

—— (1994b) "Ethics in Consumer Research," in C. T. Allen and D. Roedder John (eds) *Advances in Consumer Research*, Vol. 21, Provo, UT: Association for Consumer Research, 566–71.

—— (1994c) "The Nature of Customer Value: An Axiology of Services in the Consumption Experience," in R. T. Rust and R. L. Oliver (eds) *Service Quality: New Directions in Theory and Practice*, Thousand Oaks, CA: Sage Publications, 21–71.

—— (1996) "Customer Value – A Framework for Analysis and Research," in K. P. Corfman and J. G. Lynch, Jr. (eds) *Advances in Consumer Research*, Vol. 23, Provo, UT: Association for Consumer Research, 138–42.

Holbrook, Morris B. and Corfman, Kim P. (1985) "Quality and Value in the Consumption Experience: Phaedrus Rides Again," in J. Jacoby and J. C. Olson (eds) *Perceived Quality: How Consumers View Stores and Merchandise*, Lexington, MA: D. C. Heath and Company, 31–57.

Lee, Harold N. (1957) "The Meaning of 'Intrinsic Value,'" in R. Lepley (ed.) *The Language of Value*, New York: Columbia University Press, 178–96.

Lewis, C. I. (1946) *An Analysis of Knowledge and Valuation*, La Salle, IL: Open Court.

Lyotard, Jean-François (1984) *The Postmodern Condition: A Report on Knowledge*, trans. Geoff Bennington and Brian Massumi, Minneapolis, MN: University of Minnesota Press.

Mathwick, C., Malhotra, N., and Rigdon, E. (1998) "An Integrated Measure of Customer

Value: Psychometric Analysis, Hierarchical Structure, Predictive Power and Generalizability," Working Paper, Georgia Institute of Technology, Atlanta, GA 30332.

Morris, Charles (1956) *Varieties of Human Value*, Chicago, IL: The University of Chicago Press.

—— (1964) *Signification and Significance*, Cambridge, MA: MIT Press.

Parker, Dewitt H. (1957) *The Philosophy of Value*, Ann Arbor, MI: The University of Michigan Press.

Perry, Ralph Barton (1954) *Realms of Value*, Cambridge, MA: Harvard University Press.

Rokeach, Milton (1973) *The Nature of Human Values*, New York: The Free Press.

Taylor, Paul W. (1961) *Normative Discourse*, Englewood Cliffs, NJ: Prentice Hall.

Woodruff, Robert B. and Gardial, Sarah Fisher (1996) *Know Your Customer: New Approaches to Understanding Customer Value and Satisfaction*, Cambridge, MA: Blackwell.

# Index

*Note*: Page numbers in **bold** type refer to **figures**; page numbers in *italic* type refer to *tables*; page numbers followed by 'n' refer to notes